1993

SPECIAL EDUCATION SERIES

Peter Knoblock, Editor

(Continued)

On Being L.D.:
Perspectives and Strategies of Young Adults
Stephen T. Murphy
Toward Effective Public School Programs for Deaf Students:
Context, Process, and Outcomes
*Thomas N. Kluwin, Donald F. Moores, and Martha Gonter Gaustad,
Editors*
Communication Unbound:
How Facilitated Communication Is Challenging
Traditional Views of Autism and Ability/Disability
Douglas Biklen

COMMUNICATION
UNBOUND

*How Facilitated Communication Is Challenging
Traditional Views of Autism
and Ability/Disability*

Douglas Biklen

Teachers College, Columbia University
New York and London

Published by Teachers College Press, 1234 Amsterdam Avenue, New York, New York

The following chapters have been adapted and expanded, with permission, from previously published material:

Chapter 1: Biklen, Douglas, "Communication Unbound: Autism and Praxis," *Harvard Educational Review,* 60:4, pp. 291–314. Copyright © 1990 by the President and Fellows of Harvard College. All rights reserved.
Chapter 2: From "New Words: The Communication of Students with Autism" by D. P. Biklen and A. Schubert, 1991, *Remedial and Special Education,* 12(6), 46–57. Copyright © 1991 by PRO-ED, Inc. Reprinted by permission.
Chapter 3: "I AMN NOT A UTISTIVC ON THJE TYP' (I'm not autistic on the typewriter)." (1991). *Disability, Handicap & Society,* 6(3), 161–180.
Chapter 6: "Facilitated Communication: Implications for Individuals with Autism" in *Topics in Language Disorders,* Vol. 12, No. 4, with permission of Aspen Publishers, Inc., © 1992.

Library of Congress Cataloging-in-Publication Data

Biklen, Douglas
    Communication unbound: how facilitated communication is challenging traditional views of autism and ability-disability / Douglas Biklen
        p.   cm. — (Special education series ; #13)
    Includes bibliographical references (p.   ) and index.
    ISBN 0-8077-3222-2 (alk. paper). — ISBN 0-8077-3221-4 (pbk.: alk. paper)
    1. Facilitated communication. 2. Autism—Patients—Language. 3. Autism—Patients—Rehabilitation. 4. Mentally handicapped—Language.   5. Mentally handicapped—Rehabilitation   I. Title.
    II. Series: Special education series (New York, N.Y.) ; #13.
    RC429.B55   1993
    616.89'8206516—dc20   92-34555

Printed on acid-free paper
Manufactured in the United States of America
99 98 97 96 95 94 93   7 6 5 4 3 2 1

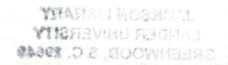

*In Memory of Burton Blatt and Mary Stewart Goodwin,
friends and teachers.*

Contents

Introduction

This book concerns a means of communication called "facilitated communication." While the book includes an appendix of "how-to" information on the method, I have written about the topic of facilitated communication not only as a technique but also as a way of thinking about people. In keeping with this theme, Facilitated Communication raises questions about the meaning of particular disabilitites such as autism, of disability in general, of education, and of change.

I have organized the book as a kind of story about my own introduction to the method, my experiences in using it and doing research on it, and the controversies that ensued. Each chapter draws on fieldwork done in the tradition of qualitative research. It is an empirical study in the sense that it is based on careful, systematically collected observations and interviews. It is more than a collection of anecdotes in the sense that the examples are drawn from observations that took place over many months in selected settings with selected individuals. The examples illustrate particular points and issues. Central to this research approach is the idea that it is sometimes best to learn about something by making few assumptions about it. In keeping with this notion, I undertook the study not to prove or disprove the effectiveness of a method (e.g., facilitated communication) or to invalidate assumptions about particular disabilities (e.g., autism) but to understand a phenomenon, in this case facilitated communication, and its implications. Among other issues, the book includes discussions on the meaning of autism, other disabilities, disability in general, and education.

It is in the nature of qualitative inquiry that the researcher generally does not know what issues will emerge as the critical ones. Rather, one begins with a general idea of what to investigate and waits to discover what will surface as critically important. Also, inherent in this approach is the idea that any effort to control or limit the variables observed would in effect negate a primary rationale for a qualitative study, which is to try to understand the meanings that people give to their worlds (e.g., concepts in their worlds, such as facilitated communication and disability) and to develop one's own understanding and interpretation of them.

I begin the book with an account of how I learned about facilitated communication from the Australian educator Rosemary Crossley, my initial skepticism about its usefulness for certain groups of people, and the struggle that I went through in trying to understand how it worked. Chapter 1 includes this story of my introduction to the method and to people using it as well as background on autism, since it was with people with autism that I first observed its use and about which I had so many questions. The chapter includes an extended example of how Crossley introduces the method to individuals. It also includes a lengthy discussion among four individuals using facilitation and myself on issues of social policy and disability, the struggles of living with a disability, and attitudes about ability and disability. Given the nature of the individuals' disabilities and others' assumptions about their abilities prior to being introduced to facilitated communication, it is a surprising as well as an exciting discussion. In this chapter I introduce a hypothesis about why facilitation works in the manner that it does.

Chapter 2 covers initial experiences with facilitated communication in Syracuse, New York. Upon return from a study trip to the DEAL Communication Centre in Melbourne, Australia, where I learned about facilitated communication, I introduced the method in Syracuse-area schools. This chapter includes descriptions of how teachers and speech therapists helped students "get started" and the literacy skills revealed. I also discuss the criteria we applied in deciding with whom the method might be useful. Numerous examples of students' typing are included. One of the surprising findings was sentence-level literacy in a number of very young children who had been presumed retarded. The chapter includes a discussion on how these individuals might have learned to read.

Chapter 3 examines the unique issues of using facilitated communication with individuals who are able to talk but whose speech is highly disordered. The chapter includes insights of people with disabilities on the meaning of independence. It also includes an extended discussion about the concept of apraxia that is the basis of the explanatory hypothesis referred to in Chapter 1.

Chapter 4 reveals another aspect of how I came to understand facilitation. It includes accounts of a number of parents and teachers who on their own discovered facilitated communication—none of them called it that or in fact had any terminology at all for it—several years prior to publication of my original article on Crossley's work (Biklen, 1990). Each of these individuals encountered considerable resistance to his or her claim that the person with a disability was communicating. From their stories, principles emerge about the nature of change and the nature of facilitated communication as well as the educational process it entails.

Chapter 5 focuses on the controversy over facilitation, including charges that the method is little more than manipulation of vulnerable people. But the chapter concerns more than issues of validity. It also concerns the social meaning of disability, the power of prevailing paradigms, the nature of science, and the difficulties of change.

Chapter 6 returns to discussions of communication unbound, examining the messages of people who for years had had their communication imprisoned. Through the words of people who use facilitated communication, we begin to get insights into the meaning of disability and the ways in which people want to be supported. This chapter includes a section on what individuals say about "not wanting autism" and on the nature and meaning of difficult behavior, including self-abuse.

In Chapter 7, I look at the place of facilitated communication in our understanding of ability and disability. As suggested at the outset of this introduction, the central issue of the book evolves to become one not of techniques but rather of perspective.

I want to thank a number of people who helped me explore and understand the issues in Facilitated Communication. First among them is Rosemary Crossley, for me both a teacher and a dear friend. Also, Sari Knopp Biklen lived and talked through every aspect of this study; I am forever indebted to her for her interest and support. I owe special thanks also to Joan Reidy and Michael Steer for helping to arrange my first visits to Australia, where I learned about facilitated communication; to Anne McDonald and Chris Borthwick for their helping me to understand the method; to Jean Meltzer for assistance in arranging for me to meet so may people associated with DEAL; to Jane Remington-Gurney and Margaret Batt for allowing me to observe them so often; and to all of the many people who appear in this book under pseudonyms. And to Naomi, Peter, Gabriel, and Rebecca White, thanks for providing a home away from home and for your friendship. I am grateful to Diane Woods and the World Rehabilitation Fund for support of the Australian part of my research. I want to thank Noah Knopp Biklen, Molly Knopp Biklen, and Burton Knopp for their support and companionship during the Australian part of these studies and for their ongoing interest and support during the subsequent American parts. Thanks, too, to my parents, Anne and Paul Biklen, and to my mother-in-law, Fay Knopp, for their encouragement. Thanks to Ian Johnson and the many wonderful

people of House M and the Ishoj Activity Center in Denmark for invit-
ing me to visit and learn from them, and to Jan Nisbet for help during
that part of the study. Thanks, too, to Lou Brown, Alison Ford, Gunnar
and Rosemary Dybwad, Emmy Elbaum, Steve Bossert, and Ken and
Mary Ann Shaw for their interest in and reactions to this research. I am
especially appreciative for the help given to me by Rosemary Alibrandi
in arranging the logistics for many of the training conferences and support groups that were crucial aspects of my work on facilitated communication and for her help on research proposals, correspondence,
and organization of data. Thanks to Peter Knoblock, Brian Ellerbeck,
and Peter Sieger for their editorial advice and for their encouragement
of this project. Thanks also to the many doctoral students and colleagues who have participated in the research, including Shri Rao, Sue
Lehr, Annegret Schubert, Arlene Knoblauch, Marilyn Chadwick, Susan
O'Connor, Carol Berrigan, Missy Morton, Nina Saha, Janet Duncan,
Stephen Drake, Mayer Shevin, Eija Karna, Sudha Swaminathan, Mar-
gret Hardardottir, and Deb Gold. Special thanks, too, to Bob Bogdan,
Janet Bogdan, and Steve Taylor for their ideas and support. I am also
deeply indebted to many teachers, teaching assistants, speech clini-
cians, and parents for their assistance in helping me to learn about facilitated communication. Thanks to Ellen Barnes for hosting our first
planning meeting on facilitation and for her ongoing interest and support. I owe a special thanks to the faculty and administration of the
Jowonio School, the Syracuse City School District, the Baldwinsville
Central School District, the North Syracuse School District, the Liver-
pool School District, and the Fayetteville-Manlius School District. Special thanks to Nancy Centra, Ed Erwin, Steve Nevins, and Geri Muoio
for supporting implementation of the method in their school districts.

COMMUNICATION
UNBOUND

CHAPTER 1

Facilitated Communication

Jonothan Solaris cannot speak. David Armbruster can say a few words, usually unintelligible. Both are young adolescents classified as autistic. I first met them in Melbourne, Australia, at the Dignity through Education and Language (DEAL) Communication Centre, an independent, government-funded organization established by educator Rosemary Crossley and her colleagues to assist people who are unable either to talk or to do so clearly. Jonothan seemed full of nervous energy and he got up from his seat frequently. His way of walking on the balls of his feet was akin to prancing. David gazed at the ceiling light, reaching toward it with his hands. Both boys relied heavily on peripheral vision. I felt that, even when spoken to, they listened to me "sideways." Also, their facial expressions did not correspond with the conversation, although David smiled a lot.

I was not surprised by how either of them appeared. Theirs were the behaviors of autism. But what I did not anticipate was that their communication with me would assault my assumptions about autism and ultimately yield important lessons for education.

On the day of my visit, Jonothan and David were present to demonstrate a method that Crossley had developed called "facilitated communication." I spent 15 or 20 minutes speaking with David's mother and several DEAL staff members, occasionally directing my statements to Jonothan and David. Then, when Crossley asked if they had anything to tell me, Jonothan began to type on a Canon Communicator (a small electronic typing device with a dot-matrix tape output). With a staff member's hand on his shoulder, Jonothan typed, ILIKEDOUGGBUTT-HHEISMAAD.[1] Seeing what Jonothan had written, Crossley asked why he thought I was "mad," whereupon he typed, HETALKSTOMELIKEIMHUMAN. By MAAD he had meant "crazy."

Jonothan and David produced only a few sentences in the several hours that we were together. But when they typed, they did so fairly quickly, without hesitation, and independently (with just the hand on the shoulder). I asked David and Jonothan if I could take some pictures of them communicating. I explained that people in the United States

1

would be interested in seeing what they were doing. They both agreed, typing Y for "yes" on their Canons. David added, NOSEY PEOPLE TO EVEN WANT TO SEE ME. Unlike Jonothan, he had put in spaces between the words. During this session, Crossley described the method of facilitated communication that had allowed David and Jonothan to communicate. In the midst of her enthusiastic and lengthy discourse, David revealed his sense of humor, typing, TURN HER OFF.

Crossley's first attempt at facilitation with a person with autism had been with Jonothan, not an "easy" student. For over a month he had resisted typing. When I asked him what had finally caused him to communicate on a regular basis, he did not answer. Then, several minutes later, he typed, IMNOTVERYQUITRHIGHTNOWBECIGOTSATONBYROSIE. Translated, he said, "I'm not very quiet right now because I got sat on by Rosie." Hearing this, Crossley asked, "Do you mean that literally or metaphorically?" Jonothan responded by typing MET.

Jonothan's easy grasp of this abstract concept "metaphorical" and David's facile sarcasm struck me as extraordinary. The content of their communication was "normal," *not* what one expects from children with autism (American Psychiatric Association, 1987). A year and a half earlier I had been similarly, if not so vividly, shocked by a letter from Australia that described Crossley's success in using a new technique to allow people with autism to communicate. The letter claimed that Crossley was eliciting "high-level" communication from her students. "Sophisticated written (typed) communication at sentence level," I was told. I did not know what to think about this claim. It seemed conceivable to me that Crossley and her colleagues had happened on a *few* people with autism for whom such communication was possible. But it made no sense that people with autism who had been classified as severely intellectually disabled would have normal or even near-normal literacy skills. By definition, people with autism who do not speak or who speak only a small range of phrases are referred to as "low-functioning" and are thought to have a severe intellectual disability as well (Rutter, 1978). Of course, one possible explanation was that Crossley's students were actually mildly disabled; in other words, perhaps they had autism but were among the group commonly called "high- functioning." This term is often applied to those people with autism who have usable, easily understood speech. Yet the letter described the method as working with students who typically might be called "low-functioning," including some who were previously thought to be severely intellectually disabled. The letter about Crossley was baffling, so much so, that, whether consciously or not, I put it out of my mind for a year and a half. But when I knew I would be in Melbourne I arranged to visit DEAL. Then, seeing David and Jonothan type sophisticated thoughts, I could not ignore the many questions their communication posed.

How, why, and with whom does facilitated communication work? Does facilitated communication work anywhere or is it more effective in certain settings, under specific educational or social conditions, and with certain people more than with others? If there were preferred conditions, how would these compare to prevailing notions about "good" schooling? Presumably, the DEAL students themselves would be able to comment on many issues, such as how society treats them and how they want to be treated. Would the DEAL students change as a result of their newfound communication and, if so, how? Equally important, would the ability to communicate lead to changes in their families, schools, and other environments? Did the success of students like David and Jonothan portend a dramatic transformation in how we think about and define autism?

TOWARD UNDERSTANDING FACILITATED COMMUNICATION: A QUALITATIVE, HYPOTHESIS-GENERATING APPROACH

In July of 1989, seven months after the session with Jonothan and David, I returned to Melbourne to study Crossley's work more systematically. I observed nearly all the students Crossley worked with both at DEAL and in the community over a four-week period. I also observed the two part-time speech therapists working with other children at DEAL, interviewed parents, and visited schools. My discussion in this chapter is based on communication efforts by 21 individuals served by the Dignity through Education and Language Centre.[2] All 21 are nonspeaking or speak only with echolalic expressions (echoes of phrases they have previously heard); all have been labeled "autistic" or display autistic behaviors; all were considered mentally retarded prior to being introduced to facilitated communication. Observations and interviews were audiorecorded; thus students' typed words were recorded as facilitators read them aloud.

In the tradition of qualitative research, I began my observations at DEAL in an attempt not to *test* hypotheses but rather to generate them (Biklen & Mosley, 1988; Bogdan & Biklen, 1991; Glaser & Strauss, 1967). Unlike studies such as clinical experiments in which one attempts to control certain variables, I wanted to understand facilitated communication in context. Through careful, systematic observation I hoped to develop an understanding of how people with disabilities, their family members and teachers or aides, and DEAL staff defined and understood facilitated communication and related issues.

The validity of an observational study rests on multiple factors (Goetz & LeCompte, 1984; Mishler, 1990), including the presence of the researcher in the setting over a relatively long period of time, frequent formulation and reformulation of interpretations and analyses of the data (Becker, 1969), constant comparisons of data, and checking of hypotheses against new data (Glaser & Strauss, 1967), including any cases or situations that might challenge the researcher's emerging hypotheses. In this study, attention to detail would prove crucially important. Similarly, mindful that my observational data might possibly be construed as unbelievable in light of prevailing assumptions in the fields of disability and communication, I recognized that I would have to present the observations in the fairest possible manner, including ample examples of data that were hard to explain and examples of seemingly failed communication as well as the more successful instances; I would need to try to explain both.

An underlying assumption of qualitative research concerning reliability is that researchers analyze data differently, depending on the perspective they bring to the analysis. Therefore the bases of analysis must be explicit and sufficiently descriptive to allow the reader to see the researchers' perspectives. Similarly, it is assumed that if researchers have a shared perspective and can establish similar levels of rapport with their subjects, they can observe the same things similarly. In this study, cross-checking of observers' data collection, perception, and analysis occurred as an ongoing process through daily discussions with participants in the setting as well as with other educators who had visited DEAL on previous occasions or who had observed individuals using facilitated communication in schools and other settings.

I entered the field not knowing what the crucial issues would be or even what concepts would prove to be particularly important. I did not assume the validity of facilitated communication or even the meaning of the term. Neither could I assume the correctness or natural validity of other concepts, such as "autism" or "mental retardation." I prepared to learn about facilitated communication, autism, mental retardation, and the educational process anew. During the course of the study, I identified topics or categories (e.g., levels of physical support, typed content on behavior, typed content on feelings, factors by which to validate that communication emanates from the student). As hypotheses and theory emerged, I looked for possible contradicting instances which might require me to modify the working hypotheses or theory.

ORIGINS OF CROSSLEY'S DISCOVERY

Crossley's discovery of literacy skills among nonspeaking people or people who have disordered speech because of autism and other developmental disabilities occurred by accident. During the 1970s, when she worked at a residential institution called St. Nicholas Hospital, she had used hand support or arm support to help people with cerebral palsy achieve greater control over their movements, to slow them down, *and* to give them more likelihood of hitting an intended target (e.g., a switch, key, button, letter, or picture on a board). The method was controversial (Crossley & McDonald, 1980) because it raised the possibility that the people's choice of letters from a language board, for example, might reflect the facilitator's rather than the learner's choice. The controversy ultimately subsided somewhat when it was aired in a court of law. Annie McDonald, the subject and co-author of *Annie's Coming Out*, went to court to win her freedom from the institution. After a dramatic demonstration of message-passing tests (e.g., Crossley left the room and returned to facilitate communication about something that had transpired in her absence), the Supreme Court of Victoria sided with McDonald and Crossley, recognizing that McDonald's facilitated communication was her own (Crossley & McDonald, 1980). Application of this method to people with autism and similar conditions was unplanned although, Crossley now believes, logical. She began with Jonothan.

By every account, Jonothan was a handsome but challenging child. He was not toilet trained. He fidgeted. To get things, he simply grabbed them. He did not look people in the eye. He nearly skipped when walking, on the balls of his feet. He had a history of fits of screaming, regurgitating food, scratching, and running away from people. In March of 1985, when Jonothan was 7, Rosemary Crossley invited his mother to leave him with her for an afternoon. That afternoon, after watching Jonothan's stereotyped repetitive play with a squeeze mop, Crossley managed to settle Jonothan on her sofa, interesting him first in a speech synthesizer and then in a Canon Communicator. With wrist support, he pressed buttons that she touched. Occasionally he pressed buttons without any assistance. She typed JONOTHAN, followed by MUM, and then asked him for "Dad." He went straight to the D, without wrist support, and then to A, where he hesitated.

"I think he completed DAD with no prompting but with wrist support," she wrote later in her notes that day. If she had prompted him, she would have actually moved his wrist toward the letter or letters; instead, she merely supported his wrist as he moved his hand toward the letters. She typed JONATHAN, whereupon he typed JONOTHAN. Crossley later checked the spelling with his mother. Jonothan had been correct. Crossley asked him if the mop was a plane when he was playing with it. He typed MOP. She guided him through the entire alphabet on the keyboard, then asked him what letter the word *good* starts with. He pressed G. She asked how many fingers she had on one hand. He pressed 5. She asked how many on two hands; he pressed 10. "If you took 5 from 10, how many would you have left?" she then asked. He typed 5. She continued, asking for 5 plus 3? He gave 8. For 3 plus 4, he pressed 6. She said try again. He got 7. She observed, over time, that Jonothan often veered to the side of a character at the last moment, resulting in a typographical rather than a cognitive error, presumably the result of cerebellar damage affecting his judgment of distance. Crossley asked if Jonothan had anything he would like to say. He spelled STOP. He was reluctant to finish the word; he made several tries and erasures before completing it.

Coincidentally, on the afternoon I interviewed Crossley about how she had discovered that this method worked with Jonothan, he came to visit DEAL. Crossley told him that we had just been talking about the first time he had typed on the Canon. She asked him if he remembered what his first word had been. As she asked the question, she held out a Canon Communicator. Independently, he typed DAD. Then he typed, JONOTHAN NOT JONATHAN. This is one child who remembers his first words.

When Jonothan's mother returned to Crossley's home that afternoon in 1985, Crossley presumed that Jonothan wanted to show her what he had been doing. But, in Crossley's words, "he completely gummed up. . . . [He] was quite unable or unwilling to give so much as a 'yes' or 'no' with her there." Jonothan's inability to communicate with his mother continued until she died in 1989. While Jonothan communicates with several other people now, much of it independently or with only a hand on the shoulder, his communication with his mother was basically unsuccessful, a fact his mother found "discouraging."

Why people who regularly communicate independently with a few people but not at all or only with support to the wrist and forearm with others is mysterious. Is it difficult for some students to communicate with people with whom they feel a close personal bond? In other words, is it harder to reveal yourself and your skills to those whose judgment you especially value? Are some people better at facilitation than others? Must the student believe that the person is an effective facilitator? Is the willingness or ability to communicate with particular people reflective of the "autistic" quality of wanting order and sameness?

OBSERVATIONS OF FIRST ASSESSMENTS

Among the DEAL students I observed were people whom Crossley was seeing for the first time. They included school-age children and young adults and ranged in age from 5 to 25. As in my first meeting with Jonothan and David, these first sessions startled me. Crossley's assessment of Louis is a case in point.

Louis was 24 years old, with reddish-brown hair and gold, metal-rimmed, rectangular-shaped glasses with thick lenses. He was wearing a black and white sweater, black jeans, and white tennis shoes when we met him at an adult training center (ATC). ATCs are considered one step less demanding than sheltered workshops, which are designed specifically for people with disabilities who are presumed to be unable to work in competitive employment but capable of working under supervision, albeit often at less-than-average productivity rates and for less than the minimum wage; people who attend ATCs are generally considered too disabled to qualify for admittance to a sheltered workshop. Louis had very little facial expression. He did not speak, except for a few phrases that seemed involuntarily uttered and out of context. As he entered the room where Crossley was to conduct the assessment, he said, "Excuse me. Get mommy on the bus. Excuse me," which did not make sense to me. Attempts at answering his statements—by saying, for example, "There is no need to be excused, you are fine"—did not quiet him. He repeated the phrase.

Crossley introduced herself and me to Louis, who sat between us. She described her work to him as helping people who do not speak find other ways to communicate. She apologized in advance for her assessment approach: "Louis, I ask people a lot of really silly questions." She began the session by asking him to press down on various pictures on a talking computer, a children's toy with a voice output that requests the person using it to press various pictures or letters and that announces the user's choice, for example, "Right, that's the apple."

As Crossley asked questions, tears began to roll down Louis's face. He was crying silently. She reassured him, telling him that she would do it with him. She held her hand on top of Louis's right arm. In response to the command, "Press the red car," Louis put his index finger on it and Crossley helped him push it down. Louis was moving slowly. He seemed tentative. The machine instructed him to find the circle, which he did. He followed with correct answers to square, triangle, circle, and triangle. He hit them all, five of five.

Crossley changed the display page on the talking computer. This time he was asked for the small rectangle. Louis started to go for the big one. She held him back and said, with emphasis, "*Small* rectangle." He then went for it correctly. She reassured him, "Yes." Louis had struggled with the demands of the machine; with Crossley's help he had gotten the right answers. When asked for the big square, Louis hesitated. As he hovered over it, Crossley encouraged him, "Go on, you've got it." He did. Next he was asked to find the small yellow rectangle. His hand wobbled between the brown triangle and blue circle. Crossley pulled him back and Louis uttered the words, "That one," and hit the small yellow rectangle.

The next page displayed a picture of grass, a tree, a car, a house, and a cat. He pressed the car on demand. He got the tree, and all the remaining pictures. Then he was asked to locate the word *tree*, as distinct from the picture. He did. Again he got five out of five of the words. On another page he had to choose pictures to go with the words *yacht, fish, dog, girl, bird,* and *boy.* For *girl* he started to move away from the picture of a girl. Crossley pulled his hand back and asked, "Where are you going?" With the exception of this help, he pressed the pictures for the words independently.

The next sheet included only words. When Crossley asked Louis to identify *clock,* his finger seemed to drop to *flower.* She said, "Hold on," and asked, "Can you point to *clock*?" He did. She followed by asking him to point to the words *hand, eye,* and *fish.* He identified each. For these, she was holding the top of his sleeve above his wrist. Louis was seemingly expressionless throughout. Next, Crossley read five sentences aloud to Louis and asked him to find words in the sentences, including, for example, "our," "on," "and," "is," and "the." He got them all. She was pleased. "Terrific. That's great, mate," she declared.

Finally, she switched to a page displaying the alphabet and asked Louis to point to specific letters, including, for example, V, G, A, and Z. He got them all. Less than half an hour had elapsed, and Crossley was ready to introduce Louis to the Canon Communicator. At this point, I wrote in my notebook, "He's sailing." Except for minor stumbling with the geometric figures, Louis had cruised through the questions. Also, he now had a slight smile at the corner of his mouth. He had relaxed.

Crossley showed Louis the Canon and went through the alphabet and numbers with him. "For starters," she asked, "can you type your name?" At this point, her hand was stretched out flat, on top of, but not actually touching, his. He typed LOUIS. As he finished, she asked if there was anything else he wanted to say. Louis started typing again. First he typed O, and then PC. Crossley pulled his hand back from the keys, saying, "I'm not sure I follow. Let's start over." This time he typed POCCO. She was confused. Then we realized what he was typing. *Pocco* is his last name. He was still responding to Crossley's first request, to type his name.

Crossley asked again if there was anything else Louis wanted to say. He typed, IM NOT RETARDED, to which she remarked, "No, I don't think you are. Keep going." Louis continued, MY MOTHER FEELS IM STUPID BECAUSE IH [he back-spaced this and crossed out the H] CANT USE MY VOICE PROPERLY. A tear rolled down his left cheek as he typed. And Crossley said to me and to Louis, "A lot of people believe that what people say is what they're capable of."

Louis was not done. He typed, HOW MUCH IS A CANON?

"They're dear," Crossley answered.

I SAVE A BIT BUT NOT ENOUGH, Louis typed.

Crossley explained that she would continue to work with Louis in conjunction with the adult training center and that she would try to get him a Canon. Then she congratulated him on his work in the session and said to me, for Louis to hear, "Anybody who starts off typing, 'I'm not retarded,' isn't retarded. First rule!"

The words of other first-time communicators, meaning those who communicated neither with echolalia nor by physical manipulation of objects, were no less astonishing. One young man typed I CAN READ for his first sentence. He had learned to read by being around words and by watching television. Crossley's students and their parents typically report that the students had had incidental exposure to language through television, magazines, and books, or with labels on foods and other items. Some were reported to have been in formal reading programs as part of early intervention and developmental training efforts. Yet until Crossley elicited typing from them, the assumption for all of them was that they had *not* learned to read.

Margaret, a 17-year-old young woman referred to DEAL by an autism center, also surprised me with her performance in her first session at DEAL. Except for "no" and an approximation of "hello," she is mute. During a two-hour assessment session, although I addressed her several times, she never once looked at me. Her first sentence, typed independently save Crossley's hand on her shoulder, was a question: CAN I COME AGAIN? Sessions with younger children were often much shorter, with the students unable or unwilling to cooperate for such long stretches.

DOUBTS: FACILITATION OR MANIPULATION?

Despite the seeming ease with which Crossley assesses some new students, she and her colleagues admit that communication is not always so easily facilitated. Initially, it has often proven difficult for students to communicate with more than one or two facilitators, especially when they are new to DEAL. They may refuse to communicate at particular moments, in particular situations, with certain people, or for specific time periods, as, for example, Jonothan did. Some are independent in some situations but dependent or noncommunicative in others, whether with the same or other people. Some then will produce obviously incorrect information. Related to this, facilitators often find themselves inadvertently cuing their nonspeaking partners to letters and therefore to words or statements. This is particularly true with people who are just learning to communicate by typing with facilitated communication. Occasionally, people who have previously demonstrated excellent facility will type only repetitions of specific letters and phrases or will produce unintelligible sequences of letters or words. None of the people I observed typing "independently," with just a hand on the shoulder, typed as well or sometimes at all for me alone or for other new facilitators. Jane Remington-Gurney, a speech therapist at DEAL, recounted that she worked with several students for months, unsure of whether the students' output was anything more than a reflection of her own manipulation of their arms. She recalled that "gradually I began to receive words from clients that were not in my vocabulary, were phonetically spelled or were . . . spelled better than I could spell." She also found that when she tried "too hard" she was even less successful.

Several facilitators, including speech therapists, teachers, and parents, encountered difficulty in identifying the source of certain communication: either it had been generated by the person being supported or by their own unconscious selection or cuing. They reported instances in which they had believed the communication to be genuine, only to discover that it reflected their own subtle cues. For instance, I asked a teenager, Bette, for example, "What is your full name? Is it Beth, Elizabeth, or Bette?" to which she answered ELIZABETH. She also declared that she prefers the name Bette. Later I learned that her full name is Beth and that her family and friends call her Bette. Another student, Geraldine, gave a staff member her family's address incorrectly. Such miscues have caused facilitators to wonder about the validity of other communication. Were the words the students' own? Or were they the facilitators'? Or were there perfectly reasonable explanations for the "incorrect" communication? Did Bette think *Elizabeth* sounded better and therefore claim it as her name? Did Geraldine not know her address and decide simply to provide any address in order to at least answer the question asked? Or had she heard the address previously—was this a typed version of echolalia, like the advertising jingles that people with autism have been known to type? Both girls who provided "incorrect" information in these instances communicated independently in other conversations, with only the support of a hand on the shoulder or a finger touching the thread of a sweater.[3]

Within the professional community there has also been a mixed reception to Crossley's work. In 1988, an ad hoc group of psychologists, speech specialists, educators, and administrators calling themselves the "Interdisciplinary Working Party" issued a critique of "assisted communication" (Interdisciplinary Working Party, 1988).

The Working Party report cited major contradictions between the nature of communication content being claimed for people with autism and prevailing theories of autism. A letter and assessment statement on DEAL prepared by staff of the Victorian Autistic Children's Association, Eastern Centre, stated, for example, "Well recognized characteristics of autism bring into question much of the assisted communication of autistic children" (Interdisciplinary Working Party, 1988, p. 91). The assessment, dated September 1, 1987, argues that children with autism would need "far more time to learn the task procedure" than just the brief moments given by Crossley, that the children would have a hard time remembering the sequence of letters they had typed into the Canon Communicator ("short-term sequential memory tasks are particularly difficult for autistic children"), and that Crossley's prompts of counting to 10 or saying "Get on your bike" would cause students with autism to forget the task and instructions. This evaluation of Crossley's work also stated that "the sentence structure used by all the children via assisted communication was not characteristic of the 'different' language used by autistic children." Only the most advanced would be capable of using *I*; they would not typically be able to use the word *by* correctly; and *why* questions would "involve cognitive processes well beyond the ability of all but a few autistic children" (p. 93). The Working Party report led to a state government inquiry entitled *Investigation into the Reliability and Validity of the Assisted Communication Technique* (Intellectual Disability Review Panel, 1989).

The Review Panel report noted that people with intellectual disabilities are "extremely susceptible to influence by people who may be unaware of the extent to which they may be influencing decisions." The panel's charge was to ensure clients' "maximum control" of decisions—

in other words, communication and the decisions made on the basis of communication. The panel argued, "given the conflict that the 'assisted communication technique' has engendered and the consequences for the client if doubt exists about his/her communication," it was essential for any disputes over communication to be resolved (Intellectual Disability Review Panel, 1989, p. 18).

In its conclusions on the validity of facilitated communication, the Review Panel equivocated. The study involved two different procedures. In the first, people were given questions that were the same as or different than those given to the facilitator (the facilitator wore earphones that transmitted the same or different information). The second procedure involved message passing. In this latter approach, people were given gifts. The facilitator did not know about the gifts. The people were then asked to tell the facilitators what they had been given. Since the Review Panel chose not to describe its subjects in any detail, the conclusions others are able to draw from the study are limited. The results of both parts of the study were summarized by the Intellectual Disability Review Panel (1989) in the following manner:

> The validity of the communication while using the "assisted communication technique" was demonstrated in four of the six clients who participated in the two studies. Under controlled conditions the data clearly indicated that the communication of one of the three clients was validated using the "assisted communication technique." The communication of the three clients who participated in the message passing exercise was also validated. The validity of the remaining two clients' communication when using the "assisted communication technique" was not established. However, the absence of data on these occasions does not automatically imply that the clients are not capable of communication. In all three cases of the controlled study, client responses were influenced by the assistant. Influence occurred with a client who demonstrated valid, uninfluenced responses to other items. It appeared that a given assistant could influence some client responses and leave others uninfluenced. (p. 40)

The Review Panel also noted that assistants appeared unaware of when they might be influencing communication. Also, some of the uninfluenced correct responses were correct in general information (category) but were not as specific as anticipated. The Review Panel concluded that the two parts of the study had produced support both for those who claimed facilitated communication had validity and for those who doubted it.

BEHAVIOR AND THE PERSON

The behaviors of people labeled "autistic" are often unusual and appear to reflect lack of attention to and/or awareness of social and communication cues and/or severe intellectual disabilities. Perhaps it is such behaviors, including the on-again, off-again ability or willingness of students to communicate, that causes some people to worry that facilitated communication is no more real than a Ouija board.

Polly is a 15-year-old high school student who attends regular tenth-grade classes. Before being mainstreamed for the first time in ninth grade, Polly had attended a special school for students with severe disabilities. As her mother rushed to catch her up on math and other school content areas, Polly grasped concepts quickly. Given a subtraction problem that would yield a negative answer, Polly hesitated momentarily and then typed, BUT IT IS LESS THAN NAUGHT. I asked one of the teachers to describe Polly's best and worst days at the high school. The teacher explained that Polly had attended the school for three months before being willing or able to communicate with her and that her "best day" was "when she typed for me!" The "worst" day was when Polly climbed a tree and pulled her skirt up over her head. Another bad day was when Polly urinated in the playground. Her mother believes that Polly was testing the school's willingness to accept her *and* that she was saying, "Look, I'm retarded—do you still want me?"

Polly has several behaviors that are not uncommon for a person labeled "autistic," including a tendency to walk on the balls of her feet and sometimes clap her hands together. At school, she will occasionally pace about 15 feet from her locker to the top of the steps and back. She has a habit of picking up items, such as a wad of dried gum, off the ground and putting them in her mouth; if asked, however, she will stop this particular behavior. When she is seated, she sometimes places her hands between her legs and rocks forward. When she types on the Canon or on an electric typewriter, she frequently appears to be looking off into space, to the side rather than forward. When I would meet her at school or at DEAL, I would extend my hand to shake hers. As I grasped her hand, she would pull back, smiling.

Another DEAL student, Bette, could be observed typing independently while simultaneously grimacing and nervously flicking her fingers between words. On one occasion she wanted to stop doing fill-in-the-blanks "set work" and demonstrate to her parents that she could say what she wanted. She typed the words, LET ME SHOW THEM WHAT I CAN REALLY DO. As she finished typing, she slapped the table hard.

It was startling and incongruous. At home, her mother explains, ever since Bette has begun to type with her mother's facilitation, "it's a little bit puzzling that . . . she can . . . have these intelligent thoughts, and yet she will . . . wet . . . the bed or [do] something like that. It's puzzling for us." Bette often needs to be prompted to keep eating or to use a bathroom; otherwise she will sometimes not eat and has toileting accidents. The same seems true of her communication. She will not initiate it. But when her mother, her teacher, or a DEAL staff person begins a conversation with her and provides some support, such as a hand on her sleeve, she will usually communicate.

Such unusual behavior was typical of the people I observed. When I reached out to shake Amanda's hand as I was saying goodbye for the day, she reeled back on the sofa, emitted a high-pitched scream, and put one leg up in the air as her arms reached backward. Another student, Robert, smacked himself on the head with his open hand in the middle of a communication exercise. Then he typed to Crossley, IM NERVOUS. When she asked him, "Are you prepared to fight your nerves?" he responded, IM FINE. Tommy, age 12, screamed intermittently while typing. His typed communication was quite normal. Joshua, age 6, uttered sharp, high-pitched cries off and on during the session. When he typed, he did so quickly. He would type the letter Z repetitively unless stopped. At the same time, he could answer questions that Crossley posed. She asked him what a cowboy does and he answered, RIDES. He typed the letters very quickly. Eric had a habit of clipping the output tape off the Canon Communicator. As he typed, he occasionally stopped to slap the table and kick at it. He also kept repeating over and over "McDogs," which his mother said meant McDonalds. It appeared to be echolalic speech.

A young man, Paul, had sores and scratches on his face one day when he came to DEAL. When Crossley asked him what had happened, he responded enigmatically, typing, I HURT MY FACE. I BASHED MYSELF. I DO THINGS I DON'T WANT TO. Throughout the session he held a handful of cloth strips. He brushed the ends of these against his nose and face. He moaned while writing captions for a cartoon and also scrunched his face into a severe grimace. In the middle of the writing, Paul got up from his chair, reached under his black sweater and ripped his undershirt off. When Crossley asked, "Now Paul, what brought that on?" he responded, I FELT HOT. Later his mother told me that when she has asked him why he grabs pieces of cloth, he has responded, BECAUSE I CAN'T HELP MYSELF.

Edward, a high school student who is mute, implied that he could use his behavior calculatingly, refusing to type for his teachers and teaching assistants, holding out for his mother to be his facilitator. When Crossley asked him what he thought his teachers should do about him, he responded with humor: SHOOT ME.

AUTISM AS WE HAVE UNDERSTOOD IT

My initial difficulty in understanding and *accepting* the claim that children with autism who were mute or highly echolalic could be literate was undoubtedly influenced by what I knew about autism. Results from Crossley's work challenged current theories; she was getting results that no one else had, at least no one else I know of.

The literature on autism is complex and sometimes contentious. (For discussions of the controversies, see, e.g., Donnellan, 1985; Rimland, 1964; Rutter, 1968). Hypotheses about its cause have ranged from the psychogenic (Bettelheim, 1967), in which mothers are blamed for treating their children so coldly as to cause them to turn inward, to the physiological (Ornitz & Ritvo, 1976; Wetherby, 1984). Yet for all the struggles waged about the "true" nature of this baffling condition or set of behaviors, there is a great deal of agreement about the behavior of people labeled "autistic." Autism is characterized by problems of speech, language, and communication, including mutism, echolalia, and perseverative speech, difficulties with social interaction, stereotyped activity, a seeming concern for sameness or constancy of order, and a lack of response or unusual response to external events or actions (see, e.g., Rutter, 1978; Wetherby, 1984). There is less unanimity, however, about the implications of the behavior.

Language behaviors associated with autism include delay in the development of language and atypical expressions of language. Capturing the range of communication (or absence of it) that characterizes people labeled autistic, over a decade ago Wing (1978) summarized the work of Kanner (1943, 1971), Rutter (1968, 1978), and Eisenberg and Kanner (1956), concluding that "simple stereotypes of the less able child have their counterparts in the elaborate repetitive routines and the stereotyped speech of the more able children" (p. 40). When some children labeled "autistic" develop more elaborate speech, she notes, "it is characterized by very special abnormalities, suggesting that it is learned by rote without understanding of the rich and subtle associations of words" (p. 40)—in other words, what we might call delayed, transplanted, or recurrent echolalia. Children with autism are assumed to have difficulty understanding abstract concepts "such as time, color, size, and feelings. . . . Questions such as who, what, where, when, and

why   are   confusing"   (Schopler,   Reichler,   &   Lansing   1980,
p. 29).[4]

To use an analogy from electronics, the brain of a person with autism has been characterized more like a tape recorder and playback device than a computer. Those who display echolalia typically produce
words that are phonologically correct but that appear to be repetitions
of other people's phrases or chunks of phrases rather than the person's
own creation (Baltaxe & Simmons, 1977; Tager-Flusberg, 1981a, 1981b).
A number of such children echo television advertisements, seemingly
without linking the words to content. Often, they repeat phrases heard
much earlier, producing a delayed echo. Prizant (1983) calls such learning and expression a "gestalt style of language acquisition," a "gestalt
mode of cognitive processing," and "gestalt forms" of expression.

Until fairly recently, the assumption has been that although the
range of children labeled "autistic" includes some who perform in the
normal range, those who do not communicate or communicate only
with very limited numbers of echolalic phrases, often seemingly out of
context, and who have a variety of other unusual and seemingly asocial
behaviors in the main are not smart (see, e.g., Bartak, Rutter, & Cox,
1977; James & Barry, 1983; Ricks & Wing, 1975). Language in the form
of stereotyped phrases, incorrect semantics, and "parrot[ed] back long
phrases" (Schopler et al., 1980, p. 29) was presumed to be the hallmark
of incompetence. If they used words appropriately, this was thought to
result from "accidental operant conditioning because these words are
closely connected with rewards, especially food" (Ricks & Wing, 1975,
p. 209).

More recently, Prizant and Rydell (1984) have suggested that the
language of people with autism occurs along a continuum from little or
no symbolic or abstract activity to higher-order thinking and therefore
more normal language, although they caution that even in its most flexible form, echolalic language "rarely approaches the flexibility of 'normal' language forms and use" (p. 191). It is presumed that "highly echolalic autistic people use echoes as a means of engaging in ongoing
discourse" (Paul, 1987, p. 77), the facility of which is tempered by their
less-than-normal comprehension/communicative knowledge (Mirenda
& Schuler, 1988). In a discussion of echolalic expressions, Wetherby
(1984) hypothesizes that the person with autism relies on the limbic system for language, accounting for the person's "proficient use of communication to achieve environmental needs, and deficient use of communication for social purposes" (p. 29); more complex, intentional
communication would require cortical control.

Other important developments in recent years concern eye use and

communication methods. Assumptions about poor eye contact, for example, are being challenged by the growing realization that people with
autism may not lack eye-to-face contact but rather may use it differently
than do "normal" people (Mirenda, Donnellan, & Yoder, 1983; see also
Rutter, 1978). Additionally, a wide array of communication literature
supports teaching alternative modes of communication to people whose
speech is limited. Wetherby (1984), for example, advocates gestural
rather than vocal communication training for people with severe autism. She believes that instruction in manual language builds on exist-
ing strengths; "the autistic child's use of communicative gestures (for
example, giving, pointing, pushing away, head shaking, and nodding)
should be the primary consideration in language intervention and
should form the foundation for teaching words, whether through
speech or signs" (p. 31). Similarly, Schuler and Baldwin (1981) also note
that nonspeech methods allow easier, quicker access to communication
where there has been a breakdown in speech; "techniques that can be
used effectively to teach nonspeech responses, such as prompting or
'molding,' by guiding the student's hands through the required responses can't be used to teach speech" (p. 250).

Despite these changing perspectives on autism, scholars continue
to ask several questions similar to the ones Kanner (1943, 1971) raised
30 years after his original elaboration of the condition or set of behaviors. Is autism attended by a global intellectual deficit? Is autism a combination of specific acquisition/detection or receptive deficits? Is it reflective of processing deficits? Does autism reflect some other problems?

AN ALTERNATIVE INTERPRETATION OF UNUSUAL
COMMUNICATION

In light of the natural language produced by Crossley's students
through typing, we are compelled to search for an alternative explanation for their mutism and unusual speech. The obvious interpretation is
that they have a neurologically based problem of expression; in other
words, their difficulty with communication appears to be one of praxis
rather than cognition. Here, I use *praxis* not as a technical term but
merely to refer to the problem people with autism have in speaking, or
enacting their words or ideas. In contrast with the recording and playback metaphor used earlier, that person's speech ability is more like a
"dedicated" computer or language device, capable of expressing
phrases that have already been introduced aurally; the more advanced
version of this speech output device can select segments of phrases and

join them with others, although it generally lacks the program to "output" verb tense and pronouns correctly. With facilitation, the person can bypass his or her problem with verbal expression and type natural language.

By saying that the person with autism has a problem with praxis, I do *not* presume a deficit in understanding, but rather in expression. This interpretation also presumes that while there may be peculiarities in vision and learning, such as involuntary attention to light or acute sensitivity to certain sounds, these peculiarities do not necessarily reflect or create cognitive problems.

There is a small body of generally ignored literature on educational methods that, at minimum, does not contradict and may well support this praxis theory. In the late 1960s, two pediatricians in upstate New York employed the Edison Response Environment (ERE), "a cubicle enclosing a multiphase electric typewriter, projector, and programming device that could respond to or direct the user in a variety of ways," also called the "talking typewriter," to teach children with disabilities, including both learning and physical disabilities (Goodwin & Goodwin, 1969, p. 557). Sixty-five of their students had been diagnosed as autistic. Some students who were generally nonspeaking, except for some nonfunctional or echolalic speech, produced individual words and echolalic-like phrases. In some instances, the typing was followed by speech development. One child, for instance, is described as using the ERE

> in a sporadic and explosive fashion, often dashing up the stairs and into the booth in which it was installed, sometimes falling down en route, jumping up on the chair, lifting up the plastic lid and typing a few keys, then tearing off the paper and rushing downstairs. This continued over a period of several months. Effort to slow him down were only partially successful. (Goodwin & Goodwin, 1969, p. 558)

One day this student, Malcolm, seemed to change. He typed his name and then COW; then he left the room. On subsequent visits he seemed to recognize letters and words, but still did not talk. He was 4 years old at the time. With his acquisition of words, he also began to talk. "At eight, he has a large vocabulary, speaks intelligently with slight articulation defect, and is doing well in the second grade of a home instruction program" (Goodwin & Goodwin, 1969, p. 558). Another student, John, also with obvious autism, first produced only stereotyped typing. His teacher had described him as "hyperactive, jams food in his mouth, laughs in a peculiar cackle, won't mind, pushes other children, mimics, screams, never says I" (p. 560). At the Goodwins' clinic he typed the words on labels or signs, for example, UTICA CLUB (a regional beer) and WORK ZONE AHEAD. Later, John successfully completed the fifth grade.

It is difficult to discern from the Goodwins' notes and article how unusual or typical of their total subject group these students may have been. Many of the children with whom they worked remained institutionalized, were placed in special schools, or stayed at home with no education. In their concluding remarks on the ERE treatment and studies, the Goodwins argued that the ERE did not cause the students' intelligence but rather provided the means of expressing their intelligence: "The E.R.E. was the instrument that showed us abilities not measured by conventional psychological tests" (1969, p. 562).

Another approach to teaching academic and communication skills seems to have coincidentally built on and confirmed the Goodwins' experiences. In her book *Effective Teaching Methods for Autistic Children*, Oppenheim (1974) described "hand-over-hand" work with autistic children as a crucial aspect of first efforts at manual communication with students at the Rimland School for Autistic Children. Oppenheim's approach apparently used handwriting rather than typing, but the support she provided closely resembles Crossley's facilitated communication. She concluded that "the autistic child's difficulties with writing stem from a definite apraxia just as the nonverbal child's troubles with articulation do when speech finally develops" (p. 54). This communicative apraxia to which she referred has been described in a rare autobiographical account by Temple Grandin, a person with autism: "Up to this time, communication had been a one-way street for me. I could understand what was being said, but I was unable to respond. Screaming and flapping my hands was my only way to communicate" (Grandin & Scariano, 1986, p. 21). To overcome the student's apparent problem with "motor expressive behavior," Oppenheim (1974) found that it was "usually necessary to continue to guide the child's hand for a considerable period of time" (p. 54). She reported:

> Gradually, however, we are able to fade this to the mere touch of a finger on the child's writing hand. "I can't remember how to write the letters without your finger touching my skin," one nonverbal child responded when he was asked why he would not write unless he was touched. (p. 55)

Oppenheim concluded that students' problem with communication was "not recognition, but rather execution, in retaining the mental image of required motor patterns. Ultimately . . . finger-touching can be elimi-

FIGURE 1.1 Attitudinal Dimensions of Facilitated Communication

Presentation/Intention

1. Don't patronize people with nervous jokes, excessive familiarity, or babying. Be candid.
2. Be reasonably vulnerable and self-effacing (e.g., make note of your own errors, personal limitations, etc.).
3. Be apologetic about the assessment process. Invariably it involves asking questions that are too simple for the person being queried; apologize for speaking about the person in front of him or her (e.g., when asking a speaking person something about the person who is nonspeaking).
4. Being a dynamic support means being able to subordinate your own ego or, at the very least, being able to carry on a two-sided conversation, rather than imposing a one-sided dominant relationship. You have to be comfortable touching, being close to people, and supporting without taking over.
5. Don't use labels (e.g., rather than referring to people as having a particular disability, talk about "students like so-and-so").

Assumptions/Beliefs

6. Assume the person's competence. "It's far better to overestimate than underestimate a person's ability."
7. Believe communication is important; conveying this belief will help convey to the person that you see him or her as important, as your peer, as someone worthy of being "heard." Respond to what is typed as if it were spoken.

nated, and the child does write without it, *although some children want the touch of a finger on some other bodily surface such as the head, in order to write"* (p. 55, emphasis added).

Typing overcomes many of the difficulties of handwriting by simplifying the communication motion to pointing at or pressing letters or numerals. Oppenheim used some pointing at pictures and multiple choice captions and some typing, although it appears that she used typing mainly with the students whose "eye-hand coordination is sufficiently developed" (p. 58). Some educators have encouraged the use of language boards or symbol systems as other accessible means of communicating; but typing has the advantage of giving people access to nonprogrammed, nonpreselected communication symbols (for instance, the alphabet and numbers), thus making the communication their own.

Like the Goodwins, Oppenheim presumed a potential competence in her students, no matter how stereotyped or unusual their behavior.

She suggested that teachers ignore the behaviors and focus on teaching academic materials.

> The immaturities and/or deficiencies in the child's general functioning—
> including the fact that the child may be nonverbal or noncommunicative—
> should never be used as an index of the likelihood of his being able to
> absorb and benefit from teaching at higher cognitive levels—specifically,
> his ability to learn reading, writing, and mathematics. (1974, p. 90)

PRINCIPLES OF FACILITATED COMMUNICATION

Crossley's interactions with nonspeaking and aphasic people reflect a certain attitude.[5] Like Oppenheim and the Goodwins, she expects her students to communicate. She seems to admire them. She anticipates their producing interesting or even unique statements. Figure 1.1 shows the attitudinal dimensions of facilitated communication.

Facilitated communication practices vary considerably with the student's disability, behavior, style of interaction, personality, and other factors. Consequently, the method is not a uniform approach to teaching or supporting communication that can be used with each person, but rather a range of skills as described in Figure 1.2.

CONVERSATIONAL COMMUNICATION:
A MAINTENANCE SESSION

One Saturday morning, four students who communicate with facilitation (a facilitator gives wrist, arm, or hand-on-shoulder support) gathered at DEAL for a "maintenance" session.[6] Jane Remington-Gurney, a speech therapist, had arranged an activity to focus the group. "It's your task to find out as much as you can about Doug," she explained. She wanted them to practice interviewing, to "try to get . . . [their] questions out as quickly as [they can] in the most direct way." This skill, she believed, would help them engage in school classroom discussions more effectively, allowing them to ask questions before "the teacher's passed on to the next thing." She asked the students to figure out signaling devices to indicate when they wanted their printouts from the Canon Communicators read aloud by their facilitators. Polly was to put up her hand. Amanda would speak the word "ready." Peter would make a sound that approximates "ya." And Bette would tap the table where she was typing. Amanda, Bette, and Polly did most of their typ-

FIGURE 1.2 Facilitated Communication Practices

Physical Support

1. Attend to the person's physical location: feet on ground, typing device slanted (e.g., at 30-degree angle), stabilized table, nonslip pad under device and person, relaxed atmosphere, etc.
2. Initially, and only where necessary, provide physical supports under the forearm, under or above the wrist, or by helping a person to isolate the index finger to facilitate use of communication aid.
3. Pull back the hand or arm after each choice so that the person takes enough time to make a next selection and also to avoid repeating selections.

Being Positive

4. Progress through *successful* choices of pictures, words, sentences, letters, name spelling, first sentence, pulling back and reminding the person of the question or request whenever an incorrect or nonsensical choice is about to be made. Use semantic common sense (e.g., *n* does not come after *w*). In other words, help the person avoid errors.
5. Provide encouragement verbally and avoid telling the person that he or she has made an error or mistake during assessment (i.e., don't say "No" or "That was wrong" or "Incorrect"). Relate to the person naturally, conversationally.
6. Be direct and firm about the tasks: the need for practice, staying on task, focusing eyes, etc. Redirect the person to the tasks (e.g., "I'm going to count to 10—1, 2, 3, . . . 10" or "You know the house rules—work before play.").

Other Support

7. Keep your eyes on both the person's eyes and on the target (e.g., letter keys). This helps you identify and prevent errors caused by hand–eye coordination problems. It also helps you monitor whether the person is attending to the task.
8. Facilitated communication often requires the facilitator to do several tasks at once, for example, carrying on a verbal conversation with the person being assisted or with others in the room, watching the person's eyes, looking at the printed output, thinking of the next question or activity and at the same time keeping your mind on the present activity, and so forth, in addition to providing physical support and encouragement.

Achieving Communication/Overcoming Problems

9. Communication is a process, including support, fading, training receivers, etc. It is important to see it as a process and to recognize that people generally get better (i.e., faster and more independent) at it over time. Ongoing support increases a person's speed; thus independence is balanced by need for speed. Encourage lots of practice; practice builds accuracy and speed!
10. If a person is not communicating, is producing nonsensical communication, or is producing questionable or wrong communication (e.g., when you doubt the communication and believe that it might be you, the facilitator, who is initiating the choices of letters and words), revert to set, structured curricula (e.g., fill-in-blanks exercises, math drills).

(Continues)

FIGURE 1.2 *Continued*

---

11. Look for small differences in communication style or behavior, such as (1) radial ulnar instability—when a person's index finger swings to one side when approaching a letter, thus consistently getting a typographical error; (2) habitual, meaningless repetitions of certain letters; or (3) the tendency to revert to familiar, echolalic words or phrases.
12. Stop stereotyped utterances by ignoring them and focusing on the task of manual communication.
13. Ignore "behavior" such as screeches, hand slapping on desk, pushing desk away, and getting up by asking, for example, "What's the next letter you want?"

Curriculum

14. Don't use teaching or communication situations to "test" the person (e.g., "Is this a cup or a dollar bill?")
15. Give the student choices of work to do.
16. Use interesting materials: cartoons to be filled in, captionless magazine pictures, crossword puzzles, and other activities that would not offend adults, teenagers, or other age groups with whom you are working.
17. Don't start communication work by focusing on the expression of feelings; wait for feelings to come. Allow the person with whom you are working to initiate expression of feelings at his or her own choosing.
18. Get nonspeaking people working together; group sessions can be encouraging and motivating as well as interesting to people who are developing familiarity with facilitated communication. It is often helpful for facilitators (also called "receivers") to work with people other than their usual partners in group sessions.

---

ing independently, with support by a hand on a shoulder, or hand on a sleeve, leg, or elsewhere. Peter has a severe tremor and required arm support as he typed.

Jane began the interview by telling the group that my name is "Professor Doug Biklen."

Amanda responded first: PROFESSOR OF WHAT? she asked.

"Of special education," I explained, "at Syracuse University, in Syracuse, New York."

Peter asked me what I thought about EACH AREA OF AUSTRALIA. I said that I had not actually seen each area, but that Queensland had beautiful fish, warm weather, and overly conservative politics. I was admittedly clichéd about Sydney, calling it gorgeous but "too fast moving," and a little more detailed on Melbourne, singling out its array of ethnic restaurants, beautiful flowers, Victorian architecture, and a quaint but efficient tram system.

Amanda then asked, WHY ARE YOU HERE? I explained my interest in facilitated communication.

Next, Polly, who had heard me lecture several days earlier on the topic of integrating students with disabilities in typical schools, challenged me. YOU PUT EMPHASIS ON INTEGRATION, she noted. WHAT REALLY DOES INTEGRATION HAVE TO OFFER TO SOME TERRIBLY RETARDED PEOPLE? Her question was a variation on the theme, "I'm not retarded," and at the same time a question about what I believe.

"It offers the chance to be seen as an ordinary person. Of course that depends on other people being able to see them in this way," I responded.

YOU MUST BE SO IDEALISTIC, she accused me.

"I think I'm optimistic," I countered. "I think if I were to call my attitudes 'idealistic' I would be . . . saying that I don't quite believe them."

Amanda entered the conversation, seeming to argue at once with Polly and with society. TOO MEAN TO JUDGE PEOPLE BY ABILITY, she typed.

I returned to Polly's original question: "I don't know if it's fair to call someone 'so terribly disabled.'"

Peter returned us to personal details. ARE YOU MARRIED? he asked.

"I am," I answered.

WHAT'S YOUR WIFE'S NAME? he asked.

"Sari," I told him.

FUNNY NAME, Peter commented, with a loud, nearly laughing sound.

"I prefer to call it unusual," I joked.

Amanda returned the conversation to ideas. TELL ME HOW REALLY RETARDED PEOPLE GET PEOPLE TO SEE THEM AS ORDINARY HUMAN BEINGS, she typed.

"We might ask the question differently," I countered. "Why is it that so-called ordinary people do not see people who are so-called 'really retarded' as ordinary?"

Amanda found my question to be a non-answer: THAT GIVES ME THE QUESTION BACK, NOT ANSWER IT, she complained.

"What I meant by posing another question was to say that maybe the problem of gaining acceptance is not . . . owned by people labeled different but is a problem for those who do the labeling."

MOST PEOPLE NEED PROOF, Polly declared. HOW CAN THE DISABLED MEET SUCH A GAUNTLET?

Polly seemed to be challenging my ideas about the social construction of reality, specifically concerning disabilities, but also agreeing with me—the gauntlet is not the disability as much as it is society's demand for proof that people meet a standard of normality.

Amanda accused me of being glib: IF YOU HAD THAT PROBLEM YOU WOULD BELIEVE THAT THE PROBLEM WAS YOURS.

I did not give up the argument, although in retrospect I could have been more sympathetic and less chidingly argumentative. "I guess I'm saying that all of us need to force society to abandon the gauntlet. And I do consider it a problem of mine," I added.

NOT REALISTIC, Polly insisted.

At this point, Peter reentered the conversation, relating our discussion of acceptance to his own situation. Peter lives in an institution for people presumed to be intellectually disabled. DO YOU REALLY FEEL THERE'S A FUTURE FOR US OUT OF INSTITUTIONS? he asked.

"Yes, absolutely," I responded, "for everyone."

YOU'LL STILL HAVE TO MAKE CONCESSIONS, Polly typed.

"What do you mean by concessions?" I asked.

Jane tried to turn us away from the conversation to something more concrete: "Let me just remind you people to stick to the task which is to find out something about Doug."

Of course they were finding out a lot about me, albeit what I believe rather than the usual details.

Responding to my question about concessions, Polly explained, UN-LESS DARING PEOPLE SUBJECT THEIR OWN WISHES, IT WILL FAIL. In other words, people with disabilities can only be accepted if "nondisabled" people make accommodations.

I agreed. The state builds roads for car drivers and airports for people who want to fly. These seemed analogous; "Society can take communication seriously; it can encourage facilitated communication by training communicators and by making communication devices available, even if it were to mean delaying or setting aside other projects." Similarly, I offered, "Society can organize schools to serve *all* students."

Polly was unconvinced. She brought in economics: YOU ARE IL-LOGICAL BECAUSE THERE IS NO PROFIT IN DISABILITY.

At this point, Bette asked a seemingly unrelated question. She wanted to know if she would ever be able to communicate. Peter told her she did NOT HAVE TO WORRY.

Amanda, still focused on the airports analogy, accused me of naiveté: THAT FALLS DOWN, she reasoned, BECAUSE PEOPLE CAN WORRY ABOUT US BUT STILL NOT HAVE ENOUGH MONEY TO BUILD AIRPORTS. Society might insist on funding airports before human services.

Amanda then returned the conversation to Bette's question about talking. Responding to Peter, she declared, TO YOU IT MAY NOT BE, BUT TO ME IT IS AND I THINK IT IS TO BETTE, TO A PERSON WHO WANTS TO BE LIKE OTHERS.

Next, Amanda questioned my thoughts on deinstitutionalization. HAVE YOU THOUGHT ABOUT PEOPLE WANTING TO BE IN INSTITU- TIONS? she challenged.

"I believe in self-determination" I told her. "People should have choices. My experience has been that when people have the option to live outside the institution, they choose it. But society often doesn't cre- ate those options."

As I spoke, Polly was writing about Bette's desire to speak. I was now getting used to this on-again-off-again style of conversation, de- layed by the timing of speaking through typing devices. Polly had typed, NOT IMPORTANT IF YOU HAVE TYPING. JUST TELL YOURSELF THAT DARING TO REACH OUT IS MORE IMPORTANT.

Jane interjected a bit of humor: "Now who is idealistic?"

Now it was Bette's turn. I WANT TO ASK DOUG IF PEOPLE LIKE ME WILL EVER BE NORMAL . . . ABLE TO DO MORE THINGS THAT OTHER PEOPLE DO? I told her that I considered her normal in the sense that she has good ideas, lots of interests, especially an interest in other people, and that other people could come to see what I see.

I am not sure if this comment triggered Peter's next remark or whether his statement was just a general sally. He asked, WHY DO YOU MAKE PEOPLE BELIEVE THEY CAN DO THE IMPOSSIBLE?

"There is a consistency about this conversation," I joked. "I'm con- stantly being told by school people that I'm 'unrealistic' [in reference to school integration], by which they mean 'We don't want to hear what you say' or 'It's not going to work.' And then I come here and you say the same thing, except you are saying, 'They are not going to let it work.'"

Jane came to my defense: "Is this the way the group really feels or the way you've been conditioned to feel by the response you've had?"

Peter answered, I'VE TRIED FOR 13 YEARS TO BE NORMAL AND I'M STILL WHERE I STARTED.

Polly typed that she did not object to the principle of integration, BUT THE DISTASTE THAT HAS TO BE BROKEN DOWN IN EACH CASE.

"Why am I arguing with all of you?" I asked.

Bette returned the conversation to the question about being nor- mal. I DO NOT THINK THAT. I AM NOT ABLE TO DO MANY THINGS. Then she asked, CAN DOUG BE OUT OF AMERICA FOR VERY LONG?— That is, would I be around to facilitate her communication, and to be a friend?

Polly typed about her own struggle for integration and acceptance. SOME REALLY TERRIBLE KIDS HAVE NO RESPONSIBILITY. Her mother explained that Polly was referring to the fact that the other students in her school do not have to forge their way in school or society; they can fool around, make nuisances of themselves, and act immature. Polly added that she and other students with autism have a responsibility THRUST ON US. JUST WANT TO BE LIKE THOSE TERRIBLE KIDS.

I told her I understood.

Ever the detail person, Peter asked me if I make a lot of money. Bette asked if my job makes me happy. I answered "yes" to both.

Finally, Amanda gave in and joined my side of the integration argument. HELP GET THE SKEPTICS TO THINK LIKE YOU. WE ARE SO CHEESED. AT LEAST I AM.

THE QUESTION OF PROOF

Inevitably, an element of my examination of facilitated communication involved looking for proof that the words were the students' own. Proof took two forms: (1) Some students were able to type independently, either without physical contact or with a hand on the shoulder, leg, thread of the sleeve, or other location. (2) For those who lacked independent communication, the nature of communication varied across individuals, despite the fact that a single facilitator might be facilitating; there were facial expressions, verbal noises, including laughter, or other signs of a person's understanding of communication; and/ or in some instances, the content of the communication suggested that it *really* came from the person communicating, not from the facilitator.

Instances of independent communication were numerous. A dozen students were observed typing phrases independently. Six of them communicated independently (without hand support on the arm or hand) much of the time, with at least two different facilitators. Of those who typed independently less often or not at all, nearly all had only recently been introduced to facilitated communication. Yet one of the people who was independent had only recently been introduced to facilitated communication. While it is possible in any instance of facilitation involving the forearm, wrist, or hand for the person's communication to be influenced by a facilitator, presumably such instances, if they were particularly important, could be double-checked at another time by withholding support. Independent communication of a similar level of literacy and content to that which was observed being physically facilitated was taken as validating a person's communication.

Petrov is an adolescent who attends a school for deaf and hearing-impaired students. He wears hearing aids, but he is not deaf. For years, people assumed he was deaf. As I observed him in a class at the deaf

school in which other students were all either profoundly deaf or hearing impaired, Crossley held just the cloth of his sweatshirt, not even
resting her hand on his shoulder. He typed answers to math problems.
I asked why he had hearing aids. He typed, I EXCUSE MYSELF, HELP-
ING MYSELF BY PRETENDING TO BE DEAF. In sociological terms, he was
"managing stigma"; his reasoning seems to be that his hearing aids imply a hearing loss, which explains his not speaking and also suggests
that his absence of speech is not due to an intellectual disability. He had
typed this independently, but the originality and unexpected character
of his answer also seemed a kind of "proof" that the words were his.

In instances where the person did not type independently, without
support under the forearm or on the hand, there was often evidence
that the person worked independently. Brian, for example, has little affect in his expressions. Yet he has a slight smile at appropriate moments.
In my conversations with him, his mood and comfort changed as we
communicated. Initially, his responses to me were quite formal. He
typed, for example, I AM ACHIEVING A GREAT DEAL ALREADY AND I
AM HOPING TO ACHIEVE MUCH MORE. His teacher told me it took her six
months of trying before she became able to facilitate for Brian. She held
her hand on his. When I asked what it was like before he learned to
type, he abandoned his formalism: IT WAS HELL AND I COULD NOT
EVEN BEGIN TO MAKE MY NEEDS KNOWN. At one point, his teacher and
Crossley left the room. I asked Brian if his mother and father would be
coming to the center to talk to us or if just one of his parents was coming. I asked him to type B for both or O for one. He typed B. Both
arrived a little while later. Toward the end of our conversation, with his
father facilitating him in his conversation, Crossley asked Brian if he
had anything he wanted to say to her. He responded, I'VE TALKED A
LOT ABOUT YOU [he had been speaking with me]. I DONT NEED TO
TALK TO YOU. Characteristically, Brian's face displayed its usual nearly
expressionless facade, with just a slight smile at the corner of his mouth.
Independently, Brian turned off the Canon.

Clearly, the level of proof for those people who were not communicating independently was less ironclad. Yet the indicators that communication was the person's own were strong enough, in my view, to
justify the continuing assumption of its validity.

CONCLUSION

The implications of the DEAL students' communication are enormous. Among other things, it forced me to redefine autism. While the
students in this study included some who previously had been thought

of as severely intellectually disabled and autistic, they demonstrated un-expected literacy skills. The Saturday-morning group, for example, in-stead of querying me about the concrete facts of my life, were far more focused on my beliefs. They chose to converse about concepts. Each of them obviously engages in internal conversations; each had thought about the issues we discussed. Also, they had chosen to speak about their feelings. Obviously their problem was in neither cognition nor af-fect. Rather, their difficulty has been in sharing what they know and feel.

Readers of this chapter will naturally ask whether facilitated com-munication will allow all people labeled autistic to communicate at high levels of literacy. This question is not easily answered. First, the cate-gory of autism, like many disability categories, is not as precise or as uniformly applied as we might imagine or desire. A broad range of be-haviors are defined as autistic, with the result that people who seem quite different one from another share the label of "autism." Second, it is of course not possible to prove that *all* people so labeled will achieve a particular level of communication. We can learn about their potential only through practice. Third, it is quite possible, even probable, that within the group of those categorized as autistic there will be a very wide range of intellectual ability, as there is in the general population. Nevertheless, it is especially noteworthy and encouraging that among those who are able to demonstrate high levels of literacy and numeracy through facilitated communication are people who were previously pre-sumed to be among the "lowest" intellectually functioning persons la-beled "autistic."

Before they could communicate, these students were evaluated pri-marily by their repertoires of unusual behaviors. Now that they *do* com-municate, schools, families, and society ask: Will the stereotyped and other behaviors associated with autism diminish or even disappear as students become more fluent communicators? This is not known. While there is observational evidence that some bizarre behaviors decline—Polly, for example, no longer makes a habit of climbing trees at her high school and pulling her skirt up—others persist. Paul did rip his tee-shirt off during a communication session, and he still clutches strips of cloth, occasionally brushing them against his face; Polly still puts objects in her mouth, but less often than in previous years; and Bette still slaps her work table periodically. It is noteworthy that at the time of these observations, Bette had begun communicating fluently only a few months earlier and Paul was living in a locked ward of an institution where he had no opportunities to communicate. Crossley believes that students who have been able to use facilitated communication at home and in school over a period of months and even years demonstrate fewer unusual behaviors than when they first came to DEAL. "We never could have mainstreamed [in school] so many of the students if they hadn't changed," she argues.

The question of how much acceptance Crossley's students will find in their families and schools cannot be separated from their behavior or from the perceptions and attitudes of people around them. Students in Polly's high school English class regularly volunteer to be in discussion groups with her; the teacher says they recognize that Polly has creative ideas about the readings they discuss. But she still does not have classmates whom she considers to be her friends. Polly told me that she worries about the idea of possibly having friends. She has not yet had one, other than her mother, her siblings, Rosemary Crossley, and people like herself who use facilitated communication. She is afraid. I DONT KNOW WHAT TO FEEL, she told me. David Armbruster said he wanted girls at his school to stop MOTHERING him. I WANT A GIRL–FRIEND, he declared. Not surprisingly, the degree to which DEAL students can or will reach out and communicate to others seems to depend on how others receive them.

Awareness of that fact pervades Crossley's work. She embraces the age-old, but not always honored, belief in students' capacity to learn and express themselves. From her first interaction with students, in which she always uses no-fail and open-ended assessments, to her unstructured dialogues with students about their lives, she engages them, speaking personally and directly to them, never patronizing. Her purpose, after all, is not to test their competence but to find ways for them to reveal their competence. She warns us against the persistent tendency to impose low expectations on students. Their poetry, their letters, and their statements are the text of her work and comprise both the product and the material of her teaching.

Perhaps more than most students, the students described in this chapter *demand* an education-through-dialogue approach, in which teachers and students learn from each other and in which schooling validates personal expression. It is as if these people, labeled "autistic," by *not* communicating except with certain facilitators and in certain supportive circumstances, are saying what all students at one time or another have said, if less obviously: We will reveal ourselves, we will show our creativity, when we feel appreciated, when we are supported.

NOTES

1. Jonothan left out spaces between words and repeated several letters without correcting the errors, although he later demonstrated the ability to put

in spaces and make his own corrections; like any electric typewriter, the Canon Communicator will produce the same letter more than once if the person typing lingers on a key.

2. In all I observed 27 people, 9 of whom were being seen by DEAL staff for the first time and had not previously communicated in more than single words or signs or echolalic phrases. The 6 people observed at DEAL who are not included in this account had a variety of other disabling conditions, including Down syndrome, cerebral palsy, and other physical and intellectual disabilities.

3. Crossley's recommendation in instances of doubt over the communication is to ask facilitators to return to "set work" in which the correct answers are known, at least until the person's facility with communication increases and becomes more independent.

4. The assumption has been that children with autism are unable "to analyze and categorize both linguistic and nonlinguistic data" (Menyuk, 1978, p. 115). This inability has been thought to limit the person's "performance in certain intellectual tasks and social adaptation" (pp. 114–115). Consistent with this interpretation, Wing explains the apparent "social avoidance and poor eye contact . . . as arising from the absence of any mechanism for understanding the environment" (1978, p. 41).

5. The principal differences between Crossley's approach and that of most other educators of children with autism is her addition of hand-over-hand, wrist, or arm facilitation in the initial stages of typed communication *and* the expectation that students are capable of sophisticated communication.

6. As with all observations and interviews, this session was audiorecorded. Since the facilitators spoke the students' words aloud, it was possible to develop a verbal transcript of the entire conversation. Typographical errors are not reproduced here since my record of the conversation was reconstructed from the audiotape and my handwritten notes, not from the output of the individuals' typing devices.

Part I

USING FACILITATED COMMUNICATION

CHAPTER 2

The Syracuse Experiment: Getting Started with Facilitated Communication

Upon return to the United States, I was determined to implement facilitated communication in the Syracuse area. Late in the fall of 1989, the Jowonio School called a meeting of parents, teachers, and speech therapists at which I shared the story of my observations in Australia, relating my initial questions about the method, including my skepticism, as well as my excitement at the students' literacy. Together we looked at videotaped examples of students in Australia. These videos revealed the early stages of one student's typing in which she was supported at the hand and wrist and then later examples of her typing with support of a hand on the shoulder and occasional support under the forearm. This student made noises and spoke individual words and phrases but could not carry on a verbal conversation. The video showed her conversing with public school officials by typing. They spoke to her, and she typed. Another student was shown being asked to guess the occupation of an individual who is frequently in attendance at the DEAL Communication Centre. The student surmised first that the man was a janitor and then that perhaps he was a gardener. Although his answers were wrong—the man was DEAL's computer scientist—this video sequence illustrated several aspects of facilitated communication training. The student did his spelling on a "low-tech" device, in this case a letter board with a Plexiglass key guard, placing his right index finger on letters by pointing through holes in the plexiglass; key guards ensure that students do not hit two selections at once. He did so with little or no apparent affect. He responded to a question that required a specific response; essentially this was a fill-in-the-blanks exercise, a form of set work often used in the early stages of facilitated communication training. Throughout the session, the student could be observed trying to move away and having to be redirected to the communication task. He stood up for most of the activity, with the facilitator holding his hand and arm with one hand

and holding him around the shoulders with her other hand. A third student on the DEAL video typed on an electronic typing instrument with a facilitator who held just a thread of her sweater. When the student gazed at the facilitator's hand holding the thread, the facilitator remarked, "That's right, I'm holding just a thread of your jumper"—*jumper* is a colloquial term in Australia for "sweater."

In addition to these Melbourne videos, I explained facilitated communication as being comprised of several basic elements (see Section I of the Appendix), providing essentially a streamlined version of the figures in Chapter 1. I described the range of physical support that would be required, varying with individuals: Some would need assistance in isolating the index finger; nearly all would need to have the letter board or keyboard located at a comfortable height, at or below waist level, and would require assistance in pulling back after each selection; a few individuals would need backward pressure or resistance applied to their arm as they typed, to help them achieve stability and to overcome impulsive, echoed typing of "canned" expressions. As for the content of first sessions, we discussed the value of using a variety of set-work activities, that is, structured materials with predictable responses, such as multiple choice, fill-in-the-blanks, yes/no, spelling and vocabulary, and sentence-completion exercises. While such activities could be designed for any level of competence, the format allows the facilitator to hold the individual back from obvious errors, thus allowing for error-free practice and the consequent confidence building that flows from it. Perhaps one of the most controversial aspects of the method was my recommendation that facilitators not "test" individuals as to whether they were in fact doing the typing; I believed that we needed to help build their confidence and that premature efforts to validate students' communication would make this impossible. At the same time, I hoped that even in early sessions, facilitators could work on reducing the amount of physical support provided.

After an evening discussion of facilitation that lasted less than three hours and was attended by approximately 50 parents and educators, people began to try the method. The mother of a 4-year-old reported back at the next evening meeting, a month later. Using facilitation, she had discovered that her son knew the alphabet. She had asked him to point to letters and he had responded. Now she wanted to know how to teach him to read. She did not know if he could read or not, but she assumed this would have to be taught. The discussion group recommended two things: Treat him as you would any child, by pointing out words to him, by showing him how they are spelled, by labeling objects at home, and by reading to him; and encourage him to communicate through writing, in other words, facilitate him in pointing to letters, either the first letter of words or whole words, to make choices of foods, to indicate activities he wanted to do, or to make other selections that are a normal part of home life, and to spell out his thoughts.

This parent's report of beginning literacy skills gave other parents and teachers encouragement that facilitated communication might work in Syracuse. One of the people present at this second meeting was a speech therapist from a local elementary school, who began to use facilitation with a boy named Mark and several other students.

ONE OF OUR FIRST STUDENTS

Mark Gordon is 7 years old. He attends a first-grade public school class at the Edward Smith School, a public elementary school in Syracuse, New York. He is classified as autistic and has many of autism's classic characteristics. He does not speak. He often looks away when people speak to him or when people are conversing. He fidgets with objects, flicks his hands, and has poor muscle tone. Sometimes he claps his hands together in front of his face and smiles, seemingly when he is excited or pleased. At other times, he hits himself, grabs and pulls other people's hair, and pinches and hits others. In response to loud or high-pitched noise, he covers his ears with his hands. Prior to January 1990 he had very limited communication. He could use two signs, for "eat" and "more"—efforts to teach him additional signs had been unsuccessful; and he would grab objects, cry, and have tantrums. But that appeared to be the extent of his communicative ability. His parents and teachers could only guess at what he felt, what he knew, and what he might want. In January 1990, when Mark was 6 years old and enrolled in one of the Smith School's regular kindergarten classes, he was introduced to facilitated communication. Over time, Mark revealed unexpected thinking and literacy skills similar to the abilities of students I observed in Australia.

Mark communicates using an Apple IIe computer, a Canon Communicator (an electronic typing device on which the alphabet is displayed sequentially—A, B, C, etc.), and a laminated 7″ × 5″ alphabet board. His speech therapist or teacher supports his hand from underneath, helping him to isolate his index finger. On occasion they are able to reduce this support to holding his arm at the wrist. With hand and wrist support, the therapist or teacher slows down his movement toward a selection; when Mark has made a selection, the facilitator pulls his hand back about 8 or 10 inches from the target—otherwise he presses his selections repeatedly, perseverating.

Mark's first efforts to communicate were faltering but promising. Initially his speech therapist showed him pictures and asked him questions about them. He in turn pointed to pictures that correctly answered her questions. Within days he was typing words. He pointed to a picture of a woman, a man, a boy, and a girl, and then was given a toy woman, man, boy, and house. He placed his index finger on the woman. He then spelled MOM. Prior to this, no one knew he could read or spell out words. Next he pointed to the boy. The therapist asked him what he wanted to call the boy. He typed, MARK. A few moments later he took the people out of the house and did not seem eager to continue working. The therapist asked him if he was all done with the picture book and toys. He did not respond with typing but stood up and picked up some balloons from a shelf. "You could tell me 'balloons,'" the therapist explained. Mark spelled BAL and stopped. The therapist finished the word by typing LOONS. Mark tried to blow up a balloon but was not successful. The therapist then did it for him and asked, "Who blew up the balloon?" He typed SCHU and gave a broad smile. The therapist's last name is Schubert.

At a subsequent communication session several days later, the therapist asked Mark what he wanted to play. He typed MARB L, then looked away. He glanced back at the letters for an instant and completed the word, ES. She asked what color marble he wanted first. Mark spelled RED. Then she asked, "What color do you want next?" He typed GREEN and laughed gleefully. Next he typed BLUE. She then asked if he wanted to continue playing with the marbles. He again typed BLUE and stood up. Then he spelled ECBBD. The therapist explained that it was hard for her to understand what he meant. He then spelled MOOJ. She still could not understand him. Such words or sequences of letters occasionally slipped into Mark's work, two or three such instances in a half hour session; yet most of his typing is easy to understand.

Mark's ability to point to letters and construct words marked a dramatic shift in his ability to communicate. Prior to the time when we introduced facilitated communication to him, he had no means of expressing himself precisely. Now, when asked if he wanted a drink, he was able to type YES and to add TANG or another specific choice. When asked what he wanted to eat, he typed RESINS. Within two months of beginning to communicate, he moved from structured questions and fill-in-the-blanks work, where the answers were predictable, to words and sentences that he initiated.

On March 21, a little more than two months after beginning to type, Mark and another student were involved in a role-play about going to a restaurant. Mark typed to the therapist, HE CAN BE THE WAITER. The next day, his sentences concerned how he was feeling. He typed to his therapist, YOU TELL MOM IM SAD MISSING DAD. His father has to be away from home for long periods because of his work. By June he was typing sentences at each of his daily therapy sessions. One day he announced that he wanted to move from the kindergarten to the next grade: I WANT TO BE IN GRADE FIRST. On June 5 he typed, I FEEL LONELY WHJEN I HAVE NO KIDS AT MY HOUSE. I WANT MY MOM TO KNUOW THAT I LIKE TO BE WITGH KIDS. These statements revealed his ability to share his feelings. He told his speech therapist that he had begun to have toileting accidents because he was anxious that the school year was coming to a close and he would not have her as a facilitator anymore: I AM WETTING CBECAUSE I DONT WANT TO LEAVE YOU. In reference to the next year, he typed, I WORRY ABOUT THEPIST NOT TALKING WITH MEP. His therapist explained that the new therapist would use the same method with him. He typed, I WANT TO MEET HNESR HER. Then he typed, I WANT TO WRITE LETTERS TO YOU. I WANT TO GIVE YOU A HUG.

The June issue of the school newsletter included Mark's first poem:

>   ME
> I like to play
> And have my way
>   Mark

Mark's ability to type sentences and to use typed communication to engage in conversation has given us cause for considerable excitement. In other ways he has not changed. He still has tantrums, including bouts of hurting himself. He still does not speak. He still does not play in typical ways with toys. He still has autism. But now he communicates with words and sentences, not because we taught him how to read or what to say but merely because he now possesses a means to express himself.

Mark is not an isolated case. During the same six-month period in which *he* began to communicate, 20 other students, all of whom are classified as autistic and either do not speak or speak only echolalically—repeating words and phrases they have heard in the immediate situation or in previous contexts—also began to communicate through pointing and typing. All of these students attend typical pre-, elementary, middle, and high schools. All of the preschool and elementary students attend classes that include nondisabled students and are taught by both "regular" and special educators (Biklen, 1992a). Table A.1 in the Appendix describes the students from our Syracuse studies in terms of their ages, verbal communication ability, communication systems prior to the introduction of facilitated communication, communication level with facilitation, and level of support provided by facilitators; the 21 students with whom we worked during the first six months are identified by an asterisk next to their names.

OBSERVING STUDENTS USING FACILITATED COMMUNICATION

The 21 students who were the focus of our initial efforts to use facilitated communication were selected by their parents and teachers. These students were identified as autistic and had major communication disorders, including being mute or using echolalic speech (no one asked us to work with any students labeled autistic who *were* able to communicate conversationally with speech). Those who had speech were limited to greetings, echoed words or phrases, and some labeling. None of the students had socially useful speech; in other words, none could carry on an oral conversation.

From the outset, including the first presentation of facilitated communication to the 50 or so parents and teachers, I treated every discussion, parent or teacher report, and observation as part of our research project (see Section II of the Appendix). With nine graduate students and one faculty colleague, I began to gather data, including audio-recordings of the initial discussions/training sessions for parents and teachers on facilitated communication, observations of the students in their classrooms when not using facilitated communication, observations of the students when using facilitated communication with a teacher, teaching assistant, or speech therapist in the classroom and/or in separate speech therapy sessions, examples of students' typing from such sessions, videotapes of the students using facilitated communication in their classrooms and in therapy sessions, and interviews of selected parents and teachers. The purpose of the videotapes was to enable us to observe facilitation sessions over and over again, allowing us to develop insights about the nature of the support provided, students' interactions with teachers and others, students' and facilitators' positioning, and individuals' responses to facilitation sessions.

Our 11-member research group had extensive background in qualitative research, although this particular study differed from any of our previous studies in that we were involved both in creating the subject of our inquiry—we had introduced facilitated communication to the Syracuse area and would continue to consult on how-to aspects of the method throughout the course of our observations—and in studying it. In other words, we ourselves were subjects of the study as well as researchers. In contrast to most qualitative research, our role as participants was central to the inquiry, at least at the beginning stages.

FACILITATED COMMUNICATION:
WITH WHOM SHOULD WE TRY IT?

Traditional assumptions about autism (see Section III of the Appendix) seemed to be of little value in guiding our work with facilitated communication. For example, if we had assumed that many individuals with autism had receptive and/or processing problems, had specific or global cognitive deficits, and had difficulty analyzing language, then there would have been no reason to believe that facilitated communication would be helpful to the majority of people so classified. Similarly, if acquisition of language skills had been presumed to be related to an ability to play with toys and to engage in imaginative play, given that we had no evidence that either was possible, we would have had to presume that facilitated communication would have little likelihood of success. Other assumptions about autism include the following: Many individuals are unable to analyze language effectively and therefore use pronouns and verb tense incorrectly; people with autism learn best through rote exercises, reproducing language without understanding it; many lack internal language; many cannot tolerate change, demand order, and fail to understand change; many appear to be sensitive to touch (tactile defensiveness); and most important, people with autism have difficulty recognizing or appreciating others' feelings. These assumptions pose a formidable barrier to facilitated or any other means of augmenting or supporting communication. In fact, because of these assumptions, many of the teachers and parents who attended the first meetings about facilitated communication at the Jowonio school found it hard to imagine that the method could work with many of the individuals they knew. Yet the weight of examples that I had brought from Australia suggested that our best approach was to place all such assumptions about autism and related disabilities in abeyance as we tried the method.

Obviously, not all people with autism are perceived as possessing all of the qualities listed in the above-mentioned assumptions. And not all people in the field of autism would subscribe to all of these assumptions. Nevertheless, these are assumptions that many parents and educators mentioned to us. Little by little, we would come to question nearly all of them. Indeed, the examples of Mark's communication mentioned above contradict many of these assumptions.

With facilitation, it becomes obvious that the students *do* understand and process language and that absence of usable spoken language does not justify an assumption of intellectual deficit, noninterest in social contact, absence of normal emotionals, or lack of other typical affective and intellectual abilities. We could not assume that students were incompetent in language, thinking, or feeling simply because they appeared to be so. Obviously, if students could respond to abstract questions and have conversations by typing, they must surely possess internal language. Some of the students with whom we have used facilitation do appear to be sensitive to touch some of the time, but this was not a problem overall and did not impede our supporting people's hands or arms. (For an excellent discussion of tactile defensiveness, and suggestions on how to introduce supportive, firm, but not engulfing or suffocating touch, see Grandin & Scariano, 1986.) And some do report sensitivity to certain sounds as well as visual stimuli.

Similarly, students' behaviors do not predict with whom facilitation will succeed. Students with autism do not seem to respond normally to the world around them: They often appear inattentive to external events; they have difficulty with speech; they often show compulsive concern for order; and some of them abuse themselves by hitting, biting, and head banging. Yet Mark exhibits these behaviors *and* types effectively with facilitation, revealing normal intelligence and a strong desire for social relations. The unusual behaviors are not predictors of students' communicative potential. The behaviors are merely that—behaviors.

In fact, many "autistic" behaviors can be observed in so-called normal people, albeit with far less frequency and intensity. Recently, I asked a group of teachers, parents, and university students to look at a list of "autistic" behaviors and identify similar behaviors of their own. My purpose in suggesting the exercise was twofold. I wanted to deflate the importance that is often attributed to such unusual behaviors, and I hoped that the activity would help the group see that people with autism are not terribly unlike other people, including themselves. The exercise was a strategy consistent with the qualitative researcher/ethnographer's orientation toward perspective taking. We were attempting to put ourselves in the position and perspective of the person with autism. The group of parents, teachers, and university students listed numer-

FIGURE 2.1 "Autistic" Behaviors and Analogous Behaviors Observed in the Nondisabled Population

- *Eye gazing over a broad range of objects:* Often, when people are preoccupied or nervous they will glance flittingly over their surroundings.

- *Desire for order (everything in its place):* A typical response to being overwhelmed with too many things to do, when it is hard to decide what to do first, is to neaten one's office, place papers in piles or file them, and so forth.

- *Hand flicking, spinning and other repetitive movements:* Many people report tapping their fingers, moving one leg up and down, and humming as unconscious activities.

- *Gazing at lights or objects for a period of time:* Sometimes, objects give off interesting light patterns or look different from different vantage points and thus attract protracted attention.

- *Jumping, hand clapping:* Nearly everyone can think of a time of excitement when he or she has jumped up and down or clapped their hands together.

- *Getting up from seat:* When studying or trying to write a speech, essay or other composition, people often get up, expending nervous energy or simply to think about what they are learning or trying to write.

- *Echoed speech:* Often one utters words associated with events going on around him or her or that one may be privately daydreaming about but which are not the words one intends to speak. Similarly, when not paying attention, people often call others by a wrong name, label an object incorrectly, or complete a task incorrectly (e.g., putting a butter dish in the kitchen cabinet rather than in the refrigerator).

- *Need for facilitating touch:* A hand on the shoulder can help a person focus or to not feel alone.

- *Seeing with feet (i.e., walking as if blind, placing one foot ahead of another tentatively, as if checking one's footing):* Whenever one feels unsure of his or her footing, for example when walking down stairs at night, it is common to put out a foot tentatively and feel one's way.

- *Need for a stabilizing touch:* When a person's hand is shaking, perhaps as a reaction to being hungry or having too much caffeine, it is common for the person to steady the hand with his or her other hand.

- *Desire for "compression":* Many people report feeling secure curled up in their bed, when sitting in an easy chair, or held in the arms of a friend. Children can be observed covering themselves with couch cushions or wedging themselves in the cracks of a large couch.

- *Biting of fat at the base of thumbs:* Many people bite their fingernails or callouses on their hands.

- *Screeches and gleeful laughter:* It is not unusual for a person to give a yelp at a moment of excitement or to groan to indicate unhappiness.

- *Ability to say one thing and do another:* Often people hum a tune or sing a song while reading a book or writing a letter; this can be accomplished as long as one does not try to think about the tune or song.

(Continues)

FIGURE 2.1 *Continued*

- *Problem of initiation and praxis (i.e., apraxia):* Many people hesitate to begin a physical activity that they do not feel confident about, such as trying to rub one's stomach clockwise with an arm while moving one foot counterclockwise on the floor.

- *Doing better for people who express confidence:* A person frequently performs better for a superb coach or teacher in whom she or he feels confident.

- *Hitting self, slapping self:* Many people hit themselves when excited (sometimes in happiness) or upset.

ous examples. These are displayed in Figure 2.1. It thus appears that the behaviors of people with autism, while unusual, are only so in intensity and prevalence.

Since these "prefacilitation" assumptions about autism and the behaviors of people with autism are not useful guides for determining with whom to try facilitation and since it is unhelpful and apparently incorrect to presume that so-called higher-functioning people would be better candidates for facilitation than those presumed to be less competent, we devised a set of criteria for selecting people with whom to try facilitation (see Section IV of the Appendix) that basically ignored the traditional assumptions about autism. The criteria included: (1) Students with autism or related developmental disabilities who do not speak *or* whose speech is not very functional; (2) students who have these problems with speech *and* who may be presumed to have severe intellectual disabilities; (3) students who have these problems with speech and for whom we may have no evidence of literacy and numeracy skills; and (4) students who have these problems with speech and who may also exhibit poor eye-hand coordination, low muscle tone or high muscle tone, index finger isolation and extension problems, perseveration, use of two hands to do a task only requiring one, tremor, instability of the finger, hand and arm, problems of initiating an action (long delays), and unusual responses to what is going on around them (Crossley, 1990).

Inevitably, irrespective of these or other criteria, some people asked: Aren't there some individuals for whom facilitation will not work? When do you decide that it is not working and just give up? Parents and teachers who raised these questions seemed driven by two motivations. Many wanted reassurance that the method *would* work with particular students; they were skeptical that it could really work with certain students who met the criteria but with whom other teaching methods had produced minimal results. Others simply wanted to know for whom facilitated communication would *not* be successful. In other words, they wanted a finer, more precise guide.

The questions about people with whom facilitation might not work and about when to give up are at once difficult and simple questions to answer. Obviously, there are some people with whom facilitators will have less or no success and some people with whom facilitators will have to struggle for months, perhaps even more than a year, to achieve fluent communication. My own experience was that people with very stereotyped, obsessive speech were sometimes most difficult to work with; they tended to type their obsessive language.

It is important to remember that a person's failure to communicate may as easily derive from limitations of facilitators and of teaching technique as from disability. Since we cannot change the latter, we must work on the former. A psychologist recently heard my colleagues and me give a presentation on facilitation. She subsequently tried the method with her 24-year-old brother, Chris, who has autism and who previously was assumed to be severely intellectually impaired. He does not speak. With facilitation, he was able to identify foods, colors, and objects and to write simple sentences. But he did not progress beyond these rather simple communications. His sister became frustrated, reporting to me, "He's at a plateau; he's started just doing anything, just pressing keys." Then he would become obsessed with the memory button on the Canon Communicator, pressing it on and off and watching its light change from green to red and back again. She wanted to know: If his problem of autism was truly a problem of praxis or of expression, then why was he not progressing to more sophisticated communication when facilitated? Probably it was a combination of factors, one of which was that his obsessive behaviors got in the way of his communicating; he needed to be told to stop them and he needed to be encouraged to do something more interesting. "The fact that he engages in compulsive or obsessive behaviors," I told her, "doesn't mean that he does not understand what you say to him or that he cannot understand abstract concepts. We can't assume that the obsessive behaviors have anything to do with what he knows, thinks, or wants to say." Interestingly, she had evidence that this might be true, that the obsessive behavior did not at all reveal his state of mind, but she could not be sure. When she took him to the dentist to have his teeth cleaned, instead of becoming very agitated and needing anesthesia, he needed only a supportive hand on his shoulder to stay calm. Staff at the dentist's office were shocked. "What did you do?" they asked, incredulous. Prior to the visit to the dentist, his sister had talked about the dentist, had explained what was going to happen, and had asked if he liked the dentist. He answered by typing YES. But then he had lapsed into his obsessive pressing of the memory button, watching the light change from red to green and back again. Eventually his sister gave up her efforts to communicate with him that day, feeling as if she were carrying on a one-sided conversation, not sure if he was listening at all. But his demeanor at the dentist's office suggested that he had been listening all along.

In the various communication sessions with her brother, this psychologist typically asked him to type picture captions, for example, naming people in pictures and labeling objects. It seemed obvious to me that he might be bored. I suggested that if he was not yet plunging into fluent conversation, she should at least build the communication sessions around topics that were of genuine interest to her and hopefully to him as well. I asked if she knew what kind of music he liked. She said, "Yeah, but he only has one tape that he will listen to, one particular Beatles tape." I asked if he had typed that he only liked one tape. She said, "No, he grabs it." It seemed to me that his constant use of the Beatles tape might be just another obsessive behavior, not indicative of his full range of interests in music. In fact, when she went with him to a music store, he typed for her that he wanted to buy a Billy Joel tape.

Some individuals may feel intimidated by requests for them to leap into fluent conversation; they may require weeks or even months of practice at simpler communication, for example, sentence completions. So, while the method can be assumed to work less well or not at all for some people, failure to work cannot be presumed to reside in the person labeled "disabled." A few weeks after Chris had seemingly reached a "plateau," reverting often to his obsessive pressing of the memory button, he wrote me a letter, revealing that his obsessive behaviors were no clue at all to who he is:

DEOGIHI HOW AREYOOOUU
IAFM FJNEE [I am fine] . . .
YIT IS SCARYXY TO TYPP PPE MY T TMTTSHKK [thoughts?]
BABEECAUCEAA FFBBRI (*Since his sister could not understand this, she asked him to start again.*)
I LIKE TO TYPE BECAUSEE IT TELLS HOWE IE FEERL I THINTK QPEOP [people] DDOO DIJSMIESS [dismiss] MYEE FEE (*Here his sister asked if he meant "dismiss my feelings," and he typed* YEW, *or "yes."*)

The next day he wrote more:

DOUG
IN HOWXX IT ISXXTO BLLLDEUU (*His sister said she didn't follow*)
BEEEAAUTISTIC [be autistic] IIIT IS DAEMSIE [damn] LIKKE

BEIENG IN SI DE [inside] AA mosinmacHINE [motion machine]
THET YPINGIISLIIQLKEEE [the typing is like] TRYING TO STAND
UPIN ACHHEDHER HHEREEBCAMEPVW *(Asked if he was trying to spell*
hurricane, *he typed* YS).

Finally, when his sister asked him why he wanted to type to me rather
than to other people closer to him, such as his family and friends, Chris
typed, HE TRUSTS I CAN TYPE. Then he typed a letter to his mother:
MOM I CAN TYPE I LOVE YOU CHRIS. Several months later, after seeing
a nationally televised program about facilitated communication, Chris
typed to his sister: WORLDZZ LIKEMEJINE NEEECD VUTO BB EI YYLL
OXPLOREEDH I Y YELL VT YELL INSIEEDEMYSEELF TODUUG [worlds
like mine need to be explored. I yell inside myself to Doug].

The question of whether or not all people will prove able to communicate with facilitation or other methods recalls the perennial debate
over educability. While we may lack evidence that each individual person is educable, while we may encounter plateaus or barriers for a short
while, as with Chris, and while we may have numerous examples in
which all efforts to demonstrate educability have failed, as a matter of
educational philosophy and practice, we must nevertheless assume educability. Simply put, the assumption of educability is a better assumption than its opposite (for an extended discussion of educability, see
Blatt, 1987).

Similarly, the educator in us has to assume communicative potential. Anything less optimistic negates our role as educators. Our task is
not to identify or decide who cannot learn or communicate, but to try
to educate and to help make communication possible. The good teacher
never gives up or stops trying. The good teacher never stops looking for
signs that the person is communicating. In terms of strategy—for example, what to say to Chris or when to ask him to type—facilitators will
probably decide on the basis of their own perseverance quotient, the
degree of support they feel from colleagues and friends, and the absence or presence of any signs of communication. But if a student has
pointed to a few letters (for instance, the first letters of words) but not
to whole words, if a student has typed one word but not additional
words for weeks or even months, or if a student has typed a few simple
sentences but then seemed to plateau or to stop typing, we are obligated
to recognize and remind ourselves that the student *has* revealed literacy
skills and that therefore the question is not whether the student has
literacy skills but how to enable the student to express him- or herself
more. The question for the facilitator is not whether facilitation may be
helpful, but how it can be adjusted to be *more* helpful, perhaps with
alternative, more motivating materials, with set work that may be less

intimidating than open conversation or, conversely, with more challenging, open discussion. Trial and error afford the opportunity to find the correct approach.

Where the student has given some sign of comprehension or of literacy, we should not judge the person by how he or she appears most of the time; instead, any sign of sophistication should be our guide to the student's potential—such as Mark saying that he is worried about his therapist not talking to him or Chris's saying that typing is like trying to stand up in a hurricane. Throughout the Australian study I was constantly forced to remind myself of this rule. In dozens of instances I had seen particular students communicate effectively with just a touch to the shoulder or elbow; I would then encounter situations in which these same students would type seemingly random letters, echolic expressions, or incorrect responses to questions—or no responses at all. It was baffling. If I had failed to recall that I had seen them communicate effectively, it would have been easy to define them as incompetent or as incapable of communicating effectively. Giving their sophisticated moments preference, we could persist.

GETTING STARTED

I begin with a working hypothesis that people with autism are capable of communicating. Following Crossley's example, I assume that the individuals with whom we try facilitation are perfectly able to understand what we are saying and that we do not need to simplify our speech—indeed, that people want to be treated as competent and that when so treated they are more likely to respond in kind. I assume that their communication difficulty is in expression, not in understanding or processing. Similarly, it helps to convey a positive, expectant attitude. Presumably everyone appreciates encouragement.

This exhortation to be positive does not always meet with complete acceptance. Some people ask: How can you be sure? Why must one believe the student can communicate in order for facilitated communication to work? Well, of course, we cannot be sure it will work. But it *is* important to act as if we are sure. Hearing people's questions about why it was important to convey an expectation of success, I searched for analogous situations that might help justify my demand for optimism. Parallels can be found in other areas of teaching. Getting started with facilitated communication is a lot like coaching a sports team or teaching reading. Positive or successful coaching is nearly always associated with a "winning attitude." Similarly, good teachers are said to raise their students to higher-than-expected levels.

Imagine a first grade reading teacher who addresses his class at the beginning of the school year, saying: "I am going to try to teach you to read this year. This may be easy for some of you. For others it may be difficult. Some of you may not be able to learn to read. I will test you from time to time to see how you are doing." We would expect that upon hearing this rather pessimistic outlook, at least some students would begin to assume that learning to read is difficult and that they may well fail at it. Now imagine another scenario, one in which the teacher exudes optimism: "We are going to learn to read this year. First grade is when you learn to read. First we are all going to learn to read and write our names. You'll learn all of the letters of the alphabet and how to spell your favorite words. I'm going to be reading lots of exciting stories to you each day; and before long you'll be reading stories yourselves. By the end of the year, we will all be reading books from the library. We're also going to write our own stories." This second approach lets the students know that the teacher expects them to succeed. While he or she cannot *know* that the students will all succeed, the teacher assumes that students will find an expectant attitude encouraging.

Section V of the Appendix summarizes the physical support, educational content and process, and motivational elements of getting started. While an expectant attitude deserves special emphasis as a crucial aspect, indeed, a sine-qua-non, of facilitation, inattention to any one of the elements can cause a breakdown in communication. Fortunately, though, false starts do not appear to jeopardize ultimate success. Time and again, we observed facilitators and individuals with communication disabilities struggle to find success, adrift over what materials to use (i.e., the kinds of structured activities), searching for ideal positioning (e.g., whether to stand or sit, the location of the keyboard or letter display), attempting to overcome highly impulsive speech and/or physical behavior, or stalled with problems of initiation (i.e., getting going physically). Yet eventually perseverance, adherence to a process of trial and error, and attempts with a variety of materials can often lead to success. It is important to bear in mind that nearly every individual seems to require initial successes with predictable, structured activities (i.e., set work; see Section VI of the Appendix), such as fill-in-the-blanks, multiple choice, labeling, and math problems, before moving on to unstructured, fluent typed conversation.

While set work is generally part of any introductory facilitated communication session, like all elements of facilitated communication training, it is a transitory stage. It is important to move beyond set-work when the facilitator and the person with autism are able to do so. Staying forever on set work confines the person with autism to circumscribed communication; it does not allow the person to set the agenda of communication or to shift the agenda, except with great difficulty. Thus facilitators are encouraged to keep open the possibility of original work. This may occur by asking the person if he or she has anything more to say, thus opening the door to open conversation. Or it may occur in the context of set work. For example, in one first session, a facilitator asked a young man with autism to describe the shirt of a man in the room with them. He typed, BLUE and then added, WITH PRETTY FLOWERS. This was a fill-in-the-blanks activity where the responses were not entirely predictable.

Figure 2.2 provides examples of letter displays on typing devices we have used with students in Syracuse. While individual students do express preference for certain devices, the type of letter display is generally not critical to success. A few students with very poor muscle tone have difficulty with electric (i.e., not electronic) typewriters, apparently because their keys require more physical pressure to depress. Other students who have considerable instability in their hand movements benefit from typing devices, such as the Canon Communicator, that have a key guard. Interestingly, the students with whom we have worked seem able to shift with ease from a standard typewriter/computer keyboard display (i.e., "QWERTY") to a serial display (i.e., A, B, C, D, E). The teacher's main challenge generally lies in providing the correct amount of physical support, instructional pacing, and encouragement—doing all this at once. Over time, facilitators become comfortable with the task of integrating the various elements of getting started.

FACILITATING WITH GEORGE

George is 4 years old and has autism. He has echolalic speech, but he cannot speak conversationally. He has poor muscle tone and appears clumsy and uncoordinated. Thus his teacher often needs to hold onto him to keep him from sliding down to the floor, away from an activity such as reading or typing. With facilitation at the hand—George has difficulty isolating his index finger—he can type words on a communication device or point to letters on a letter board, respond to specific questions with single words, copy words presented to him, and do fill-in-the-blanks and sentence completion exercises. One day, his teacher, Charles, read him a story and then asked him questions about it. The

FIGURE 2.2 Sample Keyboard Layouts

teacher's remarks below were all spoken, and George's were all spelled by pointing to letters on a letter board. This interaction occurred during the early stages of George's facilitated communication training.

> CHARLES: One day Hattie was standing by the bushes and what did she see? *(Put up picture of eyes)*
>
> GEORGE: EYES
>
> CHARLES: What did she say?
>
> GEORGE: GOO *(pause)* DNESS GRA *(stopped)*
>
> CHARLES: That's a hard word to spell. *(Helped to finish spelling* CIOUS *by coactively moving George's hand to the letters)*
>
> GEORGE: ME
>
> CHARLES: That's right, she said, "Goodness gracious me." And the goose said . . . *(Filled in two more animals)* What did the cow say?
>
> GEORGE: MOO *(and spoken:)* Moo!
>
> CHARLES: At the end the cow said, "Moo!" But what did the cow say first?
>
> GEORGE: MMY MY.
>
> CHARLES: That's right! Now, Hattie saw two eyes, and then what did she see? *(George did not respond, so Charles waited and then repeated the question)*
>
> GEORGE: EAMNO *(and spoken:)* Oh, my. *(Charles then repeated the question while putting up a picture of ears.)* EARS (spoken as well as spelled)
>
> CHARLES: Good. What did the goose say?
>
> GEORGE: WELL WELL
>
> CHARLES: Good job! What did Hattie see next? Two eyes, and two ears, and a _____.
>
> GEORGE: NO
>
> CHARLES: What did Hattie see next? N O _____ What's the next letter? *(Waited, but with no response from George)* I don't know if you were spelling no or going for what I think was next. *(Put up picture of nose)* I see two eyes, two ears, and a _____.
>
> GEORGE: NOSE
>
> CHARLES: Good. What did she see next?
>
> GEORGE: GO TO
>
> CHARLES: You know what, George? It's not time to go anywhere now. It's time to finish the story. Then you can tell me where you want to go. Hattie saw two eyes, two ears, a nose, and a _____.
>
> GEORGE: HEAD *(This was technically correct—she could see the whole head—but it was not part of the story.)*

CHARLES: Yes, but what does this animal walk on? Two _____.
GEORGE: LEGS
CHARLES: Good. What came next? What else did Hattie see?
GEORGE: O PON
CHARLES: I'm not sure what you're spelling. Why don't we try again? She saw . . . and _____. That's a hard question, but I bet you can answer it. *(George tried to squirm out of Charles's lap. Charles pointed to the picture of the body.)* If you're not going to answer this part, tell me about this part. *(Pointing to tail.)*
GEORGE: BOO *(stopped)*
CHARLES: Now what?
GEORGE: DY
CHARLES: And do you know what that animal was? What do you think that animal was?
GEORGE: FOX
CHARLES: And the goose said, "Oh no," and went flying off. *(Makes goose picture fly away)* And the other animals went flying off. *(Makes them fly away)* But what did the cow do?
GEORGE: MNMOO
CHARLES: Oh, the cow said, "Moo." Did the fox stay?
GEORGE: FOX ON
CHARLES: What happened to the fox? Did the fox stay?
GEORGE: SCARED
CHARLES: Good job! What did the fox do when he was scared?
GEORGE: GO A *(hesitated)*
CHARLES: Go what? Keep going.
GEORGE: WAY
CHARLES: Good work, George! You helped tell the whole story! Now, do you want to do something different?
GEORGE: NO
CHARLES: What do you want to do? Go?
GEORGE: DOWN TO EARTH ROOM
CHARLES: Okay, let's go to the Earth Room.

THE STUDENTS' WORDS

The youngest student with whom we tried facilitated communication was age 3 years, 9 months at the outset. Left alone, unsupervised in class, he engages in stereotyped play, repeats several words or approximations of words that he hears others say, and does not play with his peers. Before he began using facilitation, his echoed words included his name, *cow, bus, stop, bus-stop, HBO, TBS,* and various logos. Describing his difficulties with peer play, one teacher wrote in his school records, "Bobby functions best during circle time when placed in his stroller . . . without direct physical intrusion and when given manipulatives. Without an activity to manipulate, he becomes extremely frustrated, struggles to leave, and screams." Bobby's mother reported at the time that "he showed no awareness of being wet or messy" from toileting accidents; toileting was part of his program at the preschool. As with a number of children with autism, he seems fascinated by order; one day the teachers observed him organizing number cards sequentially from 60 down to 1.

Bobby's teacher facilitates his typing by resting a hand under his right forearm, supporting his arm as he selects keys on an Apple II computer keyboard, and pulling back his arm after each selection. Recently, when given fill-in-the-blanks questions related to the story of *The Three Little Pigs*, he spelled the words HOUSE, STICKS, and BRICK. The teacher showed him a wolf, and he typed WOLF. Actually, the teacher's "wolf" was a Walt Disney Goofy doll. Immediately upon typing WOLF, Bobby reached unassisted for the key on the keyboard that scrolled the word processing program into a mode in which he could type another word. With the teacher's hand underneath his forearm, he typed GOFY, a creative spelling for "Goofy."

Bobby's typing is at once "normal" and unusual. His literacy skills surprised us. Even for a student without autism, written vocabulary such as his would be considered precocious. Further, here is a child seemingly unable to engage in ordinary play with peers and with objects such as toys; yet his typing is not echoed language. In fact, at one point in the exercise, the teacher gave him a fill-in-the-blanks question: "a house built out of _____"; Bobby said "house," echoing his teacher, but typed the word STICKS. This has been a common phenomenon among the students with whom we have worked; those that have echolalic speech will frequently *say* their echoes but *type* perfectly ordinary language.

The communication of this student, like Mark's communication described earlier, challenges traditional assumptions about autism. First, it appears that Bobby listens quite well. And he can think about what he hears. Despite the fact that he cannot speak responses that reflect his thinking abilities, he can communicate them through another channel, typing, albeit not yet in sentences. Second, his echoed speech may well have been learned by rote and may well be parroted back, but it is not reflective of his intellectual abilities, specifically his ability to engage in analysis of abstract ideas, for example, that his teacher wants him to imagine the Disney character Goofy as the wolf. Third, far from closing the world out, he has let it in. He does not play with objects or peers in typical ways, but he is observant. Among other things, he has focused his intellectual energies on understanding language and on learning to read. He has demonstrated that he knows the words *sticks, house, bricks,* and *wolf*. One possible hypothesis is that he may even give *special* focus to such intellectual activity, in effect compensating for not being able to play normally. Or perhaps his disability in some fashion causes him to focus on certain activities such as ordering numbers, noting spatial designs, and reading. Either hypothesis, or both, may explain his seemingly precocious written vocabulary. Perhaps words are his toys.

As explained earlier, some students who do not speak, type echoes. This phenomenon has been reported in the literature (Goodwin & Goodwin, 1969). Even with facilitation, students in our own study occasionally type echoes, for example, HBO, MOM, OPEN THE CLOSET, and other words that we interpret as echoes because they appear to be unrelated or only tangentially related to what the students are being asked. The prevalence of such typed echoes decreases as students gain experience and practice with facilitated communication. Except for one student who explained by typing that she speaks less now because her echoed speech makes her appear dumb, we have not observed a reduction in students' spoken echoes, although such a reduction might occur as the students become more proficient with typed communication. It is also common for students to type letter combinations that are difficult to understand and that in some instances are not words. Occasionally students combine both meaningful and seemingly extraneous words. When asked what his favorite sandwich is, for example, a 14-year-old student, Evan, typed, LATTUCE TREE FOR THE PLATED AND TUNJA.

Within several months of beginning to type with facilitation, Evan told us that he wanted to take typical academic classes at his grade level and that he wanted to practice his typing over the summer so that he might do well in regular classes the next year. He had never before been in any regular academic classes. He was thought to be moderately retarded and severely learning disabled. He has not spoken since he was 4 years old. Without facilitation, his typing is limited to echoed words and seemingly noncommunicative selections of letters. With facilitation, he communicates conversationally. For example, when I mentioned to him that I would be visiting Denmark and meeting people like himself who are labeled "autistic" and who type their thoughts, he typed, I WANT TO SAY CONGBRATULATION S,L. "Congratulations for what?" I asked. GETTING FREW#E, he typed. "Said like a poet," I remarked. Then he added, I WANT VTRO GO WITH DOLYUG TO DEBHMARK. Aside from the typographical errors, which appear to result from instability of his index finger movements, and aside from a minor grammatical imperfection, this is normal, conversational language.

Five months after beginning to type, this student wrote a poem entitled MY DAD:

```
JOKING, PRETTY GOOD AT FOOTBALL, HANDSOME
LOVGES MOM,, BOBBIE, MME
WHO SOMETIMKES FEELAS WIOPORRIED, POROUD AND HAPPY
WHYO  BFEARS  MEETINFTS,  HNAVUINGT  NO  MONEY,  MDYIKNFT
[dying]
WGHO WOHULED LIKE MDRE TOL NOT GTBEE ATGISTRIKC


RESIDENT OFR BA,LDWINSVILLE
MY DAD


BY EVAN, MJAY 24, 199o0p.
```

Evan's typing reveals ordinary social interest and emotions. In contrast to traditional assumptions that the person with autism is withdrawn, highly egocentric, and aloof, Evan is not consumed with immediate needs or desires. He demonstrates care for the people around him. For example, he can observe, understand, and feel compassion for his father.

Naturally, the communication of the first 21 students varied. After six months only one did not yet reveal a knowledge of words; this student was 4 years old. However, this student was able to point to pictures that were the correct answers to questions we asked, and he knew his colors. Most often, he did not point with his index finger but moved his entire upper body toward the correct answers to his teacher's or speech therapist's questions. Two students typed individual words that were ordinary language, as contrasted with echoes, and 18 students produced sentences; two of the students who typed sentences produced only a few simple sentences and typically typed single-word responses to questions. All of the students demonstrated unexpected awareness of their environment and unexpected social awareness and interests. Evan's thoughts and expressions, like Mark's, reveal an inner life of the mind that extends beyond concrete concerns. His communication reveals more flexibility of language than the dimensions—such as demands, turn-taking, and rehearsal abilities—described by Prizant (1983). Further, Evan seems proficient in sharing ideas—for example, when he asks to tell people in Denmark congratulations for "getting free"—as well as in acquiring knowledge from others rather than merely from trial and error (Wetherby & Prutting, 1984, p. 374).

Shortly after beginning to type with facilitation, several students typed, IM NOT RETARDED. One kindergarten student, for example, typed YELL T KIDS THAT I CAN TALK. I NOT RETRDED. Speaking of his newfound skill of communicating through typing, he typed, I THINKIT IS GOOD, I THIKNING IT HELPFS ME TALZKK. I LIKE THEEN TYPEWRITER AND THE COMPUTER AND THE BORD. The phonetic and creative spellings are not surprising, especially since this student is 6 years old. A week after commenting on his typing, he complained about other students' behavior: THE KIDS CALL JONAH RETARDED. I HEARD THAT ON THE BUS. I THINK IT IS RONG BECAUSE JONAH IS NOT RETARDED. He also told his speech therapist that the other students were bad for running in the hallways: THEIR TEACHERE HADB TO TTELL THEMN TO WALII. Another 6-year-old student wanted to carry his complaints to the school principal: I WANT TO GO TO THE OFFICE AND TELL MRS. H. IT WANT TO TELL HER THAT THE KIDS ARE BAD. THE KIDS TOLD ME THAT I AM STUPID. IT HAPPEN TODAY.

Implicitly in their complaints about others, these students are declaring themselves competent. By "telling on" nondisabled peers, they announced their own relative goodness. Their comments are reminiscent of the Australian student, Polly, who complained that her nondisabled peers seem to enjoy a wide berth for misbehavior, while she must run a gauntlet of discrimination and has the responsibility for good behavior and for succeeding "thrust" on her.

WHERE DID THE STUDENTS LEARN TO READ AND DO MATH?

One 9-year-old student who cannot speak, except for a few sounds that approximate words, sometimes makes high-pitched sounds, flops on the floor, and has tantrums. Before she was introduced to facilitated communication, her teachers assumed she could not read. On the first day that she was encouraged to type, she spelled her name, leaving off only the last letter. Two weeks later she correctly spelled her second grade spelling words. When her teacher explained that she could take the weekly spelling tests, the student typed, I WANT A SPELLING BOOK TOO. She also revealed that she knew simple fractions and that she could add, subtract, multiply, and divide. Such skills raised an obvious question. Where did she learn them?

Prior to being introduced to facilitated communication, few of the

21 students had had any formal instruction in reading. They had been presumed incapable of academic learning. Their limited communication skills made it seem reasonable to assume that they could not comprehend language. Yet the typing of all but one student revealed unexpected literacy. Where and how had they learned it? Many of their parents are surprised at their skills. Several parents recall having used flashcards with their children when they were young; eventually, when their children seemed unresponsive, the parents had abandoned the cards. Others never used flashcards. Some parents mention that their children might have watched siblings doing schoolwork. Others note that their children have been exposed to "Sesame Street" and other educational television programs. And a few mention that their children with autism habitually collect books and leaf through them. But only a handful of parents thought the children were reading them.

Traditionally, in instances in which children with autism have demonstrated reading skills, particularly when they have done so at an early age, researchers have discounted these skills as isolated, "hermetic," hyperlexic (i.e., overability in reading), and often performed without full comprehension (Goldberg, 1987; Silberberg & Silberberg, 1967; Whitehouse & Harris, 1984). A few children with autism have also demonstrated exceptional writing abilities, termed "hypergraphia," which have similarly been thought to exceed presumed intellectual ability (Whitehouse & Harris, 1984). Even very young children have been observed to be "preoccupied with alphabet blocks, frequently looking at books, and in one instance taking books rather than soft toys to bed" (Whitehouse & Harris, 1984, p. 285). Whitehouse and Harris identify three cases in which children were observed "decoding" words by the age of 2; they use the term *decoding* to suggest that the ability to identify and even say words or point to them correctly is different from reading; reading presumes understanding. By school age, these early readers/ decoders were observed reading road signs, telephone directories, and catalogues. Despite these skills, their cognitive abilities have been discounted, presumably because of their inability to speak conversationally: "Their decoding ability was often taken as a sign of unrecognized intelligence, although the majority of parents realized that the child could not comprehend. On school entry the word-calling ability sometimes led to inappropriate classroom placement" (p. 286). Presumably, had these students been introduced to facilitated communication, the researchers for whom they were subjects would be able to see that their so-called decoding skills were in fact reading skills and that they were not hermetic or isolated; rather, the children simply lacked an effective means of expression. Labeling such skills as "decoding" and "word calling" seems little more than an elaborate and not so subtle way of denying the students' competence, saying in effect: They are not reading.

We can only hypothesize that many, if not most, of the students with whom we have used facilitated communication and who have demonstrated literacy abilities developed these skills informally, that is, they are mainly self-taught, presumably from television, signs, advertisements, and other available reading materials, such as newspapers, books, and magazines. It is important to recognize that early, self-taught reading has been observed in many children before they attend school (Doake, 1988; Ferreiro & Teberosky, 1982; Holdaway, 1979).

As noted earlier, all of the students of preschool and elementary age are integrated partially or full-time in regular classes with nondisabled peers, and all of the students of secondary age attend regular schools and have some interaction with nondisabled students, despite the fact that they all have severe disabilities and none had an effective means of communicating prior to using facilitated communication. Presumably, the practice of placing students in academic classes benefited their acquisition of subject-matter content. As one fourth-grade teacher remarked, "I always felt that we were doing the right thing by having the students integrated in regular classes, but I had no idea just how right!" Her point was that she now believes the integrated classrooms continuously provided opportunities for these students to learn academic content, unbeknownst to their teachers! Responding to this point, a high school student who has autism and echolic speech and was always (i.e., prior to being introduced to facilitated communication) assumed to be severely intellectually impaired, recently explained that he learned math, including Roman numerals and simple algebra, by hearing and observing it taught to nondisabled students in his integrated classrooms. This is perhaps a lesson for educators. We should not underestimate the possible benefits of informal learning in schools, at home, and elsewhere of either academic or social skills.

CONCLUSION: RECURRING QUESTIONS

In retrospect, our experience of using facilitated communication with beginners was remarkably easy. It would have been more time-consuming, possibly more discouraging or even daunting, if most of the students had not revealed that they could already read; we did not need to teach them. For many of the students, words and sentences seemed to virtually explode out of them; we were there to catch and admire them.

Concurrent with our near euphoria over the students' progress, questions about the method abounded. Many of the questions that had arisen in my Melbourne study (see Chapter 1) remained. In the early stages, we often wondered if we might be cuing students to their selections of letters and words. Related to this concern, we felt we still did not fully understand why students seemed better able to facilitate with some people than others, why it sometimes takes a new facilitator days or even months to succeed with a student who has been typing fluently with others, and why students continue to want or need a touch to the elbow or shoulder, even though such contact appears to provide no physical support in terms of stabilizing or slowing the students' arm movements. At the same time, other questions began to emerge.

Some of the students have highly echolic speech. We wondered if in the process of typing their words these students might experience an improvement in their ability to speak what they wanted to say rather than seemingly disconnected, unrelated words or phrases. Further, we began to wonder about the echoed language. Is it an entirely separate language from the written word, emanating from a different region of the brain than the cortex? Some of the echolic language seemed appropriate and meaningful—for example, when a student would say hello to someone and say his or her name—but much of it was seemingly unrelated to the circumstances in which it was said. Do some of these students have "word finding" problems, such that when they search for a word they want to say they find and speak a related word, not exactly the word they are looking for? Is this a version of a problem that all people have, but which in the case of some people with autism and related disabilities is more severe and more apparent—perhaps the person with autism lacks the average person's ability to cover up a word-finding problem with a pause or with a completely different phrasing of the same, intended idea. Many of our early successes with facilitated communication came with students who had little speech. Would the method have the same value for people with much speech, albeit not very functional speech?

Perhaps most intriguing, six months after beginning to use facilitation, we wondered what the students would be able to tell us about autism. We wondered what we might learn about their outbursts of self-abuse or hitting others and screaming. When students did these things, were they acting out of frustration? Where they trying to communicate something? We also wondered about their emotions. It appeared that students were telling us that their emotions are remarkably typical and that they cover a very broad range. Would this finding persist?

Finally, we wondered how far facilitated communication would spread, not only among people with autism, but to people with other disabilities. Since the method appeared to work with people labeled "autistic"—we were having some success with each person with whom we tried it, although since teachers and parents were nominating those with whom we would try the method, we could not claim a random sample—it seemed logical to suspect that the method would be applicable to a larger group. But how large? We could not help wondering if the method would force us to question the very nature of disability. Already we seemed to be finding that many people had previously been presumed to be intellectually disabled or retarded because they *appeared* to be so. They could not use speech effectively and they could not physically respond to questions and other examinations of their competence, so they had been presumed incompetent. But the evidence of their incompetence was limited and flawed; the tests had not provided a method whereby they could reveal their thinking. We were discovering that this was true for many people with autism. How far would this finding extend? We knew that was a question unlikely to be answered in the immediate future, but it was an intriguing one.

CHAPTER 3

I AMN NOT A UTISTIVC OH THJE TYP
(I am not autistic on the typewriter)

ECHOES

In the opening scene of *Family Pictures*, novelist Sue Miller (1990) describes a not uncommon event in the lives of families with children who have autism. The Eberhardt family sings "Happy Birthday" to one of the children, Mack. When they finish singing, the narrator's brother with autism, Randall, speaks the words, "Happy birthday, dear Mackie." One of his sisters is astonished: "Did you hear him? My God!" The father is *not* astonished. "I wouldn't get excited," he counsels, "that's about his annual quota of words, isn't it?" The father's frustration, revealed in his instantaneous discrediting of Randall's speech, exemplifies the enormous social disadvantage experienced by people with autism, due mainly to their problems of communication. Randall's momentary expression is not atypical of people with autism who are essentially mute. In the first published account of autism as a distinct disability, Kanner (1943) described mutism as one of the qualities characteristic of some persons with autism, a mutism that may on rare occasions be broken by a momentary expression, believed to be brought on by stress or excitement. Because echoes appear to be based on other people's words, even words heard years previously, and because people with autism appear to have differing levels of ability in mediating them, their communication may include pronoun reversals, repetitive (perseverative) speech, seeming insistence on certain phrases including a demand for particular words in particular situations, lack of temporal correctness in responding to others, and seeming fixation on a topic, phrase, or sentence pattern—all resulting in an apparent unease or stilted quality in social communication. Randall Eberhardt's momentary, "annual" expression typifies echolalia; he literally repeats a phrase of the song, "Happy birthday, dear Mackie." Echolalia can take the form of immediate or delayed echoing (i.e., repetition of words or phrases heard days, months, and even years earlier).

In a fascinating account of "bedtime soliloquies," Baltaxe and Simmons (1977) concluded that where their subject was able to *use* echoes to accomplish functional communication, the resultant language appeared to be based on "a limited but usable linguistic system" (p. 392). The child was thought to mediate echoes by breaking down previously heard language into "quotationlike or rote-learned echolalic patterns" or "individual chunks of varying size," then joining them to form new utterances, or what Baltaxe and Simmons (1977) term "delayed mitigated echolalia" (p. 392). Such expressions typically sound "autistic" because, although they may be context-related, they are also in some way out of context and usually display ungrammatical form or atypical syntax.

As noted in Chapters 1 and 2, such communication was thought, until recently, to be barely communicative for most people who could speak and only modestly useful for others. Prior (1979), for instance, concluded that even among people thought to be "high-functioning," such language "is characterized by concreteness, repetitiveness, recognition without analysis, and a mechanical, noncommunicative approach" (p. 372). It generally breaks down in social interaction, since unusual grammatical forms may elicit confusion on the part of the listener/responder. Or it may be limited to a few predictable, customary interactions (e.g., greetings, yes/no responses, repetition of one choice from among several offered).

Other researchers interpret such communication, looking to decipher communicative intent. In one of the first studies to attribute social meaning to echoed language, Prizant and Duchan (1981) categorized 1,009 "immediate echoes" of four children with autism into the following categories:

1. "Turn-taking," whereby the person with autism uses the echo to fill the space in a conversation that would normally be taken up by a meaningful response
2. "Declarative" expressions, used to label an object, action, or location
3. "Yes answers," used to affirm other persons' statements
4. "Requests," used to seek an object or action
5. "Nonfocused" expressions, which seem to be without intent, except perhaps to indicate anxiousness or other arousal
6. "Rehearsals," or add-on phrases to statements, indicating comprehension
7. "Self-regulatory" expressions, which are words or phrases stated in conjunction with actions

In a related study of delayed echolalia, Prizant and Rydell (1984) found even more elaborate communicative functions, expanding the list of functional language types to include "providing information," "verbal completion," "protest," "calling," "self-directives," and "directives." Again, however, if using these linguistic responses in a relatively more sophisticated fashion than the mere repetition of a word or phrase—that is, mitigated echolalia—the person with autism is described as lacking ease of communication. Prizant (1983) describes these limits: "Regarding discourse and social interaction, it appears that autistic persons often initiate interaction motivated largely by the need to ensure predictability by maintaining an established routine" (p. 299). Such communication is characterized by "incessant questioning, preoccupation with specific topics, an inability to shift topics, and poor perception of listener needs" (p. 299). Prizant notes that such language gives the impression of an inability to use "creative and generative linguistic processes" (p. 303), resulting in limited manipulation of previously heard chunks of language or gestalts. The assumption is that the limitation in communicative ability derives from "cognitive limitations" (p. 303).

Wetherby (1984) hypothesizes that the person with autism may have insufficient cortical control of the limbic system. Since it is presumed that the limbic system "is capable only of transmitting vocal signals of low informational value, and is thought to mediate vocalizations that are emotional reactions or self-stimulatory responses" (p. 29), failed control of it could conceivably explain the observed eruptions of unusual language in some people with autism. Physiological studies of people with autism, using autopsies and magnetic resonance imaging, reveal anomalies in the limbic system (Bauman, 1991) and in the cerebellum (Courchesne, 1991), but not in the cortex. Schuler and Prizant (1985) hypothesize that "more sophisticated cortical mechanisms appear involved in intentional forms of echoing serving a range of communicative and cognitive functions" (p. 179). Not surprisingly, given that most people with autism experience difficulty producing useful spoken language, it appears that nonlanguage communication is common—whether through crying, tantrums or aggression; moving toward a listener for attention; gazing at objects, such as food; pointing; shaking one's head or nodding for refusal or agreement; or pulling others to an object or location (Prizant & Schuler, 1987, p. 290).

While facilitated communication reflects the presumption that gestural communication holds more promise than modeling spoken language, it derives from premises radically different from notions of autism that assume social and cognitive deficits. Training in facilitated communication helps the communicator overcome neuromotor difficulties of instability and apraxia. It is easier to point than to form spoken words. It is easier to point with a single finger than with multiple fingers. And with individual pointing, a facilitator can slow the person down.

Apraxia does not necessarily imply cognitive deficit (see, for example, Darley, Aronson, & Brown, 1975; Hagen, 1987; Kelso & Tuller, 1981; Miller, 1986). Nonstereotyped expressions, particularly those comprised of several words or phrases, are more difficult for the person with autism than labeling with single words, greetings, or commonly heard multiple-word expressions, such as advertising jingles. In typing, production of original, multiple-word communication improves when the person is stabilized and slowed. This is analogous to many sporting activities or to playing a musical instrument. For example, the average skier stands at the top of an expert slope filled with moguls (i.e., mounds of hard snow), contemplating how to get through or over them. He or she typically will be able to plan the moves to navigate two, three, or four of the moguls successfully before either stopping or skiing out of control. It takes a great deal of practice to be able to ski a hill full of moguls flawlessly. Similarly, the person learning to play the piano may be able to play a few notes or chords without error, but not a whole song. With practice, going slowly at first and then over time speeding up, the person succeeds in playing an entire song. In the case of both the skier and the pianist, confidence plays a part. Facilitation allows people with autism a similar opportunity with communication. It is possible to go slowly, to gain confidence, and eventually to produce words and sentences, with individual words and simple communications preceding sentences and paragraphs.

In our experience, even students with highly echoed language appear able to produce appropriate, natural-seeming language when using facilitated communication in the context of structured academic work. For a few, open-ended fluent conversation persists in being problematic. The difficulty of moving from appropriate language in structured contexts to appropriate language in open-ended situations is a challenge for facilitators to address. It is further complicated by the fact that individuals' success with more open-ended expressions may appear variable; that is to say, their "good communication" may come and go. Whether this results from stress, different levels of motivation, tiredness, or other factors is not known.

The fact that many people with autism can produce normal written language using facilitated communication supports the hypothesis that they have apraxia, a difficulty in getting their bodies to do what they want when they want. Even most persons who are nearly always mute have produced normal text while typing with facilitation (Biklen, 1990; Crossley, 1988); thus suggesting the presence of inner language. Many students with echolalia are able to produce normal typed language that contrasts with their echoed speech; hence their echolalia appears more "automatic" than volitional. It is not the automatic language, but rather the difficulty of engaging in voluntary action, that signifies the apraxia. After looking at the unique problems of communication by people who have highly echolalic speech, we will return to this matter of apraxia.

STUDENTS WHO SPEAK IN ECHOES

Mustafa, age 12, has a wide range of echolalic expressions. He will say aloud words that he has seen around him. For example, while looking at the cover of a puzzle box he spoke several words that appeared on the box: "100 pieces," "puzzle," and "sign." As he spoke these words, alternating them with giggles, he nevertheless responded to the speech therapist's questions correctly. He pointed to letters to type CALIFORWNIA. He pointed to the outline of New York on the map and spelled NEW YORF. For Texas, the therapist prompted him by saying, "I think it starts with T"; he finished it. As with other students who have echolalic expressions, Mustafa typed natural language when his spoken language was ignored; he often spoke one thing and typed another. Thus even though his spoken words were highly echolalic, his typing was not. When given a cartoon picture story about two birds and a hat, he produced a series of sentences appropriate to the cartoon frames: HE FOUND A HAT. HE PUT IT ON. HE WENT FOR A WALK. HE SAW A BIRD. THE OTHER BIRD LAUGHED. HE DROPPED THE HAT. THE OTHER BIRD LOOKED. THE BIRD PICKED UP THE HAT. HE WALKED AWAY WITH THE HAT. HE SAT ON THE HAT. HE ON HAT. THE FIRST BIRD GOT MAD. HE GRABBED THE HAT. HE PUT IT ON HIS HEAD. THE BIRD HAT HAD A LITTLE BRD IN IT.

Communication by Mustafa and other students progressed over time. As with students who are mute, the facilitators attempted to move the students who have echoed speech through series of set work, such as filling in blanks or answering questions that had a limited range of answers. The set work is especially helpful in working with students who have echoed speech because the facilitator can immediately distinguish between original and echoed language. In a typical early training session, a speech therapist asked Todd, a 17-year-old high school student who has echolalic speech and occasional, apparently natural language, what he bought at the grocery store. Todd typed FLOUR. She asked what he was going to make. He answered, COOKIES. After he had typed these words, she asked with whom he was going to make cookies. Todd did not answer. When the therapist tried to coax him to type by taking his arm, he pulled away. She asked him if the noise of the other students was bothering him. Allowing himself to be facilitated on the forearm, near the wrist, he typed, NO. She asked him what he was going to do on Friday. He returned to an earlier question, typing, COOKWI. The therapist said, "Cook w i . . . ?" He typed WITBH. The therapist then said, "with. Cook with," and Todd finished the statement, MBOM [i.e., mom]. A few minutes later, he typed responses to opposites, for example, DOWN in response to "up," NO for "yes," SPOON for "fork," an unusual choice of GIRL for "brother," and YES for "no." Then he typed a sentence: I WANT TO STOP. Before ending this session, the therapist asked him to date his work; he correctly typed, MAY 8.

Several students have persisted with echolalic speaking at the same time that they type ordinary language. Todd, for example, answered a series of questions about a brief story by typing them on a computer keyboard, yet throughout the exercise, he intermittently spoke the words, "I do not like it." At no time did he pull away from the typing or in any other way indicate that he did not like the activity of typing. It was as if the echolalia was extraneous. Apparently, someone else in the setting had said "I do not like it" previously, several minutes before he began the typing session with his teacher. Another student, age 6, typed answers to his speech therapist's questions about a book they were reading, including, for example, the sentence, THE BOY HELD THE MOUSE UP while he simultaneously sang "A, B, C, D, . . . Now I know my ABC's." The singing did not appear to interfere with his ability to type perfectly responsive answers to the therapist's questions. The singing was analogous to the humming, whistling, or unconscious singing that many people engage in while they work. Anyone can do this and still successfully accomplish an intellectual task, such as writing a letter or essay or answering questions, so long as he or she does not think about the song being hummed or words being sung. The minute one thinks about the humming or singing, it becomes impossible to complete the other intellectual work.

In another session the six-year-old student typed I WANT T YELL [tell] THE STUDENTS I NOT RETARDED. When the therapist asked him if she should tell the other students what he had just typed, he said "no" but typed YES.

Todd, who, as noted, often speaks echolalic phrases at the same time that he types ordinary, conversational language, was asked by a nondisabled student why he does this. I DONT KNOW, he typed. His teacher asked how it made him feel. He answered, IT MAKES ME FEEL FRUSTRATED, adding, I FEEL LIKE I AM TWO PEOPLE. "You mean when you use the board?" the teacher asked. Todd added, AND WHEN I TALK. (Todd and many other students have typed to us that we should pay attention to what they type, not to what they say.) Later Todd explained that when people respond to his speech as if it is what he wants or means to say, PEOPLE THINK I AM STUPID. The nondisabled student told him she thought this response by people was merely the product of their ignorance. She said she hoped he was proud of himself. "You are very smart," she concluded. I AM PROUD, Todd spelled.

One of the most interesting exchanges we had with students came on a day when I was escorting two officials from the Norwegian Ministry of Education through several public schools, showing them examples of inclusive schooling in which students with disabilities are educated with nondisabled students. As we drove out of Syracuse to the Baldwinsville School District, I told the visitors about one young teenager who has a condition called Klippel Trenawny Weber syndrome, a disability that has been presumed to be associated with retardation and that causes the person to spew automatic (i.e., echolalic) language. This student, Joseph, speaks clearly and easily, but most often with phrases that are repetitive and typically are not specific to the conversation; this spoken language usually includes only general content. The following are my observational notes of the visitors' interchange with Joseph:

> Today I brought two visitors from the Norwegian Ministry of Education to visit Joseph in his speech class.
>
> After I introduced Ida Drage and Tove Lindberg to Joseph and his teacher, his teacher asked Joseph if he had a question for the visitors. He said aloud, "All right. You might want to look at this." As he spoke, he typed, CAN YOU TELL ME ABOUT NORWAY? Ida and Tove explained that Norway is a cold country, with high mountains, snow, and an extensive seacoast. Joseph typed, THAT SOUNDS A LITTLE DIFFERENT FROM HERE.
>
> Ida asked Joseph if he would like to see a picture of her family. He said, "Okay, that's all right." After looking at the picture, which included Ida's children and the family dog, Joseph typed, I LIKE YOUR FAMILY.
>
> Joseph's teacher asked him if he wanted to say anything more. Joseph said "Okay" and typed, DO YOU LIKE OUR SPEECH CLASS? As he typed, Joseph continued to speak, saying, "How are we doing so far? See if we can keep it up here." The visitors responded

quickly to Joseph's question: "Yes, we like it very much. And you are typing very well." At this point, Ida walked over to me and whispered, "What would happen if no one held his arm?" The speech therapist was supporting Joseph at the wrist as he typed on an electronic typewriter. I whispered back that he would not be able to respond to them the way he was, at least not yet. Ida commented quietly, "It's very strange, isn't it."

Next, the Norwegians asked Joseph if he could tell them about his family, whether he had any brothers and sisters and so forth. Again, he responded verbally, but not revealing what he would type, "Okay, just a minute." Then he typed, I HAVE A HOUSE ON A STREET IN BALDWINSVILLE. As he was typing the name of the town, he said, "It's a long word to get through, huh?" and then hit the carriage return, saying, "Got it now."

Joseph's speech teacher asked him if he could respond more directly to their question. "Remember, they wanted to know about your family," she reminded him. At this point another student came by the classroom door to give the speech teacher an attendance list. The student messenger is labeled "handicapped" and is a friend of Joseph's. When Joseph saw him, he said, "Alex." Then to us, "That was Alex by the way." While Joseph was talking he continued to type, writing, I HAVE A MOM AND A DAD. Trying to get more detail, Ida then asked, "Do you sleep in your own room?" Joseph said, "All right, we'll take care of that," then typed, I HAVE MY OWN ROOM.

Joseph typed at a reasonably fast pace, using the index finger of his left hand. After telling his guests that he had his own room, he asked them, WHERE ARE YOU STAYING? They responded verbally, "We are staying at the Sheraton University Inn." IS THAT A NICE HOTEL? Joseph asked. Their negative response caught me by surprise, especially since I had recommended the hotel to them. "No," Ida said, "it smells of smoke. But it doesn't matter. We are going to New York this afternoon." Joseph was obviously warming up with his typing and the conversation, for now he told them, YOU NEED A BED AND BREAKFAST.

. . .

The end-of-period bell rang and Joseph said, "That's the bell," and typed, THANKS, apparently ready to leave for his next class. However, Ida squeezed in two last questions: "How long have you been typing? And how do you like it?" He answered both questions quite specifically. WE HAVE DONE THIS SINCE SCHOOL STARTED, he

typed. IT LETS ME COMMUNICATE LOTS BETTER BECAUSE I DON'T
SAY EXTRA WORDS. As he was typing, he said, "Okay, I'll end
about there." It was time for his next class.

Ironically, despite his newfound communication abilities, at the time of
this class session in which he conversed with the visitors, Joseph was
still attending a self-contained special class for students labeled "mentally retarded." Apparently, because his automatic speech sounds so
normal, albeit not specifically responsive to what others are saying,
most people presume that he does not really understand a great deal,
in other words, that he is not smart. They treat him kindly, but more
often than not as a sweet fool rather than as someone of considerable
sophistication. A year later he entered regular grade-level academic
classes with nondisabled students his age.

STUDENTS WHO TYPE ECHOES

With each of the echolalic students, teachers and speech therapists
attempted politely to ignore the spoken echoes, saying to them, "Why
don't you type what you want to say." This approach generally succeeded, although one therapist reported continuing difficulty with two
students. One of them spoke *and* typed echoes of the therapist's words
as well as delayed echolalia; the other student, a 14-years-old who had
not spoken for ten years, typed echoes. To address their difficulties, the
therapist stopped speaking herself and began to converse with the students through typing. She typed her thoughts or questions and facilitated the students' responses. This led to their communicating in ordinary language. The following is a four-way conversation (all typed)
involving one of the researchers, the speech therapist, and these two
students, Maggie and Evan:

THERAPIST: TODAY, MAGGIE, I BET THERE WILL BE A LOT OF
             TALKING. WE WILL FOCUS ON WHAT YOU SAY WHEN YOU
             TYPE. OK?
MAGGIE: I WANT TO ASK EVAN ABOUT FOR.
THERAPIST: THAT WAS DIFFICULT FOR YOU TO SAY. WOULD YOU
             TRY AGAIN?
MAGGIE: EVAN. HOW DO YOU FEEL ABOUT AUTISM.
EVAN: I FEEL AWFU.
THERAPIST: DO YOU WANT TO SAY ANYTHING MORE ABOUT THAT?
EVAN: YES I AM NOT HAPPY TODATY.

THERAPIST: PLEASE EXPLAIN.

EVAN: IK THYINK TYOU ARE POITGE BJUUT NOT LOKIKE ME MAGGVIE

RESEARCHER: HOW DO YOU THINK MAGGIE IS DIFFERENT THAN YOU?

EVAN: I THOINBK SHGBWE IS 1/4POLITGE.

RESEARCHER: OK

MAGGIE: I LIKE TO ASK EVAN WHAT EDOES HE SEE IN HIS FU-TURE?

EVAN: I WANTN TO GO TO CPOLLLEGE.

MAGGIE: YOU ARE INTELLIGE NT.

EVAN: YES I AM SO ARE YOU.

RESEARCHER: THERE IS NO MODESTY HERE.

EVAN: YOU ARE RIOGHT.

RESEARCHER: IS THERE ANYTHING THAT YOU WANT TO TELL MAGGIE?

EVAN: PLEASEW TELL ME ABOUT HYLW YHOPU FEEL ABOPUT AU-TISEM

MAGGIE: I FEEL TERRIBLE

RESEARCHER: WHAT DO YOU THINK YOU CAN DO TO OVERCOME SOME OF ITS EFFECTS ON YOU? ANYTHING?

MAGGIE: I DONT KNOW

RESEARCHER: I AM HOPING THAT BY TYPING AT LEAST YOU WILL HAVE A MEANS OF COMMUNICATING WHAT YOU ARE THINKING AND FEELING. HOW DO YOU FEEL ABOUT THAT, EVAN?

EVAN: I FEEL YI THAST YUPOU ARFED MY FRFIKEEND,. I AMN NOT A UTISTIVC OH THJE TYP

The numerous typographical errors that Evan makes are due to his hitting keys next to or near the ones he intends. His typing improves when he slows down. It would improve even more if the typewriter had a key guard so that only one key could be hit at one time.

Several days later, Evan and Maggie elaborated on their feelings about typing. Evan explained that he worried about not being able to communicate effectively with more than a couple of facilitators. He volunteered his own solution to this problem, allowing that he would have to PRACTICE DAILY. Maggie characterized the typewriter as a much-cared-for companion: I CAN TRY TO YTPE UNTIL YOU TAKE AWAY MY LOVE. Unclear about this, I asked what she meant. Maggie explained, I RALLY NEED THE TYPEWRITER. i AMERAGTGER [i.e., eager] TO GO TO ALL SIXTH GRADE CLASSES. At this point, I typed back,

ARE YOU SAYING THAT THE TYPEWRITER IS YOUR LOVE? Maggie answered YES.

Over time, the speech therapist was able to speak out loud to Maggie and Evan without their reverting to echoes of her speech. Thus the strategy of having to type to them was only a stage in the training method, not an ongoing mode of dialogue. After six months of training in facilitated communication, given for approximately 40 minutes a day, five days a week, both students were enrolled for the first time in academic classes at their grade levels. They both immediately demonstrated that they could do grade-level work. Examples of their work appear in Chapter 6.

OVERCOMING PERSISTENT, FORCEFUL ECHOES

Students who have highly echolalic spoken language often type the same echoes if allowed to type independently (i.e., without facilitation) but all the students with whom we have worked have demonstrated the ability to produce at least some connected discourse through typing when facilitated. For a few students, their ability to type ordinary language was dependent on their being given highly structured communication opportunities—such as fill-in-the-blanks exercises, math problems, or questions that can be answered only with specific and limited responses—and on being slowed down in their typing; if they were not slowed down, their typed echolalia reemerged. The latter strategy was particularly essential for students who displayed seemingly compulsive typing of certain echoed phrases, usually on a limited number of topics. (Section VII in the Appendix describes the assumptions and practices for facilitating with students who have echolalic speech or typing.)

Jerome, who is 21 years old, speaks a great deal, but generally on only a few topics and almost always repetitively. Among his usual topics are the police garage, which is the location of his supported employment work-training site; the Syracuse Chargers, an athletic club he has been part of; mommy; and home. To overcome this problem, his speech teacher selected a highly structured, fill-in-the-blanks activity. The content was neither functional nor suited to his age level, but nevertheless, the interchange is highly instructive, for it shows Jerome producing both normal and echolalic language and suggests the difficulty that his teacher had in helping him get past the echoed expressions; fortunately, the highly structured format proved a successful strategy for enabling Jerome to produce some nonechoed responses. I have provided this extended example because it demonstrates the strategy of using structured work to enable a student to get beyond echoed expressions *and* because this student was the most challenging to his teachers of all the individuals in this study; it took eight months before he began to demonstrate any clearly nonechoed responses:

JEROME: SOMEDAY WILL GET PICE GARAGE OKAY EEE
FACILITATOR: We need to get the calendar. Stay right here. I'll get the calendar. (*At this point, Jerome jumped up from his seat and ran over to a teaching assistant in the special class. Jerome began at once to speak to the assistant and to straighten the teaching assistant's collar. He said, several times, "talk about police garage." The teaching assistant redirected him by standing up and moving toward the facilitator, saying, "I'll talk to you after you work with April. First work, then we will talk." Jerome sat down again.*) Look, Jer, I wrote "police garage" down [on the calendar].
JEROME: Ferris wheel, ferris wheel, car ride mommy. (*Jerome started screaming. The facilitator ignored the screams. Jerome turned to her and spoke.*) Talk to Dan, yes.
FACILITATOR: Come on Jer lets do this paper. Children like to go _____ in the pool.
JEROME: SWIMMING
FACILITATOR: Great.
JEROME: Swimming. GREEN WATER
FACILITATOR: He forgot to _____ his dog.
JEROME: TALK TO
FACILITATOR: I _____ 50 dollars for the lamp. (*There was silence, so the facilitator said "paid."*)
JEROME: PAYD
FACILITATOR: We _____ to fix the leak in the roof.
JEROME: TRY (*Jerome then screamed and hit the table, saying, "talk about roof." He then typed more.*) WE TRY
FACILITATOR: What would the answer be?
JEROME: We try. MOMY WANT TO (*Jerome started screaming again, hitting the teacher, and getting up and down from his chair. He put the letter board on the floor and touched it.*)
FACILITATOR: Jerome, let's do more, then we'll talk about mommy. The little boy lost his two front _____.
JEROME: Teeth. TEETH FRONT TEETH FIRST TEETH TETH
FACILITATOR: Okay good.

His typed addition of GREEN WATER and FIRST TEETH TETH appear to be add-on echoes to his correct spoken responses. The response TALK TO is an unusual, but nevertheless reasonable, response to the sentence, "He forgot to _____ his dog." More predictable responses would be "feed" or "walk." He spelled *paid* wrong, although it is possible that when starting to type the word, the Y merely slipped in as a naturally occurring effect of typing too quickly, a phenomenon that nondisabled typists also experience—they begin to type one word and another or a combination of two comes out when both words start with the same letters.

Jerome's echoes appear extremely impulsive and automatic. As soon as a question is asked, he often responds with an echo, sometimes related to the context or question and sometimes off target. As we have noted, he often types echoes after giving appropriate typed responses, as if it were difficult for him to hold back the echoes.

Similarly, automatic, echo-like expressions can be observed in anyone's speech. Word-association tricks provide a convenient example: If you ask a person to tell you the color of a white house, the person says "white"; if you then ask the person the color of a swan, the person wiil again say "white"; and if you then ask the person what a cow drinks, the person will automatically say "milk" rather than "water." Similarly, if you ask a person to spell *coast, roast,* and *boast* and then ask him or her what goes in a toaster, the person will usually say "toast" rather than "bread." Because of the prior associations, the person gives an automatic response that is not the same response that would likely be given if he or she was "thinking" about it. It may be that when the facilitator slows the person with autism, that person is better able to type intentional rather than automatic words.

It took more than a year for Jerome to begin to type a few non-echoed conversational sentences. As we will see in Chapter 6, we learned that he had a sense of humor, something that we had not been able to discern until he communicated with facilitation. The fact that it took more than a year before Jerome produced original, conversational language was certainly as much a reflection on the fact that we were learning about how facilitation works as it was a reflection of Jerome's autism, that is, the intrusiveness of some of his obsessive behaviors, such as his getting up and down, his insistence on fixing people's collars and pulling down sleeves, his hitting, and his quick, echoed speech and typing.

GENERALIZING COMMUNICATION TO ADDITIONAL FACILITATORS

One of the most baffling behaviors is some students' selectivity, or ability/inability to communicate with different facilitators. All but two students with whom we worked in the first year and a half in Syracuse could communicate with several facilitators. Most students are most fluent with one or two facilitators, with physical support faded back and with greater language production. For none of the students has physical support yet been faded completely. Ironically, students would comment to the effect that the facilitator with whom they were most fluent really "knows how to hold my arm." Yet logically, this explanation does not make much sense, particularly when the person may be supported only minimally, for example, with a light touch to the elbow. It is even more puzzling that with new or other facilitators, the same person may need to have his or her hand or wrist held. It appears that students feel confidence in their most seasoned facilitators or in certain people who convey a particularly supportive attitude toward them. Part of being supportive may lie in knowing how to help the student develop confidence, by first engaging in simple interactions, such as choices (e.g., "Do you want milk or orange juice?" "Do you prefer the computer or the Canon?"), before moving on to open-ended communication. A first-grade student spoke to this issue when he typed, i cant spell with him [his father] because he doebvsnt know how to put good boacrd questions.

Because generalizing to multiple facilitators is often problematic, we developed a series of suggestions, drawn from the experiences of dozens of teachers, parents, teaching assistants, speech therapists, and other facilitators (see Section VIII of the Appendix). The suggestions included confidence building, physical support, and step- by-step progression of the content format. Specifically, we found that it was important to recognize that many individuals experience difficulty with generalizing to multiple facilitators; it is a natural problem. Confidence building is important for the person communicating through facilitation as well as for the new facilitator; for some people it can take several months or more to achieve generalization. Being persistent and optimistic appears to help. If an individual is facilitating more fluently with one or two people and not well with others, it is important not to blame the individual but rather to problem-solve with the person to make it work. Invariably in this situation, individuals with disabilities have indicated that the most supportive thing for the new facilitators to do is to keep trying and to try to relax.

Regarding physical support, teachers and parents have tried a variety of strategies, including having a seasoned facilitator place his or her hands over those of the new facilitator and then to withdraw that support slowly. In every instance, new facilitators have had to give support at the hand, wrist, or other point where the person with autism began when first introduced to facilitation. Once facilitation has begun with a new facilitator, the process of fading back the physical support may occur more quickly than it did with the person's first facilitator.

Considerations regarding content are not different from those involved in getting started in general. That is, new facilitators generally must begin with structured set work and then progress toward fluent conversation, even though the person with autism may have exhibited fluency with others. Obviously there will be exceptions to this principle, but in general it appears to pertain. It has proved particularly useful for new facilitators to begin facilitated communication with a particular person with everyday functional choices (e.g., selection of foods, choice of clothing, choice of activities).

INDEPENDENCE/INTERDEPENDENCE

During one session with Maggie, a student mentioned above, the speech therapist faded her support back to Maggie's elbow. In response to a question, Maggie typed, YOU SAYR YREAM. The therapist did not understand and so typed, WHAT DO YOU MEAN? Maggie responded, typing, I AM UNAG. The therapist, who was still providing support only at the elbow, typed, I'M NOT CLEAR YET. TRY AGAIN. Maggie then typed, I AM FSRUA, and stopped. The therapist asked, DO YOU MEAN FRUSTRATED? At this point the therapist returned to supporting her by resting the palm of her left hand under Maggie's left forearm. Now Maggie typed, I AM FRUSTRSYOU ARE NOT HOLDING MY ARM. The therapist apologized, typing, I'M SORRY. I WAS EXPERIMENTING. And I sheepishly added, ITS PARTLY MY FAULT. I'VE ENCOURAGED YOUR TEACHER [the therapist] TO TRY TO HOLD LESS SO THAT YOU CAN BECOME MORE INDEPENDENT. To this Maggie responded, I AM NOT READY. The therapist typed, WE UNDERSTAND. And Maggie finished, AM OK.

Several months later, even though she did become fluent with just a touch at the elbow from this facilitator, Maggie challenged the importance her teachers placed on independence. She typed, I AM QUITE HAPPY RTO BE DEP [i.e., dependent] ON PEP [i.e., people] MUCH OF THE TIME. She also explained to her speech therapist/facilitator that if she became equally fluent with other facilitators she might lose her close relationship and time with the speech therapist.

During the year in which this research project proceeded, a student in Australia who had been one of the students observed in the study of the DEAL Communication Centre (Biklen, 1990) wrote me a letter in which she questioned society's definition of *independence*. If she were permitted to reconstruct the social meaning of independence, it would be "the way that I am offered big choices and then helped to behave in a reasonably accepted way." But she knew all too well that society's idea of independence—the "accepted" independence—"is doing things for yourself," she wrote. "But that was too dreadfully frightening and so I do not make a big effort to achieve this." Her goal was to be able to make "big choices" and to be "reasonably accepted," not necessarily to do things for herself, which she regarded as a "beastly threat." To her, society's notion of independence, doing things on her own, meant settling for lower levels of accomplishment than she was willing to accept: "independence required a lack of achievement. For example, the autistic repetitive words [what we have termed *echoes*] are so intrusive when the assistant is not firm." The facilitator provides her with confidence "that I was not going to mess up," whereas society's "independence" often meant being plagued by "a lack of control of my silly directly autistic behavior." A "light touch on my elbow tells me that I am totally safe and that success is a constant and real possibility."

This student's point is a critical one. By whose standards should the relative "competence" of people with autism and other disabilities be measured? Is nonengagement with other people the measure of independence? Does *independent* mean being able to do something with mechanical supports as contrasted with human support? For this student, independence has less to do with the nature of supports she uses than with the measure of self-determination she can achieve.

WHEN ECHOES REINTRUDE

As students become more proficient at typing what they want to say, one cannot help wondering why it is that on certain occasions the echoes return, even if briefly. Similarly, even though individuals prone to echolalia could type appropriate, seemingly nonechoed communication within the structure of set work, it is curious that for some of them, echoes still dominate their attempts at open-ended communication. Two factors seem to play a part in this type of communication breakdown. One is excitement or nervousness; the other is confidence in and familiarity with the facilitator.

When students are excited or nervous they are likely to type their common echoes. Such is the case when Jerome, mentioned above, types about the topics—the police garage, the Syracuse Chargers, mommy, and home—that he repetitively speaks about. This can happen to students who have become quite independent in their communication with certain facilitators and who have demonstrated the ability to type long conversations flawlessly. For example, a year after Maggie began typing, she was interviewed by an Australian television crew. As she began typing to them, she typed, `yzwwy tree leave gra y`. This was not clear to us. But from here on her typing was quite clear. She typed to the interviewer, `what do you want to kneow`. The interviewer asked what facilitated communication has meant to her. She responded by typing, `learning to type has been my rebirti as a nosrmal person.` When asked what she meant by "normal," she typed, `someone who d oes anything tiey want with their life`, and added, `people understand that i am an intelligent person. e very one wants to be treated with respect.` The interviewer then asked Maggie what it had been like for her before people recognized the person inside her. She responded, typing, `i was a clown in a workled that was not a circus.` This statement so flabbergasted the interviewer that she ended the interview, thanking Maggie. Maggie concluded, `you are wellcome thatnk you very much.`

A few weeks later, several other filmmakers visited Maggie as well as many other students to plan a documentary on facilitated communication. In this instance, extra words appeared in her typing; it was difficult always to understand what she was typing. She explained that she was VERY NERVOUS. Also, she was typing with the aid of a new facilitator, who cupped her hand under Maggie's elbow. When asked how long she had been typing, Maggie responded, ABOUT A YEAR NOW. Then one of the visitors asked how the facilitation helped. She typed, REASON AND WITH FACILITTION I CAN FIND THIS MORE COMFORT-ABLE. One of the filmmakers asked how school was different now than before she use facilitated communication. Maggie explained, I FIND THINGS WASTE IN MY HEAD ARE NOT WASTED ANYM [i.e., anymore]. THERE USED TO BE READING TIME NOT WRITING TIME. Her phrasing was not as fluid as usual, although her metaphors were as sharp as ever. She explained that communication is difficult for her but that facilitation helps: I THINK ONE NEEDS ANY WAY THEY CAN TO GET INFORMATI OUT THIS WHICH WOULD WORK FOR ME. Asked what its like to communicate by typing and why it is sometimes difficult, Maggie explained, GET SAYING THINGS IN HEAD BUT TYPE WRITER I GET LOST.

On still another day, when I first facilitated with Maggie myself, she was able to respond to questions with single words, but not phrases or sentences. She told me that she got her best grades in SCIENCE, that one of her friends is named JENNY, and that she would be going to JUNIOSR HOIGH SCHOOL next year, but when I asked her the name of her science teacher, she typed MARSH, the name of her speech therapist, not the name of her science teacher. Maggie's difficulty with producing the correct name is typical of the word-finding problems, a type of aphasia, that we observed in a number of students. When asked for specific information, such as the name of a restaurant where they ate or the name of an object they had observed—even the names of siblings or of the family dog—individuals would often give incorrect answers. This appears to be a version of a problem also exhibited by many non-disabled people, who may say several incorrect names before producing a correct name or identify an object by the name of a related object (e.g., refrigerator for air conditioner). Unfortunately, this can be a particularly intense problem for people with autism or other developmental disabilities. From our experience with Maggie and others, it appears that even the slightest nervousness or anxiety, such as may occur when communicating with a new facilitator, may increase the word-finding problem; it is noteworthy, however, that in our observations we saw this problem emerge even when individuals were typing with familiar facilitators.

In contrast to these examples of Maggie struggling with communication, when facilitating under less stressful situations and with her speech therapist providing only light support at the elbow, Maggie can type abstract thoughts excellently. The following letter, written to the same Norwegian visitors who had conversed with Joseph, reveals this:

```
NOVEMBER 15, 1990
DEAR VISITORS FROM THE NORWEGIAN MINISTRY OF EDUCATION,
     I AM SORRY THAT WE DID NOT HAVE A GOOD CHANCE TO
DISCUSS THE FACILITATED COMMUNICATION. I AM WRITING TO
TELL YOU ABOUT IT.
     THIS HAS CHANGED MY WHOLE LIFE. I CAN NOW TELL
PEOPLE HOW INTELLIGENT I AM INSIDE. I CAN EXPRESS THE
PLANS THAT I WANT EVEN THOUGH I DONT ALLWAYS GET WHAT I
WANT. I CAN TELL PEOPLE MY DREAMS AND GOALS IN LIFE.
     I CAN MAKE REAL FRIENDS.
     I CAN TELL PEOPLE WHAT I LIKE AND DISLIKE. I AM ME
AND EVERYONE CAN LOVE ME NOW BECAUSE I AM A GOOD AND
VALUABLE PERSON.
     SINCERELY,
     MAGGIE
```

APRAXIA AND VOLUNTARINESS

Our experiences with facilitated communication tend to support Crossley's (1988) and Oppenheim's (1974) hypothesis that people with autism experience global apraxia, affecting literally all aspects of voluntary physical activity. To explicate this, it is instructive to relate our experiences with facilitation to characteristics associated with apraxia (see, for example, Darley et al., 1975; Hagen, 1987; Kelso & Tuller, 1981; Miller 1986). As noted earlier, apraxia does not necessarily imply cognitive deficit; in fact, the thinking abilities of people with apraxia far exceed their capacity for expressive language. The typing of individuals in our investigations reveals communication abilities reflective of sophisticated thinking, or at least abstract thought. As with people identified as apraxic, all the individuals in our studies found it more difficult to produce complex or multiple-word expressions than simple words or familiar multiple-word phrases (i.e., echoed multiple-word production); their performance appeared to be aided when their movements were slowed through initial facilitation training. The normal written language observed in people with autism using facilitation (e.g., Maggie's letter above) is also consistent with apraxia, where the individual "demonstrates . . . that he has the word clearly in mind. He may be able to write it" (Darley et al., 1975, pp. 251–252). Even most individuals who are nearly always mute produced normal text while typing with facilitation, thus suggesting good receptive comprehension skills. With apraxia, "speaking performance . . . [is] significantly poorer than their performance in listening, reading, or writing" (Darley et al., 1975, p. 252); individuals with echolalia were able to produce normal typed language that contrasts with their echoed speech (although for a few, this required the structure of fill-in-the-blanks, cloze, and similar set work); hence their echolalia appears more "automatic" than volitional. Familiar words, such as greetings or names, and words perceived both visually and audially may be more fluently and correctly stated, while less familiar words or ones not presented visually or verbally to the person may be stated with articulatory errors—or not at all. Again, this seems consistent with the notion of apraxia, where the person may be able to state greetings, advertising jingles, and songs with ease but experience breakdowns in producing nonautomatic speech (Darley et al., 1975, pp. 281–282). The physical support provided in facilitated communication, particularly in the early stages, may serve as the mechanism for helping individuals to overcome apraxia. Also, typing with only the index finger is a relatively simpler motor task than multiple-finger typing, speaking, or signing.

In Figure 3.1, the left-hand column summarizes characteristics associated with apraxia, as presented by Hagen (1987). The right-hand column lists analogous behaviors observed in varying degrees among individuals in our studies of facilitation.

In addition to the observed problems in language, the hypothe-

FIGURE 3.1 Comparison of Communication Characteristics Associated with Apraxia and Those Seen in People Using Facilitated Communication

*Communication Characteristics Associated with Apraxia**	*Communication Characteristics Seen in People Using Facilitated Communication*
• "The person exhibits multiple articulation errors."	• The students in this study who speak often speak some words with difficulty, producing parts of words and omitting syllables.
• "The frequency of errors increases as complexity of the speech motor task or word length increases."	• The students who have some spoken language can sometimes imitate one or more words immediately upon hearing them, but rarely a whole sentence and never several sentences.
• "The speech pattern is dysprodic, labored, hesitant, and often perseveratory."	• Thirteen students cannot speak at all; other students produce perseverated speech, sometimes using a few words and other times whole phrases, often with unusual stress, pitch, or rhythm.
• "There is a poor ability to imitate sounds and words, yet automatic speech is often near normal."	• The students who can speak cannot repeat long phrases or sentences said to them but do speak repetitive, "automatic," "cocktail conversation" perfectly, as if effortlessly or compulsively.
• "Inner language processes are intact."	• When facilitated, students in this study produced typed language that discloses excellent inner language; they could not have discussed their feelings, likes and dislikes, aspirations and frustrations, and other complex concepts if they had lacked the ability to understand linguistic concepts.
• "Auditory comprehension is normal to near normal."	• The students' written communication revealed good auditory comprehension of language around them.
• "Reading comprehension is demonstrably better than speech production."	• None of the students has demonstrated high-level or mediated spoken language, yet with facilitation most were able to type normal language revealing unexpected literacy abilities.

* From Hagen, 1987, p. 35.

sized apraxia appears to affect all other aspects of the lives of people with autism. A standard indicator of apraxia is the observation that a person can blow out a candle if a candle is present but cannot imitate blowing out an imaginary candle. The individuals in this study appear generally unable to make their bodies do what they want when they want, except for some stereotyped or routine tasks. For example, we observed a teacher tell a student to pick up his biology text and come with her to his high school biology class. He stood staring at her. She repeated the statement and walked over to the table where the book was located. He then picked up the book and walked slowly, several yards behind her, to the biology class. Another student was seemingly unable to shake hands with one of the researchers but could, with facilitation, type sentences attesting to his pleasure at the researcher's visit. Researchers commonly had to grab individuals' hands in order to shake them, although a few could respond quite appropriately. More perplexing, however, was the observation that individuals often seemed capable of doing something when not asked, but to be unresponsive or very delayed in response when asked. Such displays of physical competence seemed automatic, as if a physical analogue to echolalia. The individuals in this study required some form of facilitation to do nearly everything. Several members of the research team reported that some individuals appeared to walk to class more easily when a classmate or teacher was holding their hands or resting their hands on their shoulders. Similarly, students were repeatedly observed requiring some facilitation (e.g., hand-over-hand or hand-on-the-shoulder support) as they played games, sat in groups, or participated in other classroom activities. Although he worked with patients diagnosed with postencephalitic parkinsonism, Sacks (1990) described several of his patients as requiring a similar supportive touch in order to initiate physical movement, to keep from falling over, or to continue movements, for example, walking down a hallway; at the same time, some of his patients displayed another similarity to some people with autism, namely, seeming preoccupations or compulsions to do math problems—he terms this arithmomania—and to contemplate ordering and reordering objects: "such oddnesses, such twists, are also characteristic of Tourette's—and of autism" (Sacks, 1990, p. 132). As we observed the individuals in this study developing greater independence in typing, we imagined what it must have been like for them to learn to feed themselves; we hypothesized that they must have been facilitated. When we asked parents about this, they confirmed our hunch. Further, several added that they still have to do some facilitating at the dinner table when their son or daughter stops in the middle of a meal or progresses exceptionally slowly, usually by providing verbal encouragement or a touch to the shoulder. While the facilitation for helping a child become an independent eater is essentially the same as facilitation for writing and communication, the former guarantees physical sustenance, the latter intellectual and emotional expression.

Many parents report on apraxic-type difficulties encountered by their sons and daughters with autism. And some of these parents describe facilitation-like strategies for helping their children achieve independence at tasks that were initially difficult or impossible to initiate and complete. For example, many parents tell of having to cup their hands over the child's as the child attempts to brush his or her own teeth. Others describe their children having difficulty buttoning clothes (Barron & Barron, 1992) or tying shoe laces (Barron & Barron, 1992; Eastham, 1992). In a classic example, Park (1982) described her efforts to help her daughter, Elly, to learn how to turn the faucet on and off. Park put her hands over those of her daughter on the faucet handle, initially providing both the pressure and twist. After doing this several times, she let Elly take over:

> Imperceptibly—I hope it is imperceptibly—I lighten my pressure. The small hand beneath mine is no longer quite limp. It seems there are muscles there after all. I move my hand a quarter inch up hers as I turn the water on again. Another quarter inch. A half. Infinitely gradually I withdraw my hand, up her fingers, up her wrist. *She goes on turning on the water.* My hand moves up her arm. Finally all that is left is one finger on her shoulder. (p. 52)

Whether or not the apraxia hypothesis holds up over time, it is difficult to predict the futures of the individuals in this study. Presumably physical activity, particularly initiating and stopping action, will continue to be difficult. On the other hand, improvement may be accomplished through practice *and* through facilitation. Clearly teachers, parents, and the individuals with autism share the goal of increasing communication independence. While it is difficult to predict what proportion of the individuals will achieve the ability to type without any physical touch, it would most likely seem to be a possibility for the preschoolers: They have the chance to learn to communicate earliest, to practice the most, and perhaps to avoid developing other behaviors that impede effective communication. As for future employment prospects or the likelihood that the individuals will be able to live independently, we simply cannot predict; this and other forms of participation in society will depend as much on thoughtful and skillful support from the people around them as on their own capacities. The prospect of maturing in a world that may view autism and related disabilities differently from the past, and the resultant potential for emotional growth once freed from the debilitating onslaught of low expectations, suggest greater possible opportunity than was even conceivable just a few years ago.

Part II

THE DIFFICULTIES OF CHANGE

CHAPTER 4

Many Breakthroughs

As word began to spread throughout the United States concerning our work on facilitated communication, I began to get phone calls from several people who on their own had discovered facilitated communication. In this chapter I will describe what these people told me about facilitation—none of them had a term for what they were doing—and about the reactions they reported from the professional community. I will describe a visit I made to a group in Denmark that was also using the method. The experiences of these pioneers of facilitation are instructive, both about the method *and* about the meaning of disability.

ONE THING LEADS TO ANOTHER

Gayle Marquez lives in Nashville, Tennessee. Her 15-year-old daughter is labeled "autistic" and "severely retarded" and appears to have coordination problems, almost as if she also had cerebral palsy. Gayle Marquez called me shortly after my first article on facilitation appeared in the *Harvard Educational Review* (Biklen,1990). She was excited to hear that someone else was doing something similar to what she was doing, and she said she was hopeful that I might be able to lend credence to her daughter's abilities.

Gayle Marquez describes her efforts to communicate with her daughter, Lyrica, as a process of trial and error:

> I started by using word cards with her to make selections at home for meals, the very functional things that you do during the day, what you want to do, what you want to eat. I finally figured out that she could type because I got tired of making enough word cards for every choice. It was too hard to keep all those word cards around. I reasoned it would be a lot easier if she would write it out herself. If she can read, why can't she spell?

When Gayle Marquez put a computer keyboard in front of her daughter, Lyrica would point to the first letter of words but would hit the same letter or letters repeatedly. So she pulled Lyrica's arm back after each letter selection. Unbeknownst to her at the time, Gayle Marquez had discovered facilitated communication.

Recognizing Lyrica's ability to read, Gayle Marquez asked the Nashville school district to shift her from a class for people with severe disabilities/mental retardation to an academic curriculum in a regular fourth-grade class, with a facilitator. She reports being told that this was impossible and inappropriate.

Gayle Marquez removed her daughter from school and began a program of home instruction that included phonics, early reading work-books, reading stories, multiple-choice questions about the content of reading, and so forth. Among other things, Gayle Marquez discovered that while she herself took more than a minute, and often two or three minutes, to read a page, Lyrica seemed to read the same page in a mat-ter of seconds: "She is a much, much faster reader than I am. How she does it I don't know. She gives it two or three quick looks, that's all." Such remarkable ability was all the more surprising when contrasted to Lyrica's minimal self-help skills. Despite the fact that her special edu-cation program at the public school had focused nearly exclusively on learning to wash her hands, brush her teeth, and other "functional" tasks, she was still not good at them. This was probably less the fault of the school program than of Lyrica's apraxia.

Lyrica can type with just light support under her wrist. Gayle Mar-quez asks questions, and Lyrica answers. As she types, Lyrica often looks away. While she may use peripheral vision effectively, not even peripheral vision can succeed when she looks completely away from the keyboard or reading material. In such instances, her mother reminds her to return her eyes to the keyboard or book. Several years after be-ginning to type with facilitation, Lyrica still depends on her mother's support at the wrist. This level of support can probably be faded back considerably, so long as Lyrica is given encouragement and prompted to look at the keyboard.

Of course, the very fact that students like Lyrica need physical sup-port at all causes some people to believe it is the facilitator doing the spelling. Such disbelief has been a common experience for parents and teachers who on their own have discovered facilitated communication. But if the disbelief breeds frustration, it also gives rise to determination. A parent of a child in Pennsylvania wrote to me, saying: "I cannot si-lence the child, or neglect his education. I want to get through to the authorities: If he can only learn upside down, then he has to learn upside down."

Gayle Marquez's determination led her to file a legal action against the Nashville public schools. In a due process hearing, a legal proceeding afforded parents and school districts under P.L. 94–142, the Education for All Handicapped Children Act, she appealed to a hearing officer to order the school district to recognize Lyrica's abilities and to place her in a school where she would be given an academic program. In his report of the case, the hearing officer described Lyrica's history of behaviors and labels:

> L has engaged from a very young age in behaviors often associated with brain damaged and autistic individuals. These behaviors include flapping of the arms, tantrum behavior, self-abusive biting, obsessive destruction of books and papers placed in her care, and making guttural noises. Further, L possesses very few self-help skills. For example, she does not dress or groom herself. Nor is she able to control her bladder for any significant period of time. (L. v. Public Schools, 1991, p. 2)

No one, not even Lyrica's mother, disputed this description. Her complaint was with the school's assessment of Lyrica's thinking and communicating abilities, not her other behaviors:

> The Public Schools have expressed skepticism as to whether or not the child is in fact communicating. The Public School officials were reluctant to say that they did not believe that communication was taking place. However, it is clear that the Public School's [sic] position is that there is a significant possibility that the communications reportedly made by L are little more than a parlor trick.
>
> . . .
>
> In this regard, the Public Schools point to the fact that the child has not been able to communicate with her Public School teachers using this method, the fact that to communicate in this manner the child's hand must be held by another and pulled back from the keys to keep her from perseverating on an individual key and the fact that the child does not look directly at the computer keyboard while engaging in this communication. The implication is that the parents' contention that the child has ability to communicate in this manner is a ploy to garner the child greater services. (pp. 3–4)

The Public Schools' psychologist "testified that the child definitely was moderately to severely retarded and that any other position on the matter was ludicrous" (p. 4). But Lyrica's parents did take another position.

They produced examples of her typing. Commenting on these, the hearing officer remarked, "If in fact reflective of the true abilities of the child, these exemplars evidence that the child has learned to read on the fifth-grade level without any significant instruction in reading" (p. 4).

Faced with an apparent deadlock of perspectives between parents and the schools, the hearing officer appointed his own independent expert. This expert was to assess Lyrica's level of reading comprehension and the level of performance reflected in the written samples provided by the parents, as well as to determine whether or not Lyrica could in fact communicate by typing on an electronic typing device. In his report to the hearing officer, the independent expert admitted to having approached this evaluative task "rather skeptical as to whether the results of the communication by Lyrica were in fact her own. It did appear to me, especially after viewing the video tape, that Lyrica was somehow being prompted by her mother" (L. v. Public Schools, attachment dated May 1, 1991, p. 2).

Evaluating Lyrica's performance levels as revealed in the quality of the written materials was simple. The expert concluded, "Lyrica's responses to the material were nearly at 100% level using material that I would judge to be at an upper intermediate level, either 5th or 6th grade" (p. 2). The issue of whether or not Lyrica was typing on her own or whether she was in some manner prompted by her mother was more complex. To develop a conclusion on this matter, the expert observed Lyrica's typing carefully. He found three types of evidence compelling:

> (1) At least on two occasions during my observation, Lyrica's wrist was not in contact with her mom's in any fashion when she struck the appropriate key; (2) Lyrica's index finger did, on approximately twenty responses, thrust forward in an action that appeared to me to be independent of the mother's wrist support and; (3) on approximately twenty occasions, Lyrica's forefinger struck a corner of the template between four letters and, in my judgement, she, independent of mom's wrist support, moved her index finger to the appropriate key. (p. 3)

Based on these findings, he concluded that Lyrica appeared to understand her mother and be able to respond to her questions. Further, he observed that while Lyrica appeared not to be reading "in a way in which a non-handicapped person would," her responses suggested that "either peripherally or in some fashion she was able to read and comprehend the presented material" (p. 3). The expert admitted that this method of reading "looks extremely incongruous" but concluded, "regardless of how bizarre the situation appears . . . it does seem that Lyrica does, in fact, read and respond with understanding and true cognition" (p. 3). Like any good researcher, the expert qualified his conclusions, in this case saying, "It is possible that this report of my observations is incorrect and that, in some fashion, Lyrica's mom has subconsciously been responsible for the level of performance" (p. 3). But he nevertheless admitted to having been won over to Lyrica's side: "however, it is my judgment that Lyrica's performance does indicate that she is able to read and to communicate at a level significantly higher than a retarded individual" (p. 3).

The hearing officer decided for Lyrica's parents. He chastised the schools: "Although the Public Schools' skepticism is understandable," he wrote, "what is not understandable is the Public Schools' lethargy in attempting to ferret out the truth in this matter" (L. v. Public Schools, 1991, p. 5). The hearing officer found that however remarkable the assertions—that Lyrica could communicate via typing, that she has at least average intelligence, and that she is capable of abstract reasoning—the evidence was "overwhelming" (p. 8). More remarkable still, she had developed her reading abilities "without any significant instruction in reading" (p. 4). He ordered the Nashville schools to place Lyrica in a special school for six months while the special school and the public schools developed an appropriate educational program for Lyrica in the least restrictive environment. It appeared that Lyrica would eventually receive the academic instruction that her parents sought for her.

WRITING VERSUS TALKING

At about the same time that I heard about Gayle and Lyrica Marquez's experiences, I got a letter from Ruth Sullivan, parent of a young man with autism, Joseph, and a pioneer in autism services. She enclosed a packet of useful articles and clippings that she thought related to facilitated communication. Among these materials was a description of how a West Coast couple, Aurelia and Arthur Schawlow, discovered that their son, Artie, could type, albeit with support to his arm or hand. The Schawlows' discovery is described in the next section of this chapter. Ironically, although Ruth Sullivan told me that the Schawlows should be credited with discovering the concept of facilitated communication, a number of years earlier she herself had also happened upon the usefulness of manual communication.

Among the articles in Ruth Sullivan's packet was one entitled "Why Do Autistic Children . . . ?" which she had published in her "Parents

Speak" column of the *Journal of Autism and Developmental Disorders* (Sullivan, 1980). It concerns the difficulty posed when her son speaks in repetitive questions, as if he has not heard the answer even when it is given, "in much the same manner as senile persons" (p. 231). "I used to pray that one day my autistic son would be capable of making a sentence, asking a question, and engaging in conversation," Sullivan writes (p. 232). No one had warned her that one day "his prolific sentences and questions would constitute a troublesome annoyance and even a barrier for his social development" (p. 232). The sentences that Joseph could speak often seemed devoid of meaning, for example, "'It's an upside-down staccato'" and "'Oh nine.'" When speaking questions repetitively, Joseph appeared to ignore answers given to him. Then one evening, Ruth Sullivan decided to try to converse with her son through writing rather than speaking. On this particular evening, Joseph and his family were intending to go out to dinner. But then Sullivan noticed that Joseph had pulled the tongue of his sneakers up so high and his laces so tightly together that his toes curled up, "like Heyerdahl's Ra II" (p. 232). Reluctantly, she canceled the outing, precipitating a barrage of angry questions from Joseph, which he repeated over and over again, as if he had not been answered. It was then that Sullivan decided to write to Joseph. She was surprised to find that his mood changed dramatically: He stopped shouting; he even stopped talking. He watched as his mother wrote, and then he wrote back. They exchanged sentences several times. Joseph still formed his part of the contributions as questions, but they were more conversational, a bit less repetitive:

> Joseph: "Mother, why are we not going to Burger Chef?"
> I: "Because you did not loosen your shoes when I told you to. Also, you were sassy, and you shouted in an unpleasant way."
> Joseph: "Mother, when are we going to get something at Burger Chef?"
> I: "We will go tomorrow night *if* you're nice. Joe, are you sorry you misbehaved?"
> Joseph: "Mother or Father, what will happen if I leave both of you at home while I walk off to Burger Chef at 29th St. and 3rd Ave.?"
> I: "You will get into trouble unless we give you permission. Would you like to go tomorrow?"
> Joseph: "Mom or Dad, why are we eating food here instead of Burger Chef?"
> I: "Because you were sassy, so we canceled the trip."
> Joseph: "Mom or Father, what will happen if I walk off & rob food from the Burger Chef without paying for it?"

> I: "You might be put in jail."
> That was all. He quietly left the room. (Sulllivan, 1980, pp. 232–233)

The format of the "Parents Speak" column is for autism experts to comment on the parent submission. In this case, Ruth Sullivan's example of Joseph's writing was responded to by Warren Fay and Adriana Schuler. Fay suggested that spoken perseverations are a response to an inability to understand the meaning of what has been said:

> From the child's perspective, the only options in the face of noncomprehension are rephrasing, silence, or repetition. The linguistic demands of rephrasing and their tendency to maintain sameness militate against this option. And presumably, the greater the emotional investment in the communicative exchange, the less attractive is silence. Repetition results. (Sullivan, 1980, p. 233)

Fay attributed Joseph's greater success with writing "in part to the change from the auditory to the visual" and to the possibility that a written exchange "invites further analysis," whereas in spoken dialogue, "transient sound signals allow little time for decoding" (p. 233). Similarly, Schuler attributes the repetitions to lack of understanding: "It has been well established that the continued repetition of utterances is related to poor comprehension" (Sullivan, 1980, p. 234.) Further, she finds, "the written word may be a mode more accessible to the autistic individual for transmitting information. Many autistic people seem better equipped to learn to discriminate words presented in a written form than in spoken or signed forms" (p. 234). Both Schuler and Fay suggest that the students cannot understand spoken dialogue but may comprehend language they can see.

Another interpretation is that Joseph can communicate better by writing than by speaking and that he writes best when in the presence of an especially supportive, familiar person. Recently, when I mentioned this possibility to Ruth Sullivan, she said, "Yes, exactly. It wasn't a physical touch I gave Joseph but a psychological touch." It seems possible that by feeling supported by his mother (i.e., his communication partner), Joseph was enabled to write what he wanted to say. Interestingly, this instance of Joseph's writing still seems unusual in that it is all in the form of questions and reflects dogged determination or a fixation on going to Burger Chef, even if that meant going alone and walking off with a tray of food. The act of writing his responses or questions probably allowed him to slow down enough to partially or perhaps completely escape from the repetitive, routinized, verbal conversational patterns in which he was trapped.

WHO WILL BELIEVE?

On the same day that Ruth Sullivan's correspondence arrived, so did a letter from Arthur Schawlow. A Nobel Prize winner (in physics), Arthur Schawlow began his letter with an account of the disbelief he and his wife, Aurelia, faced when they began to publicize their success in helping their son Artie to communicate through typing:

> I am enclosing copies of the articles which we wrote in 1963 and 1965 [sic; actually it was 1983 and 1985] about our son's acquisition of communication. A few people believed and tried it. Some others thought we were faking. A speech therapist who had been helping us, and had indeed taught us how to use communication boards, told us we should stop using the Communicator, evidently believing that we were deluding ourselves. Needless to say, we stopped trying to use her help. (A. L. Schawlow, personal communication, September 4, 1990)

In retrospect, the Schawlows' efforts to find a means for Artie to communicate was an odyssey. When he was of preschool age, he became incontinent and was judged not acceptable by his nursery school program. At age 5 he was accepted into a program that had been started in California by another parent. But when that parent moved away, the school became less accepting of Artie; he withdrew more. Later, finding that "the public schools had nothing for him in those days" (Schawlow & Schawlow, 1985a, p. 7), the Schawlows placed Artie in a residential setting in a rural area. He proceeded through several different residential placements, eventually being asked to leave each because of occasional tantrums, ripping of his clothes and sheets, and staff fears that he might become even more difficult. Reluctantly, the Schawlows placed Artie in an institution, which, instead of providing him with many promised educational programs and activities, "insisted on drugging Artie until he looked like a zombie" (p. 8). Eventually, the Schawlows succeeded in forcing the hospital to stop the medications. In the continued absence of educational programming, the Schawlows began to provide their own programs for Artie. First they hired a sign-language instructor to work with him. To their surprise, he responded by showing that he could make a number of signs, although signing was never easy for him. Then Aurelia Schawlow, Artie's mother, began to work with him herself. She would drive 65 miles each way to visit him in a new placement, a residential home. Using a Texas Instruments Touch and Tell, Aurelia discovered that Artie knew the alphabet. He could point to letters on demand.

During a 1981 trip to Sweden, where Arthur received his Nobel Prize, the Schawlows learned about a person with autism who was typing, using a Canon Communicator. Back in California, they bought a Canon. Initially, they thought the Canon proved a total failure for Artie, who was then 27 years old: "He would hit just a few keys over and over, like X X X X Z Z Z Z, and would not type words" (Schawlow & Schawlow, 1985b, p. 4). Aurelia Schawlow shifted to presenting him with alphabet and word cards, attempting to build up to fluent communication. Eventually Artie began to type words and sentences on the Canon. Among other things, he typed to his mother, I WANT TO GO HOME (Schawlow & Schawlow, 1985a, p. 15). He also spelled that he had learned to read when he was 10 years old. When asked why he had not revealed this skill previously, he typed, TOO HARD (p. 15).

A key to the Schawlows' success in helping their son to communicate was the emotional support they provided. "Our autistic son lacked confidence," Arthur Schawlow wrote, "and wanted a reassuring hand on his" (Schawlow, 1985, p. 2). The fact that they needed to touch Artie's hand or arm in order to reassure him and to keep him pointing at letters or numbers paralleled what they had learned from the family in Sweden. Viola and Magnus Ronnlund, the parents of Mats Ronnlund, wrote to Arthur Schawlow in 1983 about their son's successes with communicating. "He has written some letters . . . though I must hold my hand lightly on his. Right now I am trying to make him write by hand without any support. Every now and then it works" (Schawlow & Schawlow, 1985a, p. 12). Similarly, the Schawlows provided Artie with physical support: "We found it good to help him when he hesitated, to ensure success. At times, I could not be quite sure whether he was doing it or I was. But, in the end, it was overwhelmingly clear that he knew the answers" (Schawlow, 1985, p. 2). Interestingly, in a comment that is strikingly reminiscent of something said 16 years earlier by Mary and Campbell Goodwin (Goodwin & Goodwin, 1969, p. 562), Arthur Schawlow concluded: "We really were not teaching him, but rather finding out what he knew already" (Schawlow, 1985, p. 2).

Aurelia Schawlow died in an auto accident in the spring of 1991. A few months after her death, Arthur Schawlow sent me a copy of a videotape that showed Aurelia facilitating Artie's typing in 1985. The tape showed his typing, usually with seemingly little attention on his part to the keyboard. "He does it often without looking at the keyboard," Aurelia noted; "Don't ask me how he does it but he does." She assumed that he might be able to do it as a result of his seemingly exceptional peripheral vision. In addition to Artie's appearing not to look directly at the keyboard, except when specifically asked to, he frequently interrupted his typing to cut up magazines, each time cutting five or so pages from bottom to top, about three inches from the magazine fold. He cut each group of pages in this location despite his mother's complaint that if he would cut closer to the margins he would get the full pictures rather than partial ones. But Artie smiled and kept cutting in the same location. Aurelia gave up asking him to do otherwise and remarked that he obviously could do it however he wanted.

FACILITATED HANDWRITING

Not surprisingly, at the same time that I was hearing from parents, I also learned of teachers who had discovered the method. For example, Carol Berger, a teacher in the Eugene, Oregon, schools, had discovered that a number of her students with autism and autistic behaviors could successfully type and write; she was surprised to discover that the method had not previously been widely recognized, researched, or adopted. Until she met Arthur Schawlow, she had not been successful in getting the profession to pay attention to what she was saying about her students' literacy skills. Another teacher, Mary Bacon, encountered a similar lack of interest or *quiet* (i.e., not enthusiastic or public) acceptance for her use of a method similar to that of a parent, Rosalind Oppenheim (1974).

Mary Bacon is a special education teacher in Tucson, Arizona. She did not use typing devices; instead, she had her students communicate by handwriting. She describes her early work with one of her students:

> I got a little perturbed with him when he wouldn't point to the ABC's for me. I slapped my hand on my side and said, "Garrett, you know the ABC's as well as I do. Now point to the W." That he did. He pointed to each one of them. I turned the page over and I said, "now, we're going to write the ABCs and I'll help you." All I did, I put my hand on his and my god, he wrote them all. (M. Bacon, personal communication, 1990)

Then she asked Garrett how he felt about being mainstreamed in regular classes. At that point she turned over the paper and he began to write in sentences, "capitals at the beginning, the period at the end."

Mary Bacon reported that the more her students were in "with normal kids, the more they want to be in there." At the same time, her students would seek out her help against name-calling and similar problems. One student wrote to her, "the children are telling me I'm autistic. I can't talk. I can't write. Please Mrs. Bacon, help me. I don't want to be autistic." They discussed how he might handle such problems, and the student reported later that things were getting better. Similarly, one student wrote a letter to Temple Grandin (mentioned in Chapter 1), an adult with autism who developed quite usable speech as a child and later earned a Ph.D. He wrote,

> Dear Miss Grandin,
> I am autistic and want to be like you when I grow up. I like the squeeze machine [a device designed by Grandin to help people with autism to relax] because it helps the buzzing stop and helps me relax when I get upset. I wish I could be like other children so I could play like they do.
> Love,
>   Fred

Although Mary Bacon recalled having heard of Oppenheim's book about handwriting with autistic children (Oppenheim, 1974), she had in fact forgotten about it by the time she began to work with her students in the late 1980s, using what I would call "facilitated handwriting." Naturally, since the method was relatively unknown—it had never received significant support or mention in the autism literature—Mary Bacon worked with little external support. A number of her colleagues and the children's parents found the literacy abilities reported by Bacon unbelievable. Yet she persisted.

On a number of occasions, students gave her information that made it absolutely clear, at least to Mary Bacon, whose words had been written. Their words offer insights into the feelings and behavior of students with autism. One student wrote often about his parents' divorce. Another, when asked why he was upset, wrote, "Because I will not be with you next year and I don't want to go to another school." When asked how he knew he was going to a different school, he wrote, "Mrs. S. and a lady said it and I don't like it. Why didn't you tell me I was going to a different school?" Another student explained to Mary Bacon that he had pulled her hair and scratched her "because you were working with other children and not paying attention to me." One student who had run out of the classroom later wrote, "I ran outside because I wanted to go outside and play." When asked how he could be helped to obey the rules, he wrote, "Make me stay in the room." Mary Bacon asked if she should do this even if it made him upset. He answered, "Yes." Still another student explained his being upset about his attire: "it makes me upset when the shoestrings don't match . . . they bother me." All of the students made very large words, writing only several words to a page.

COMMUNICATING THROUGH LYRICS

By far one of the most surprising and intriguing accounts of alternative communication means to come to my attention is described by Katie Dolan (personal communication, February 20, 1992), whose son Patrick is diagnosed as autistic. In a letter written to Dr. Bernard Rimland, Director of the Autism Research Center, she described her son's apparent use of record lyrics to communicate (K. Dolan, January 14, 1992). As she explained, Patrick's method is "*un*facilitated":

> We only discovered it [Patrick's communication method] in 1968 when he was 18, though we realized after our discovery, that he had been trying to communicate with us since he was very young. His method is similar to the communication on a keyboard, but much more complex. He uses a three speed child's record player. He must have 33⅓ vocal music records which he plays on 45 speed while placing the needle strategically on key points to make sentences, phrases, etc. similar to the kind of philosophical statements that have been reported in computer facilitated communication only he does not have as wide a range of choice. He doesn't seem to be able to process the words at slower speeds. Nor does he look at the record as he places the needle.
>
> We first recognized his "words" in 1968, after I returned from my first NSAC [National Society for Autistic Children, since renamed the Autism Society of America] conference. . . . It was the first time I had been away from Patrick for a week and he was strangely alert that night. As I unpacked, I heard him playing his record player with the usual chipmunk sounds, but now warbling, "If you loved me" over and over again. I said out loud, "Patrick, do you think I don't love you and that was why I was gone last week? No, it's because I do love you." And then I said to my husband, "What am I doing talking to a record player!" We went to bed thinking nothing more of it, but on Sunday morning, when Patrick rarely awakens early, his father passed his door to hear him up and playing, "Don't ever let her leave me again," which caused him to yell to me, "Come on down here and listen to this!" As I entered Pat's room, he deftly switched the needle on the same record to, "I'll never let you go, I'll never

let you go, I'll never let you go!" I yelled, "Patrick, have you been trying to talk to us on that record player all these years?????" And he clenched his fists and nodded his head and his body in one big yes!!!!!!!!!. We cheered and yelled and danced around and cried a little, too, because then he soberly and swiftly pulled out another record from a tall black stack and without looking at it, played, "I give thanks," "I give thanks." "Are you thanking God, because we finally figured this out?" And, he again, much more slowly, nodded yes.

We remembered as a child, that he used to play, "When I worry and cannot sleep," over and over, suffering as he did from insomnia, but doctors had discarded the sleeping problem as a part of his hyperactivity or disturbed behavior, so we neglected to pay much attention, too. How ashamed we felt that day.

On that same Sunday, he played a lot of phrases, including a mischievous moment of, "I'm leaving on a jet plane, don't know when I'll be back again" and when I asked if he was going to leave us now after I'd left him, he smiled and nodded quickly to the affirmative.

He has played many comments since then. A recording studio for whom I made commercials generously made a 33⅓ record for me with scores of taped sayings on it, which I had his favored, same-age attendant record. Phrases such as "I'm hungry," "I'm mad," "I don't want to do this anymore," "I want to take a bath," "Let's go for a ride," "I want to be alone," etc., etc., etc. . . .

When I brought the record home, Patrick immediately began shaking his head "no"! "Whadya mean 'no,' you haven't even heard it yet!" I screamed at him. He continued to push me and the record away shaking his head back and forth. "Look," I said, panic welling up in me, "a lot of people have gone to a lot of trouble and expense to make this record for you, and you can at least listen to it." He didn't want to, but he did put it on the record player and put the needle to it once and then whipped it off and threw it in his big closet shelf. That wasn't too unusual as he threw all the records, but they never broke. I continued to beg and plead and sometimes I would play the record myself on both sides all the way through, but he wanted nothing to do with it. Finally, one day, he put the needle right on "I don't want to do this anymore" and that ended that. He played everything but that record for many days, maybe weeks, but one night upon returning from a meeting, I found my husband on the front porch waiting my arrival. "Guess what he did tonight?" "What?" "He got that record you had made for him and put the needle on 'Let's go to Baskin and Robbins,' and boy, we jumped in the car and were there in twenty minutes!!!!" He has used that record spasmodically since, but not as much as I had hoped.

In her letter, Katie Dolan recounts additional examples. For instance, at the end of a week when she had been actively campaigning for changes in special education and vocational rehabilitation, "sud-

denly . . . I heard him playing the old Davy Crockett record he hadn't
played since he was 5 or 6 years old, the one where Davy goes to Washington, D.C. and the words . . . [are] 'Making right the government,
Making Right the Government.'" On another occasion, Katie Dolan told
a television reporter of Patrick's ability and of the fact that once when
she asked Patrick if he understood that through her advocacy she was
trying to help him and other people with developmental disabilities, he
"played from a Beetles record, 'She gives me everything,' skipping to
another part of the record to say 'She's so sweet, so kind, I'm so proud
of her.'" But when the cameraman asked Patrick if he would play it for
him, Katie explained that "he would never do it on call or in another
part of the house." But,

> to my shock Patrick brought his record out and played the exact piece
> again, even skipping to the second segment. They used it as background
> music for the TV piece and the cameraman brought Patrick a brand new
> Beetles record as his was badly scratched from his skipping over the ridges.

Patrick's use of record lyrics is inherently limited. As his mother
explains in her letter, *"he has very limited choice of words!"* Also, some of
his communication could be analogous to contextually correct echoed
communication that can be observed in the verbal language of some
people with autism. I have *not* observed Patrick's use of this method and
therefore cannot attest to its exact character. Nevertheless, whatever its
precise nature, at the very least, Patrick's method deserves our attention. Unfortunately, Katie Dolan has encountered lack of interest. She
writes:

> I told a lot of people about this strange skill of Pat's . . . I announced it at
> NSAC conferences (two other parents reported that their kids were doing
> some talking on record players, though nothing as elaborate as Patrick's);
> and I pursued graduate students and professionals in hearing and speech,
> all to no avail. So, we just accepted it and enjoyed it and used it in the
> family. Many times I was condemned and accused of fantasizing about Pat-
> rick's *talking on a record player*, but that was nothing new for me in my stri-
> dent position as an activist.

HOW MANY BREAKTHROUGHS MUST THERE BE?

The fact that many people who were once thought illiterate and
severely mentally retarded can communicate far more than others had
imagined is not a new phenomenon in the annals of disability. Nearly

everyone knows of Anne Sullivan's discovery of Helen Keller's abilities (Lash, 1980). People in the disability field are also familiar with the remarkable advances in augmentative or alternative communication for people with cerebral palsy (Crossley & McDonald, 1980; Sienkiewicz-Mercer & Kaplan, 1989) and with their literary accomplishments (Brown, 1970; Nolan, 1986). Christopher Nolan's account of his emergence as a writer exemplifies an emerging literary trend of autobiographical accounts by people long presumed unable to think in the abstract and unable to express themselves. In *Under the Eye of the Clock,* Nolan (1987) calls himself Joseph:

> Nora sat watching. Spasms ripped through Joseph's body. Sweat stood out on his face. He was trying to let his mother see what he was capable of. She was not impressed. He could see that despite his ordeal. The phone rang and Eva suggested that perhaps Nora would take over from her and hold Joseph's head. The spasms held him rigid but within a couple of minutes he felt himself relaxing. Nora waited, her son's chin cupped in her hands. Then he stretched and brought his pointer down and typed the letter "e." Swinging his pointer to the right he then typed another letter, and another one and another. Eva finished speaking on the telephone and Nora, while still cupping Joseph's chin turned and said, "Eva, I know what you're talking about—Joseph is going for the keys himself—I could actually feel him stretching for them." Eva, his courageous teacher, clenched her fist and brought it down with a bang on the table. "So I was right, I was afraid to say anything, I had to be sure," she said as she broadly smiled.
>
> Joseph sat looking at his women saviors. They chatted about their discovery while he nodded in happy unbelievable bewilderment. He felt himself float reliably on gossamer wings. He hungered no more. He giggled nervously before he even bespoke his thanks. He cheered all the way up the corridor, said goodbye to dear Eva and giggled and cheered up into Nora's face all the way home.
>
> Feeble Joseph was just eleven years old, but before long he would be taking on Nora, schooling her to see what he could see, instructing her to steady his head for him while he typed beauty from within, beauty of secret knowledge so secretly hidden and so nearly lost forever. (p. 56)

Despite these breakthroughs recounted in popular as well as research literature, the idea of competence among people with certain labels continues to surprise, if only because the labels that people have had thrust on them, especially the label "retardation," convey the opposite expectation. Consider, for example, David Goode's (1992) account of discovering competence in a person with Down syndrome; the man, named Bobby, had received pessimistic diagnoses of communicative and cognitive abilities:

> Communicative assessment: ". . . Speech or language therapy is not recommended as prognosis for improvement is poor . . . client can communicate basic needs but cannot express complex ideas and understands very little . . . difficult to communicate with. . . ."

> Cognitive assessment: A quick test of intelligence yielded a mental age of approximately 2.8 years. Clinician concludes that Bobby is "severely mentally retarded. . . ." (p. 200)

When Goode and his colleagues played back a videotape they had made of Bobby interacting with others, adjusting the tonal quality of the sound, they suddenly saw a different Bobby revealed:

> When we mechanically altered Bobby's tonal qualities on the tape, many . . . formerly senseless utterances became more audible. By means of mechanical readjustment they were perceived as sensible (or sometimes potentially sensible) statements. Anyone who interacted with Bobby would perceive that his speech was apraxic. It was less obvious that his syntactically fractured talk had meaning, and especially that it was meaningfully related to the context of conversations. It had been our common assumption that Bobby did not understand much of what went on around him. But after watching the tape perhaps thirty times, a new definition of the situation emerged: Bobby's behavior seemed more like that of a foreign-speaking person than like a retarded one. Apart from his difficulties in making himself understood, the transcript of that tape revealed that Bobby had followed the direction of the conversation and had produced semantically meaningful, if ill-formed utterances. We began to appreciate that cognitively, Bobby was far more complex than we had supposed. (pp. 204–205)

Upon reading a passage such as this, one is wont to ask: Why have such "discoveries" not been more widely discussed in the disability literature? Similarly, why have Bobby's considerable reasoning and communication abilities not been taken by those in the disability field as a possible sign that many people's competence has been missed?

BREAKTHROUGH IN DENMARK

A group in Denmark has in fact generalized such a discovery from one to many people with disabilities, although, as with the instance of

Bobby, the larger disability field has not yet recognized the broader import of their success. An account from Denmark by Ian Johnson (1989) in a British journal describes how 14 residents of House M at the Danish institution Vangedehuse began to communicate by pointing at letters on letter boards. The 14 were presumed to have intellectual abilities at a "functioning level of ½–3 years" (p. 13). All but one do not speak. The one who speaks does so only occasionally. "They all have emotional disturbances which are manifested in various ways: aggressive; self-destructive; passive 'flight' of various types" (p. 14). When they began to type or to point at letters, all revealed "very correct written language, with few spelling errors," although "their styles and levels of sophistication vary a good deal from one to the other" (pp. 14–15). Johnson credits the staff's attitude: They treat the residents as people of their chronological ages and look for any signals, including facial expressions or body language, of their willingness to try communicating through pointing or typing.

The first person among the group to communicate was 22-year-old Helle, whose teacher made the discovery. Helle is described as multi-handicapped. She can stand with support and is able to walk short distances. "She has been evaluated as psychotic and possibly knowledge-concealing," Johnson writes (1989, p. 16). When she first began to communicate with her teacher, she would do so only when they were alone. Johnson reports that the teacher was not believed by colleagues. Helle only began to communicate at House M with other facilitators two years later. Then, one by one, each of the House M residents revealed literacy abilities. Johnson's description of the Vangedehuse communication method closely resembles facilitated communication:

> We hold the resident's hand so that the forefinger is pointing, hold the hand against an alphabet board and then he or she points to letters. The alphabet boards are usually quite small, even pocket size. We can easily have them everywhere and use them in all situations. Some residents need a much lighter 'hold' than others. Sometimes the process goes quite fast, but at other times the resident moves very slowly or even comes to a standstill. We encourage them to carry on sometimes by shaking or squeezing the hand just to bring their concentration back or at other times taking a minute's break and then carrying on. (p. 18)

Johnson reports that the "more aggressive" residents seemed to calm down over time. When asked how they had learned to read and spell, many said they learned from television. Many of the residents required encouragement and moral support to type or point. Eventually, many participants at an adult activity center attended by the House M residents also began to use the communication method.

In addition to everyday, conversational communication, the House M residents wrote poetry about themselves, their communication, and the world. Helle, for example, wrote a poem, "To my brother" (Johnson, 1989, p. 21):

> One day my brother
> Looked in judgement on his strange sister
> And wished his beloved Helle was normal
> My friend, I this odd creature
> Want to be appreciated as any other
> And wonder if you love my soul
> Despite my body.
>   Helle

Another resident, Pia, wrote a poem entitled "Difficult" (Johnson, 1989, p. 22):

> It's difficult
> It's really difficult!
> It's difficult
> Only the mouths that talk
> Get attention!
> Only the mouths that talk
> Give a direct kick up the arse,
> To those who listen
> Sometimes the world must realize
> That life inside is dark and difficult
> Physique gets in the way
> The world understands only talk
> May be the world is blind.
>
> Now the world experiences the thoughts of the silent
> I wonder if God Job was cold and blind
> When he gave others silence as both crazy birthright and childhood illness.
>   Pia

I visited Ian Johnson and House M residents in June of 1990. During the trip, I also visited a day training center in Ishoj, Denmark, a work-training center attended by several of he House M residents as well as other adults with severe disabilities. Through conversations and observations, I saw that the communication method being used was very much like what Crossley has labeled "facilitated communication." The people with whom it was being used include people classified as autistic and multihandicapped.

One man, Johan, who cannot talk, used a letter board to spell responses to my questions. (Because my notes of the Denmark conversations are based on translations from Danish to English of what the individuals actually spelled, the transcriptions that follow do not include any of their pointing errors—e.g., extra or wrong letters.) Johan told me that his disability was KNOWLEDGE HIDING. He said that he had learned on his own how to read: YOU THINK I AM CLEVER, BUT I AM MORE THAN THAT. I COLLECTED UP LETTERS FROM HERE AND THERE. A man at the activity center told me that he had learned by watching television and BY READING THINGS THAT WERE LYING AROUND. When I asked whether any of the residents had exhibited the problem of saying one thing while typing another, Johnson explained that they had and that one had spelled, WHY IS IT NOT THE WORDS I THINK THAT COME OUT?

Ironically, and depressingly, the life circumstances of people at Vangedehuse's House M and at the Ishoj activity center have not changed markedly since they began to communicate. True, they are generally treated as competent by most people in each setting, but they have not moved out of the institutional cottages to apartments in the community or from the activity center to jobs. They can make choices about clothing, food, and the like, yet they still spend large segments of their time doing little and being bored. One staff person at House M remarked, "They hoped for a revolution and nothing happened." This is an issue that I will discuss in Chapter 7, in relation to the experiences of people in using facilitated communication not only in Denmark but also in the United States and elsewhere.

Some seem to have lost hope that their lives can really change. In response to my question about whether he could imagine himself working, perhaps with support, one man spelled, IT SOUNDS CAPTIVATING BUT I DONT BELIEVE IN IT. Another man told me that ITS OFTEN BETTER TO NOT DO ANYTHING, TO GET PEACE OF MIND BY BEING STUPID.

Others still maintain hope. I had an extended conversation with a man named Carsten, one of those who remains optimistic. I WOULD LIKE PEOPLE TO STOP PEOPLE THINKING OF OTHER PEOPLE AS STUPID. THAT WOULD HELP PEOPLE LIKE ME TO SHOW OURSELVES, OUR PERSONALITIES, he told me. THAT FREEDOM LIES A LONG WAY AHEAD. BUT IM ON THE WAY, he further spelled. He explained that it was strange to have his words translated to another language (from Danish to English), but that it was wonderful THAT SOMEONE FROM THE GREAT

WORLD WANTS TO LISTEN TO WHAT I SAY. He spelled, I WOULD LIKE
TO TELL YOU MUCH MORE ABOUT MYSELF BUT I NEED QUESTIONS TO
BE ABLE TO AVOID DISCUSSING MY OWN NAVEL. Having said this,
though, he continued to spell:

> I THINK YOU ARE COMPLETELY CLEAR HOW IT FEELS TO GROW UP
> AS A STUPID BABY. THEREFORE I WONT TELL YOU ABOUT THAT.
> BUT I NEED TO HEAR HOW PEOPLE IN OTHER COUNTRIES CAN
> CHOOSE THINGS FOR THEMSELVES. HERE ITS THE PARENTS WHO
> CHOOSE FOR US. EVEN THOUGH WE'RE ADULTS. THAT'S SOME-
> THING I'D LIKE TO CHANGE.

I told him that although I had not had to endure such treatment myself,
the fact that I work with people with disabilities evokes condescension
in some quarters, with people telling me that I must be "so patient,"
that it must be "depressing," and that it is "noble to work with the handicapped."

I told Carsten what I knew about self-advocacy groups and asked if
he was planning on attending an upcoming self-advocacy conference in
Paris. MY PARENTS WONT SPEND MONEY ON ME TO GO THERE. THAT'S
THE FIRST PROBLEM, he explained. Then he continued:

> I THINK THERE'S A HEAVY CLOUD OF PROBLEMS THAT I WANT TO
> SOLVE. I FEEL I AM WITHOUT RIGHTS. I HAVE DIFFICULTY IN
> COMING THROUGH, FIGHTING MY WAY THROUGH THE FIRST PROB-
> LEM. I'D VERY MUCH LIKE TO HEAR HOW THE PEOPLE CAN
> REACH, BE ABLE TO TRAVEL. HAVE THEY PARENTS WHO THINK
> ITS A GOOD IDEA OR DO THEY HAVE HELP FROM SOCIAL WORKERS
> WITH FUNDS TO BE ABLE TO COME WITH THEM.

"It's probably a combination of both," I volunteered. Carsten related the
difficulty of gaining funds for travel to the broader question of being
taken seriously even at home in Denmark:

> HERE . . . WE HAVE DISCUSSIONS IN THE NEWSPAPERS ABOUT
> HOW MUCH PEOPLE CAN BELIEVE WHAT WE WRITE. EVEN IN HOS-
> PITALS TO HAVE SOMEONE WHO HELPS WE HAVE TO HAVE SOMEONE
> WITH US TO ASK FOR US TO BE TREATED AS HUMAN BEINGS,
> OTHERWISE WE'RE TREATED AS SMALL BABIES. I THINK IT
> WILL TAKE A LONGER TIME HERE IN DENMARK BEFORE WE CAN
> ORGANIZE FOR RIGHTS.

Carsten added that he hoped this would all change for young children with disabilities.

As we communicated back and forth, Carsten pointed quickly. His facilitator had to keep her eyes riveted to his small, 3" × 7" letter board to catch his words. She spoke them in Danish and Ian Johnson translated. Throughout, it was impossible not to notice that much of the time Carsten looked away from the letter board, usually looking to his left side, with the board situated below his right hand. When asked if it would not be easier to point if he looked at the board, he answered, YES YOU'RE PROBABLY RIGHT THAT I OUGHT TO LOOK DOWN BUT I'M A CURIOUS PERSON, CURIOUS IN THE SENSE OF ·WANTING TO LOOK AROUND. Carsten's facilitator pointed out that he moves far more slowly when communicating with a new facilitator. Also, she explained, he types more carefully when using a computer. Carsten added that with some people he has no success with communication at all:

> ITS AS THOUGH WE DON'T OR CAN'T FIND A RHYTHM BECAUSE THEY'RE SO NERVOUS. THEY'RE GOING TO READ WRONG OR MIS-UNDERSTAND. SO I'M NOT ABLE TO EXPRESS MYSELF. SOME OF THOSE PEOPLE I'VE KNOWN FOR A LONG TIME AND AT THE TIME WHERE I COULD ONLY SMILE AND SCREAM AND CRY. IF ONLY THEY ARE AFRAID TO ALLOW ME TO SPEAK BECAUSE THEY MAYBE THINK THAT I'M ANGRY AT THEM BECAUSE THEY, ONE TIME THEY WERE ROUGH OR AWFUL WITH ME. HOWEVER, I'M NOT ANGRY AT ALL. THEY DIDN'T KNOW ANY BETTER AND OFTEN I BELLOWED TOO MUCH.

CONCLUSION

Carsten was not alone in his bellowing. Each of the people described in this chapter was at one time or another known to make loud noises and to *not* communicate. Owing to certain factors and conditions, all now *do* communicate with words; that is, all can communicate with typed or written words and sentences, rather than with bellowing. By way of concluding this account of multiple, similar but separately occurring discoveries, it may be helpful to consider the factors and conditions that appear to have been present in each instance.

First, although at the outset none of these individuals could communicate effectively, all were approached by parents or teachers with an attitude of openness to the possibility that they might be able to communicate. Each was observed, carefully, for any sign of communicative intent or ability. Gayle Marquez read to her daughter Lyrica and placed letters and words in front of her; the Schawlows tried numerous activities and communication devices; Mary Bacon literally demanded that her students show her what they knew. Goode (1992) refers to this attitude of openness or of looking for how the person him- or herself might define his or her life and how he or she might be communicating, as an "emic" perspective, rather than the usual, professional, "etic" perspective. Several of Helen Keller's family members had the emic view. Even before Anne Sullivan arrived to begin working with Helen, Helen was observed to have developed over 60 signs; for example, "she imitated the motions of cutting bread and spreading butter" for bread and butter, and for ice cream she would pretend to turn the freezer and shiver (Lash, 1980, p. 47). When Helen's father would put down the evening paper, she would imitate him by climbing into his chair, putting the paper in front of her eyes, and putting on his glasses (Lash, 1980, p. 47). And when going for a ride in the surrey, she would refuse to wear her bonnet, untying it and throwing it to the ground, then pulling on her nurse's bandanna, indicating that she wanted a bandanna to wear instead (Lash, 1980, p. 47).

Second, the facilitators—in these instances parents, a teacher, and staff of an institutional residence—were persistent and inventive! Gayle Marquez and the Schawlows worked with their children for several years before making a breakthough. They used a simple method of trial and error; it was thus that each independently discovered the need to hold onto the child's arm in the initial stages of communication. Similarly, Helle's teacher and House M staff "discovered" the residents' communicative abilities over a period of years. Ruth Sullivan's discovery that writing could allow her son Joseph more control over his communication also derived from a combination of persistence—she was exasperated but still willing to try another approach—and inventiveness. Katie Dolan would certainly never have discovered her son Patrick's use of record lyrics for communication if she had not been a careful observer.

Third, physical touch and emotional support seem essential in helping the person with autism or related disabilities focus on original communication. For some people to be able to express themselves, they need to be released from their compulsions. The physical touch may accomplish that. Also, they need to feel they can do the task being asked of them, whether typing, pointing, or handwriting; the physical act may require a supportive hand. In some instances, the teachers or parents were battle axes, fierce, demanding, and expectant of progress—Mary

Bacon slapped her side, Gayle Marquez and the Schawlows tried a vast array of activities, and Ruth Sullivan tried writing with Joseph. But along with their demands and perseverence they conveyed support, especially the clear message that they expected these children and young adults to be able to communicate back to them. In each instance, the facilitators provided opportunities and time for the communication user to practice and thus to get better at the activity of communicating. The facilitators had relationships with the people with whom they worked, knew them well, and cared about them. It appears that individuals with autism need facilitators who *want* them to succeed!

Fourth, instances of communication were not discredited by the facilitators as islands of ability or as noncomprehending use of language. In other words, the facilitators did not allow prevailing theories of autism to invalidate the evidence of literacy and competence that they observed. When other people around them, including knowledgeable professionals, were disbelieving, uninterested, unsupportive, or even antagonistic, these parents, the teacher, and the residential staff remained steadfast in their optimism and determination.

CHAPTER 5

The Validation Controversy Returns: Are the Words Theirs?

Each of the early discoverers of facilitated communication mentioned in the previous chapter encountered disbelief or, at the very least, skepticism. Professionals and others wanted evidence that their sons and daughters or students were really the source of the typing. Some critics, in the positivist tradition, demanded that the method be tested experimentally.[1] Not surprisingly, concerns about who was doing the typing soon developed into full blown controversy.

NEGATIVE POSITIVISTS

Seven months after publication of "Communication Unbound" (Biklen, 1990) in the *Harvard Educational Review,* Melbourne's leading newspaper, *The Sunday Age,* published an "exposé" of facilitated communication under the six-column banner headline: "Experts slam disabled 'charade'" (Heinrichs, 1991). The article heralded criticisms of Robert Cummins, a Senior Lecturer at Victoria College, and Margot Prior, a professor at La Trobe University. They reportedly claimed that "on not a single occasion," had there been systematic tests showing that the claimed communication derived from the people with disabilities (p. 1). "It's time to call a halt to the charade," Cummins is quoted as saying, to "an apparent cult of deception or illusion" (p. 1).

Cummins and Prior (1991) raised three main concerns: (1) that facilitated communication involves witting or unwitting manipulation of people with disabilities, whereby the facilitator's words are attributed to the communication user; (2) that facilitated communication has never been empirically tested and therefore has not been proven valid; and (3) that claims about facilitated communication contradict 50 years of research in autism and developmental disabilities.

Manipulation

Regarding the first concern—manipulation, cuing, or what has also been referred to as the "Clever Hans Phenomenon" (Sebeok & Rosenthal, 1981)—Cummins and Prior correctly note that I reported the problem of "cuing" in the "Communication Unbound" article. But my concern with cuing involved instances during training in or early phases of facilitated communication where facilitators were not certain whether or not they were prompting certain selections. These instances of doubt about possible cuing did not invalidate the individuals' ability to spell, type words and sentences, and communicate their own thoughts. Rather, while it was true that in the early stages of training communicators might respond either to unintended physical cues or to their perceptions of what the facilitator wanted them to say, the same people who displayed evidence of being cued also revealed the ability to communicate on their own, in their own words.

At the crux of Cummins and Prior's criticism is the matter of voluntariness, which they either choose to ignore or simply do not understand. "There is . . . a problem of logic which the providers of direct motor assistance [Cummins and Prior prefer to refer to facilitated communication as "direct motor assistance" and "assisted communication"—they not only object to claims about facilitated communication, they want to rename it as well] seem unwilling to address" they argue (Cummins & Prior, 1991, p. 15). Since "voluntary control over *any muscle in the body to almost any degree* can now be used to activate a switching device to enable independent communication," they write, "it may be asked why anyone who possessed the ability for voluntary movement and the cognitive capacity to use that movement for communicative purposes would choose to be tied to an 'assistant'" (pp. 15–16; emphasis original). They answer their own question:

> The success of assisted communication has very little to do with emotional support, . . . and very much to do with physical control by the assistant; either in the form of overt control of the client's movements or by supplying covert cues which are used by the client to control his or her movements. (p. 16)

They further argue that if facilitated communication involves physical manipulation, this would explain a number of observations in my first study of facilitation (Biklen, 1990), such as the following: that a student typed, LET ME SHOW THEM WHAT I CAN REALLY DO, but could not independently communicate, either by typing or useful speech; that some students could communicate with some facilitators but not others, even if they expressed a desire to do so; that some students had been unable to progress to independent communication despite more than a year or two of communication training; and that one student used a word that was incorrect—a word that I had used in another part of the "Communication Unbound" article. While manipulation of communicators *would* indeed explain these events, so too would students' presumed neuromotor difficulties, particularly apraxia, as well as students' presumed poor confidence and need for emotional support. Curiously, Cummins and Prior seem unwilling to give serious attention to these two hypotheses, especially to apraxia, despite the fact that both concepts have been central to explanations of facilitated communication (Biklen, 1990; Crossley, 1988).

The only one of the "anomalies" raised by Cummins and Prior that is not explained by apraxia is their criticism that the word *suborn* appears in two places in "Communication Unbound," the original *Harvard Educational Review* article (Biklen, 1990), and that it is wrongly used, first by me and then by a student, Polly. In the first instance, I should have used the word *subordinate*. In the second instance, after listening more than 20 times to the audiotape of the interview in which I attribute *suborn* to Polly, I have concluded that the word was probably *subject*. The quotation from Polly should have read, "unless daring people subject their own wishes, it will fail." (I made this correction in retelling this account in Chapter 1 of this book.) Interestingly, Polly now types independently much of the time, with no supportive touch at all.

To further buttress their charge of manipulation, Cummins and Prior claim that the students I observed in Australia are reported by me as using non-Australian words, as being too sophisticated in their thoughts, as being too literate, and as being too consistently negative about their own past treatment. They charge that "some of the words are extremely rare and would not normally be part of the Australian young person's linguistic environment (e.g., nosey—this is a colloquialism not used here)" (Cummins & Prior, 1991, p. 11). The editor of one of Australia's most famous dictionaries of slang and colloquialisms, *The Dinkum Dictionary: A Ripper Guide to Aussie English* (Johansen, 1988), apparently disagrees with Cummins and Prior: "*nosey enough to want to know the ins and outs of a chook's (domestic fowl, chicken) bum (anus) . . .* (also: nosy) inquisitive; prying; snoopy" (pp. 285–286). On the cover of my copy of this dictionary, a reviewer is quoted as calling *The Dinkum Dictionary* a compendium of "the words we *really* use." The student who typed the word NOSEY did so with a facilitator's hand on his shoulder and no other support; Cummins and Prior have not explained how it would be possible for a facilitator to manipulate any person, let alone a person who has a range of extraneous behavior including hand flapping, to type out statements such as NOSEY PEOPLE TO EVEN WANT TO SEE ME through cues transmitted only by a hand on his shoulder.

Regarding the matter of students typing content that is sophisticated beyond their years, Cummins and Prior charge that the discussion with four students that appears on pages 306 to 310 of "Communication Unbound" (Biklen, 1990) is "of such an abstract and sophisticated level that it reads like a conversation between well educated adults with a strong interest in philosophical issues" and is "amazing," "likely to be characteristic of gifted teenagers," and "statistically improbable" (Cummins & Prior, 1991, p. 12). I freely admit to having been delighted at the sophisticated conversation in which four students asked me about my work, argued with me about the pros and cons of mainstreaming, and challenged my ideas about the likelihood of making society more accommodating and accepting of people with disabilities. Inasmuch as all four students have disabilities and all were treated as retarded prior to being introduced to facilitation, it is not surprising that they would have well thought-out ideas about disability and social policy. But I am not convinced that my conversation with them was terribly unlike the kinds of conversations that we may observe in schools or in other organized teenage discussion groups. I recall having conversations of a similar nature when I was in high school, albeit about different issues, generally the dangers of nuclear war, U.S. foreign policy, and modern art. Further, some of the students' comments concerned mundane matters, such as my reactions to Australia, whether or not I am rich, and my wife's name. Three of the four were able to type relatively independently, with just a hand on the shoulder or at the elbow. Thus Cummins and Prior's objection again deteriorates to the claim that because the evidence I reported contradicts dominant theories of autism, it therefore cannot be true.

At a more fundamental level, Cummins and Prior challenge the idea that students introduced to facilitated communication would suddenly reveal spelling abilities. I too was surprised by this. Similarly, our subsequent Syracuse studies revealed surprising literacy abilities, hence my use of the term *unexpected* to describe these abilities. To understand this phenomenon, I turned to the literature on early reading skills (see the discussion of this in Chapter 2).

Next, Cummins and Prior (1991) register "concern" with "the regularity with which Crossley's many subjects over the years have produced communications (exemplified in this paper) referring to years of injustice, misunderstanding and shoddy treatment, blame of previous caretakers, and prescriptions for appropriate treatment of people who are handicapped" (p. 12). I reviewed my article (Biklen, 1990) and found no such statements about years of injustice. The only quotations remotely fitting that description are MY MOTHER FEELS IM STUPID BE-CAUSE I CANT USE MY VOICE PROPERLY (p. 296) and IT WAS HELL AND I COULD NOT EVEN BEGIN TO MAKE MY NEEDS KNOWN (p. 311). Neither seems intrinsically unlikely or terribly negative. Louis's mother probably did believe he was intellectually disabled, as did most of the rest of his world; Brian could not make his needs known, at least until he could communicate with facilitation. On the other hand, it does not surprise me at all that when individuals first develop a means to express themselves they would want to make clear their wishes and feelings, especially concerning their own treatment. Is it really surprising that people who have been shut away in institutions or in disabled-only schools might complain about such treatment? Such views pervade autobiographical accounts by people with disabilities (e.g., Grandin & Scariano, 1986; Mairs, 1986; Nolan, 1987; Sienkiewicz-Mercer & Kaplan, 1989; Zola, 1982).

Empirical Testing

The draft article by Cummins and Prior (1991) in which their criticisms appear came to me from Arthur Schawlow. Schawlow reacted to it much as I did, and in so doing addresses Cummins and Prior's second major criticism of facilitated communication, that it has not been empirically tested. The issue of testing is discussed in a later section of this chapter (see also my response to Cummins & Prior: Biklen, 1992), but Arthur Schawlow's comments are presented here. In a covering letter to me, he wrote,

> Even though they [Cummins and Prior] admit . . . that "It is undoubtedly the case that some people can progress from assisted communication to independent communication," they seem to be trying hard to prove that assisted communication does not exist. . . . This attitude makes me angry because it could lead to denying the possibility of assisted communication to autistic people who need it desperately. (A. L. Schawlow, personal communication, March 31, 1991)

"Looked at in the most objective light," Schawlow wrote, the Cummins and Prior paper (1991) "indicates the great difficulty in providing objective proof of assisted communication." Schawlow's own experiences with his son who has autism shape his reading of Cummins and Prior's call for validation tests:

> Autistic people are often locked into rituals of various kinds, and a small variation in procedure can sometimes be troublesome. Moreover, they sometimes do want to please the facilitator by typing what they think he wants. Further, they often fantasize. Our son has many times told us good things that have happened, which turn out to be really just things he wishes had happened. Some questions just don't interest him, and he is likely to say just about anything then. . . .
>
> For all these reasons, and from our extensive experience, I believe that it is all too easy to devise a test of facilitated communication that will give a negative result. (A. L. Schawlow, personal communication, March 31, 1991)

Interestingly, Katie Dolan, the parent mentioned in the previous chapter whose son uses record lyrics to convey his thoughts, wrote similar comments in her letter to Bernard Rimland. She wrote to him:

> You . . . asked for . . . a test "to once and for all end the controversy" in your last Autism Research newsletter. Thank God for you scientists. But lest we forget, people with autism have never responded to any of our tests. It is wrong of us to demand that they pass tests that we have not been able to develop for them.

Controverting 50 Years of Research

The third concern, stated by Prior, is that if it is true that facilitated communication allows many people with autism to reveal normal literacy, this "would represent a major challenge to almost 50 years of energetic and sustained research into the problems of autistic children" (Heinrichs, 1991, p. 6). I addressed this challenge in an op-ed piece that appeared in the next week's *Sunday Age* (Biklen, 1991). In addition to explaining the several ways in which we learned that the students' words were their own (e.g., unique phonetic and creative spellings, students' transmission of information not known to the facilitators, students' tendencies to say things in unusual ways and to say things that teachers would not typically say in the presence of their students, including swearing, the students' remarkably different uses of language and their different personalities despite their having the same facilitators, and so forth), I reported my total agreement with Prior's conclusion: "Prior is certainly correct. Indeed, Crossley's development of facilitated communication promises to revolutionize the field of autism and more importantly the lives of people with autism and related communication disorders" (Biklen, 1991, p. 15).

Throughout their critique of "Communication Unbound," Cummins and Prior (1991) create straw arguments that, not surprisingly, they destroy easily. The most egregious of their concoctions appears in their introduction, when they say that if my finding is correct that people with autism are using language at a sophisticated level, "It might suggest that Kanner's (1943) original hypothesis is right after all, i.e., that children with autism are actually very intelligent, *but the depth of their emotional disturbance means that their abilities rarely emerge. However, that belief has been challenged by research*" (p. 3; emphasis added). I neither said that nor implied it. Crossley (1988, 1990) and I (Biklen, 1990) provide considerable detail about and discussion of the fact that the forms of neuromotor difficulties, including apraxia, experienced by people with autism would explain the difficulties of communication and the successes revealed through facilitation. It seems that Cummins and Prior want to attribute to me what their arguments would have been in this situation. But none of *their* arguments are my arguments.

A FATHER'S LETTER

As I have already noted, Cummins and Prior are not alone in their criticisms and concerns. Throughout our work of implementing facilitated communication, many people have voiced disbelief in it. How could something so simple not have been discovered much earlier? One expert on autism even asked, "Are you saying that even the severely retarded ones can read?" Bernard Rimland had heard Crossley and me make a presentation on facilitated communication and graciously pointed out to the questioner that we were not saying that, but rather that the people with whom we were working were not retarded after all. Others asked why we refused to blindfold the facilitators. Many people told us that they found our work interesting but that they were suspending judgment until they could be convinced that it is valid. Some said that they found it hard to believe. Ironically, for well over a year, most experts in autism did not initiate talking with me or any of our research group about the matter, perhaps for much the same reason that I had at first been skeptical myself of facilitated communication (see Chapter 1): Descriptions of students with autism writing normal sentences just did not fit with the prevailing conception of autism as primarily a cognitive, social, and communicative disorder. At times we felt that expertise in autism was a fairly good predictor that people would be disbelieving. While a number of parents expressed skepticism as well, there seemed to be far more skepticism from parents of older children than of younger children. Some of the parents of young children were actually not enthralled with facilitated communication, but only because they were still hoping that their children might develop effective speech.

Some critics simply called us charlatans. Six months after first introducing facilitated communication in Syracuse, I received a letter from one father distraught about facilitated communication.[2] While entirely negative, his letter captures nearly all of the concerns I have heard leveled against facilitated communication and is thus helpful for understanding the breadth of such doubts. The letter was addressed to the daughter's school principal, with a copy to me. While the principal met with the father to discuss his concerns, the father's disbelief was not assuaged; the girl's mother, on the other hand, was enthusiastic about facilitated communication and insisted on its being available as part of her daughter's school program.

The father's complaints were numerous and strong. Among them he declared, *"I have tried facilitated communication . . . many times with no results."* I faced this same problem when I first observed and tried facilitation in Australia. To learn the method I observed others using it and then tried it myself, but with only modest results; students would do structured, predictable work (i.e., set work) with me, including math problems, fill-in-the-blanks exercises, and homonym matching, but usually not anything open-ended. At least, with the open-ended work, I was not confident that I was not cuing the students. For example, with no one else in the room, one student typed for me that her favorite football team was the Blues. Yet when I asked her father what he thought her favorite team was, he said, "No, not the Blues; it's the Cardinals." Immediately I felt a wave of self-doubt wash over me. Had I inadvertently cued her to type Blues, a team that I had heard many people talk about in Melbourne?

Fortunately, I could explore the matter further. With one of the student's regular facilitators present, we could ask her why she had typed Blues. She explained that one of the staff at her group home was a Blues fan and that she had switched to the Blues. I was reassured by this response, yet I still wondered whether I had cued her to type Blues. In any case, I did not wonder whether this particular student could type sentences and communicate abstract thoughts. With her regular facilitators, she was able to type with no touch at all or with the facilitator holding onto just a hair of her mohair sweater. Similarly, in several instances I facilitated students who had worked with DEAL staff for a number of months or even years, students who were virtually independent (e.g., a hand on the shoulder, fingers on the thread of a student's sweater, a hand on the back, a familiar facilitator next to but not touching the person); thus I was able to see that they certainly could communicate effectively and nearly independently.

Since the observations by the father in Syracuse came near the beginning of our work, and since his daughter's poor muscle tone and general floppiness require support close to the wrist or on the hand, it was truly difficult to see who was responding. As noted in Chapter 1, when facilitating a person for the first time or in the early stages, especially if the person's movements are slow and muscle tone is low, the facilitator sometimes cannot be sure that the movements are those of the individual with the disability (see Remington-Gurney, 1989). As much as it bothered me to hear his severe doubts, I could understand them. When it was suggested to this father that the facilitator's confidence in the child could possibly influence the facilitator's success, he became even more offended: "I firmly believe that if [my daughter] were able to or had the desire to communicate with anyone she would do it with me. I say this not out of pride but out of a confidence in my feeling of the nature of our relationship; that it is very strong and many other types of communication take place or exist between us constantly." Unfortunately, he felt accused of being an inadequate father on the basis of his being unsuccessful in facilitating his daughter's communication: "I do not believe that this [using facilitated communication] should be a contest to see who can be the closest to [my daughter] with the 'proof' being who can produce the best results using facilitated communication."

"*Raising false hopes does a disservice . . . by creating the illusion that handicapped people must fit into our scheme of 'normal' instead of [our] accepting and valuing them for who they really are.*" This father believed that the school was attempting to show his daughter as "something she is really not," redefining how to view his daughter rather than recognizing her limitations. Instead, he argued, "savants" are exceptions, with "many autistic people . . . functionally retarded (70% to be precise with half of this group nonverbal)." It is certainly true that with facilitation his daughter was being redefined as someone of seemingly normal intelligence rather than as severely retarded. All of a sudden she was doing well in math (she was first in her class), spelling, and other academic work. Previously, although she had been integrated with nondisabled students in a regular second grade, she had not been thought capable of academic work. Claims of her academic successes offended this father:

> My child is severely handicapped. This breaks my heart; but I have learned to live with that and make it part of my joy. I cannot in good conscience allow that to be erased by the denial of others; that [she] . . . is reading and comprehending after giving her second-grade reading, social studies, spelling, science, and math texts (at Doug Biklen's recommendation) is incredibly ludicrous, not to mention a serious fabrication. To have been told to my face that this severely handicapped, brain-injured child is the top math student in her second grade class is absolutely intolerable. The onus of responsibility to prove whether this so-called method is effective should rest on the practitioner.

Again, the father's disbelief is understandable, and he is right that the burden of proof should be on those who profess particular levels of competence. Once again, however, we were in the awkward position of having to ask critics to give us and the communication users (i.e., the students) time to achieve more independence. This man's daughter had conveyed information not known to her teacher, she had sworn at her teacher, and she had demonstrated gaps in her knowledge—for example, she revealed that she did not know how Roman numerals worked—but if these evidences that the words and selections were her own did not convince him, he would have to wait for her to become more independent. In the meantime, I had to admit to being at least a little complacent in the recognition that if particular claims of a student's competence ever were to prove false, it seemed better to err in the direction of competence than incompetence. I agree with this father when he writes, "We need to communicate honestly about handicaps; otherwise the message is given that it is not o.k. to be who we are." But if we were truly honest, we would have to acknowledge that certainty about the meaning of individual disabilities, particularly so-called intellectual abilities, has always been illusive.

"Even if it were true that (my daughter) were able to communicate through f.c., I find this very impractical in a real-world setting." This father's concern is that if facilitation works only with certain facilitators, then what good is it in her real life? My response is that if his daughter can communicate only with certain facilitators—we have found that thus far students communicate with some facilitators better than with others and with some not at all or only to a very limited extent—arguably, that is still

better than not being able to communicate at all! But, the father asks, "Where does this leave my daughter? Still having to be dressed ten years from now while Dr. Biklen basks in his new-found glory?" Here, the father raises a different issue: In focusing on communication, is the school ignoring other crucial needs, for example, self-help or skills of independent living? Conceivably, his daughter may not improve remarkably in other aspects of her life, including dressing herself, for it appears that all aspects of physical activity—not just speaking and writing or typing—are difficult for students with autism and similar apraxia. Yet in introducing facilitated communication, I have never argued against helping students develop other skills, including dressing.

"You must understand how difficult it is to enter into a discussion with a proponent of facilitated communication. . . . The nature of the discussion is closed in that if the child does not produce the message for any certain person the [reason] . . . is that the child is merely choosing not to produce or give a message because he/she is 'afraid,' doesn't want to be 'found out,' doesn't 'trust,' the facilitator doesn't 'believe' strongly enough and the child 'senses' this, or for some reason only the child knows. This . . . circular reasoning . . . leaves no room for discussion." Of course the fact that a student does not communicate with certain facilitators does not explain why the person does not communicate. Some students have typed words to the effect that "so-and-so doesn't believe I am smart" or "so-and-so doesn't believe in me," or "so-and-so doesn't know how to do it." But such typing is apparently not convincing to this father, for it could have originated from the "successful" facilitator as a cover story for the student's failed communication with other facilitators. Rather, I can only argue that the issue of the communication user's confidence in the facilitator is a hypothesis for which there appears to be considerable support, especially in the fact that communication users in different schools and even in different parts of the world have conveyed this reason independently. Also, it is quite observable that even students who become independent in their communication with a familiar facilitator sitting next to them usually must start at the beginning with a new facilitator, requiring support on the hand, wrist, or arm; unless one believes that the regular facilitator is in some way giving visual signs or cues—even this would involve rather remarkable skill on the part of the communication user—this would appear to give credence to the hypothesis that confidence is important and perhaps crucial.

"The assumptions being made about [my daughter] and her condition can only lead me to believe that the people working with her believe that autism is an emotional disturbance. I and many others believe that autism is not primarily an emotional disturbance but rather a biological or perhaps a genetic problem. I

. . . challenge the assumption that inside [my daughter] there is another person who is just dying to get out and merely needs a facilitated form of communication in order to reveal her true personality." I agree with this father that autism is most likely a "biological or perhaps a genetic problem." It appears to be a neurologically based problem that affects motor abilities, including communication as well as social interaction and expression of feelings. I do not see any evidence that autism is a form of emotional disturbance. Even when a student does not facilitate with a certain person, I am not convinced that this failure to do so is entirely voluntary. Rather, in suggesting that confidence may be implicated, I imply nothing different from what has been said of people performing any number of physical activities, including sports: Confidence seems to play a part in performance.

"If she were really so proficient at using the Canon Communicator, then why does she so often just make a quick stab at gibberish and continue to go to the Handi-Voice [a typing device with speech synthesis output]. . . . Unless someone is guiding her hand she will not type anything but a random series of letters, usually within the same area of the keyboard." This father apparently tried to replicate the method, without success. His daughter was willing to point, but "pointed to the same location no matter what was there. More interestingly, she exhibited the same behavior when the test was turned upside down!" There are two responses to these concerns. First, we have found with most students that they need to be slowed down in their pointing, thus enabling them to control their selection, whatever it is. Often, their independent (i.e., without facilitation) pointing is impulsive and perseverative, *not* volitional. Second, many of the students with whom we have used facilitation will point repeatedly at the same location or at random letters unless facilitated and slowed significantly; it is for this reason that in the early phases of training in facilitated communication, we use structured work; thus the student becomes familiar with the method and gains confidence as well as skill at controlling his or her selections. Perseveration on a single selection can also be interrupted by pulling the student's hand back 8 to 10 inches from the selection before another choice is made.

"I am . . . very curious about the inconsistencies in . . . 'spelling.' She spells words that aren't spelled the way they would be (i.e., if they were spelled phonetically) perfectly (e.g., . . . 'know') and other times she spells words phonetically. . . . If [she] is a genius with a photographic memory then I would expect her to be able to spell correctly all the time." Not surprisingly, when facilitators see a student communicating words and knowledge that had previously been unimaginable from the student, some may conclude that the student is a "genius." Frankly, I find this label as potentially

harmful as "mental retardation"; it tends to convey stereotypes. But even if a student does demonstrate exceptional reading and memory skills, it is wrong to assume the student will not commit errors in writing, even simple spelling or typographical errors. Naturally, this father wonders if the facilitators' expectations may not be communicated intentionally or unintentionally to the student. This is possible. Facilitators may give cues to the student, particularly in the early stages of communication training when the student is learning the method and is not yet independent. Equally, students may use a combination of creative spellings, phonetic spellings, and correct spellings, depending on how well they are paying attention, how tired or alert they are, whether echoed words slip into their typing, how much they have worked with a particular facilitator (this may affect confidence level or nervousness), and so forth. Each student needs to be observed carefully for patterns of errors so that these may be addressed as part of the training process. In any given communication session, we generally encourage students to write first and then go back and correct or learn spelling. Similarly, we have observed that students are often more fluent in their typing with some facilitators than others, but this appears to change over time; as students become more used to their facilitators, they improve in both fluency and independence.

"When [she] 'produces' a series of letters, 'abbreviations,' 'initials' or even a couple of vocalization sounds, [they are] . . . usually interpreted in a certain way to make sense. Why could these things not just as easily be interpreted in twenty other different ways? Why is it so clear that [she] is saying 'hard math' when she says 'ha mmm'?! If people stop to think about it she says 'ha mmm' in many other situations, not just in school or around math. In fact, these are . . . her self-stim [self-stimulatory] sounds." The father has a point. We cannot assume that particular sounds or particular letters that may be initials or parts of words mean anything in particular unless we have queried the communication user. As in working with anyone who uses a communication board or other communication device, it is a standard procedure to suggest what the person means after seeing a letter or two. If the guess is correct, the person can indicate so by typing "yes," by giving a yes sign such as a smile, nod, or vocalization, or by simply going on to the next word. In this situation it is always good to remember that the person communicating may *not* mean what is suggested but may go along with the suggestion rather than correct the facilitator. At other times, the same person may insist on proceeding with something other than what the facilitator expected.

I shall never forget just such an instance when I was reading aloud the letter selections of a friend who has cerebral palsy and who independently points to letters and words on a communication board. He was speaking to an audience of over a thousand people at a national conference on the topic of architectural accessibility and was expressing his displeasure at the inaccessibility of the hotel in which the meeting was being held. He spelled, THIS IS A SH (as he spelled a word beginning with "sh," I imagined that he was going to spell *shitty* and consequently expressed concern, saying to him and the audience, "I hope you are not about to say what I am thinking," but he and I proceeded) I (and then he paused before finishing the word) NING EXAMPLE OF A SHI (here we were again, with the audience and me in stitches) TTY SO-CALLED ACCESSIBLE HOTEL.

"When asked why . . . the facilitators [can't] be blindfolded in order to show that they are not producing the message for the child, Dr. Biklen replies that this would not work because the child would 'feel' that he/she is not believed . . . or is being 'tested' and will therefore not perform!" This father is certainly not alone in asking for blindfold and other tests of students' abilities. Many skeptics of facilitated communication have asked why we don't test the students. One such test, proposed to me by a leading U.S. autism researcher as well as by some other parents and professionals who have attended our training sessions on facilitated communication, would be to have facilitators blindfold themselves while the communication users type. Such suggestions arise frequently and reflect genuine concern about the validity of a means of communication that at least in its early stages requires dependence on a facilitator.

I have not encouraged any use of blindfold testing, believing that it may cause the student to fail for two reasons: mechanical or neuromotor reasons and confidence. When facilitators work with students, watching their selection of letters, pulling them back after each selection, slowing them down, and giving verbal encouragement, often calling out letters as they are typed and saying words as they are completed, students still often hit letters next to intended letters or type echoed words or phrases as well as seemingly nonsensical sequences of letters. Thus the facilitator must be "all eyes," working hard to hold the student back from obvious errors (e.g., perseverative strikes at the keys, frequent hits of keys next to correct choices, three or four consonants in a row). In other words, the facilitator aids the student by assisting physically, but *not* guiding. Further, while I understand people's concerns that facilitators may be purposely or inadvertently guiding students' hands, uncertainty in the early stages of facilitated communication training seems a small price to pay in order to ensure that the student's confidence and the trusting, supportive relationship of facilitator and communicator are not violated.

A test with blindfolds would convey to the students that the facilitators are questioning their competence. This could undermine students' confidence in themselves and in their facilitators. Given that many students take weeks and sometimes several months to generalize their ability to communicate to new facilitators and that they report lack of confidence in and by new facilitators, anything that would detract from the facilitation user's confidence is problematic.

Actually, we *do* test the students, although not by blindfolding facilitators.

TESTING

Types of Testing

Academic testing. We test students' reading comprehension, math skills, and knowledge of science and other subjects. The majority of students with whom we have used the facilitated communication training method—we refer to it as a training method to convey the fact that for most students, facilitation is seen as a stage in the process of becoming an independent communicator—take tests and do schoolwork that their teachers evaluate. Many individuals can do multiple-choice tests with slight or no facilitation after relatively little training. And some facilitators have administered various psychological tests, including intelligence tests, modifying test protocols by giving students facilitation. Academic testing examines for knowledge of content as well as communicative ability.

Information sharing. In addition, facilitators ask students questions; although informal and unobtrusive, their questions could be construed as testing. They ask them what is new in their lives, how they spent a holiday, who their relatives are, and what they did over a weekend. In response to the latter question, for example, one boy reported that he had ridden a bike, as fast as the wind. The facilitator was a bit incredulous. She had not known that he could ride a bike. The student then explained that he had ridden an exercise bike at his uncle's home. The student's mother later verified his account. Another student described having Thanksgiving at the home of her mother's friend. A third student reported to his speech therapist and to me that he had just moved to a new apartment in a neighboring town and that he did not like the apartment: THE KITCHEN IS TOO SMALL, he complained. Revelation of such information can confirm for the facilitator that he or she is not cuing the student.

Message passing. Message passing is a more explicit test based on this same idea, namely that students will convey information not known to the facilitator. The Intellectual Review Panel government study in Melbourne, Australia, utilized such a procedure when it attempted to validate facilitated communication (Intellectual Disability Review Panel, 1989). Three DEAL Communication Centre clients were given gifts while their facilitators were not present. Then, when their facilitators returned, the students passed the message, all three relating what they had been given.

Considerations in Selecting Tests

Unless the particular test is one used with all students or is normative for the setting (e.g., home, workplace, recreational situation), any tests designed to validate or invalidate communicative ability will almost certainly convey to the student that the facilitator is questioning the student's competence or at the very least is not "with" the student. Such tests ask not only how much a student knows but whether the student knows or can communicate anything at all. The effects of this message may be to make a student excessively nervous, to undermine the student's confidence, or to anger the student enough for him or her to refuse to participate in the test. A number of students have even expressed annoyance when facilitators or observers persist in showing amazement at their reading and typing abilities, as if to say: Why do you continue to be surprised at my competence?

Lack of confidence should not be minimized or ignored. As Arthur Schawlow writes, "The gentle, encouraging, personal contact is hard to convey, but it is important. Autistic people are so frightened! They have all had discouraging experiences" (A. L. Schawlow, personal communication, September 4, 1990). Similarly, a student with autism explains her own trepidations over communicating, even with facilitation:

> I really resisted . . . finding out I really could communicate by typing because I got along fine as all decisions were made for me by my parents who provided me with a nice safe life. Typing meant I had the means of making my own wishes known. I found this scary because you can't imagine what it is like being locked inside yourself all your life and then having the key to escape your self imprisonment; sometimes the prisoner likes security.

Hope for a better life finally made me realize I had to accept typing instead of talking just as someone who can't walk accepts a wheelchair. I owe DEAL a lot because to me it gave me the direction for a better life.

Some people hope I am manipulated by my mother when I type to ordinary people but there's no way I would let this happen. My mother gives me confidence and encouragement and a reassuring hand round my waist. You would need some form of physical encouragement if you had been labeled retarded. It is devastating to your self esteem. To me it appears that to accept the reality that I am typing my own thoughts is not possible for some people because such a fact would be against all they have believed in for many years. In reality by having this point of view they are very insulting to people like me.

I would be willing to type on video if that would help to overcome prejudice affecting the willingness to believe I am actually typing.

Monica Shanahan, 1991

As noted in the previous section, to suggest that facilitators blindfold themselves is to ignore the fact that one of the main aspects of facilitation is the act of slowing down students' pointing or typing. Many of the students have unstable hand and finger movements as well as a tendency for impulsive, repetitive, even perseverative pointing or typing, both of which can be offset through the facilitators' stabilizing support; the facilitator often applies backward pressure as the person attempts to make a selection on a letter board or keyboard. The fact that many students with autism exhibit these physical/motor difficulties has been well documented in the research and education literature (Maurer & Damasio, 1982; Oppenheim, 1974; Wing, 1969; Wing, 1978). Some students with autism may already type before being trained in facilitated communication, but their typing is generally either just a series of letters, seemingly unrelated, or it is limited to certain phrases, words, or echoes of things previously heard or seen. By slowing down the person's typing, the facilitator allows the person to type what he or she wants (Biklen & Schubert, 1991). With some communication users, facilitators provide so much backward pressure that they become tired from the facilitation. If blindfolded, the facilitator could actually misdirect and throw off the communication user's intended direction.

Good testing requires that the test giver design or select a test that actually lessens the disruptive effect of poor confidence as well as of noncognitive behavior, such as the instability and impulsive movements mentioned above. Freeman and Ritvo (1976) discuss a similar concern in an essay on cognitive assessment:

> In order to mitigate the influence of . . . neuropathophysiological factors during psychological evaluations, we introduce behavior therapy techniques into the testing situation. These behavioral techniques are aimed at controlling non-cognitive behavioral factors of a disruptive nature. For example, it is impossible to meaningfully evaluate a patient who is handflapping and intermittently attending. (p. 31)

In using facilitated communication, we frequently encourage students to hold their free hand still, perhaps to put it on the table or under their leg, to be sure to look at the typing target, and to read the test questions or other schoolwork (e.g., reading, math problems) carefully. Facilitation of the typing hand in the form of assistance with isolating the index finger, stabilizing the hand, pulling the hand back after each selection, or merely providing a reassuring touch to the elbow are "interventions" designed to help the person overcome noncognitive, neuromotor, and confidence problems. Were the facilitator blindfolded, his or her "support" would turn into an impediment.

Finally, testers must ask what they are trying to test. If the purpose is to reveal, demonstrate, or validate a person's competence, the test and test procedure should be selected or designed to show the person's ability. A test should not unnecessarily disadvantage the person. For example, it would not be useful to administer the Stanford-Binet intelligence test to people with autism who do not speak, primarily because the Stanford-Binet requires verbal skills—unless, of course, the person is facilitated.[3] Similarly, it would be unfair to give a social studies examination in English to a student whose only language is Spanish. Along these same lines, any test of students using facilitated communication must not ignore the fact that the students have problems of initiating movements, of impulsive and unstable movement, and of self-confidence. Stated more positively, if a test is intended to reveal people's abilities, then it must be designed and implemented in a manner that allows people to demonstrate those abilities, not merely their unrelated difficulties.

UNOBTRUSIVE VALIDATION

There may be myriad reasons why people want facilitated communication to be validated, not the least of which is so facilitators and others can *know* that the words are the communication users' own. Other reasons derive from concern and skepticism revolving around the following issues: (1) Students demonstrate unexpected literacy, dramatically unlike the highly stereotyped and echoed language of so many people with autism and related disabilities who speak, and free of the problems of pronoun reversals, incorrect verb tenses, and other difficulties of "autistic" language—and certainly quite different than the non-speaking condition of many people with autism. (2) Students are fluent with some facilitators but *not* with others, although this problem seems to be resolvable if new facilitators are persistent and willing to suspend disbelief. (3) Students say things that are not what facilitators or others necessarily want to hear—including criticisms of school programs, parents, care workers or other students; expressions of self-doubt; and information about sexual or other abuse. One defense against such information is to believe that it must not be the students' own. (4) Some students say things that are not true about family life, accomplishments, and so forth. (5) At least in the early stages of training in facilitated communication, facilitation is given at the hand or wrist, thus naturally raising questions about who is communicating.

Partly in response to these concerns and partly as a natural process of observing the students and ourselves as facilitators, we identified seven unobtrusive indicators that the words are the students' own. Together these indicators provide as much proof of communication as experimental design tests.

Typographical Errors

Each student tends to type somewhat differently, at different rates, with varying degrees of stability or instability, and with varying results. Many students make typographical errors. Different students have different error patterns, even when they work with the same facilitator; in other words, these patterns of typographical error are idiosyncratic to the students, not the facilitators. One student, for example, often hits keys next to the intended keys. Another student frequently types two or three additional letters for each five or six intended ones. This is a problem that can be remedied by using a key guard—usually a piece of Plexiglass that fits over a keyboard, with a hole for each key—that requires the student to put his or her finger through a hole in order to reach the key, thus making it impossible to hit multiple keys at once. This problem can also be alleviated for some students by insisting that they keep their eyes on the keyboard or letter board. Still another student often types incorrect or unintended letters but then corrects most typographical errors before continuing to type, thus slowing her rate of communication significantly. Some students have a tendency to strike the same letter repeatedly unless pulled back after each selection. All of these are patterns observed in particular students, not particular facilitators.

Phonetic and Creative Spelling

Many students produce phonetic and creative spellings that are unique to them and that do not appear in the work of other students, despite the fact that the students sometimes share facilitators. A preschool student spelled *octopus* as OCTBUS and two elementary school students spelled *scissors* as SCISSOES and SISSHORS. Another spelled *words* as WERDS, and one spelled *talk* as TORK.

Style and Speed

Students vary in the physical motions and speed of their typing. One third-grade student has flaccid muscle tone and often slides off her chair onto the floor. She tends to take many seconds between selections of letters, revealing apparent difficulty with initiating movements. Facilitators must be persistent in helping her stay on her seat and must be patient in waiting for her selections; often the facilitators encourage her by saying, "Go ahead, you can do it." Another student types relatively quickly but frequently hits at the facilitator with her other hand or fidgets with plastic chips, beads, and pieces of paper or other objects nearby. This student requires strong backward pressure on her wrist or arm as she types. The pattern and speed of both students do not vary much, irrespective of who is facilitating them.

Content Unknown to the Facilitators

Students frequently reveal information not known to their facilitators. The student who told his teacher that he rode an exercise bike over the weekend is one such example. Another student typed the correct number of his house address, which was different from that listed in his school records. Unbeknownst to his facilitators/teachers, his family had moved the week before. Another student wrote comments on a book he had read, a book his teacher had not read. One student said he wanted to take photographs of himself and his teacher from school to place in a "picture kaddy" in his living room at home; his parents verified that indeed the family had a "picture kaddy" in their living room.

Unusual Expressions

Many students type phrases and sentences that are unusual and/or would not be expected from the facilitators. One first-grade student, for example, typed to me, DO YOU LIKE MY DODI NG MY SPELLING? I DO! TNY. He then explained by typing that TNY meant THANK YOU. On another occasion he typed, I WANT TO BE NOT WALKING. Several students have demonstrated excellent facility with swearing. One typed to her teacher, GO HOME BITCH. Another typed FBC and then, when queried about the meaning of these letters, began to spell out a swear word, FUC; she was told she could stop after the C; initials of the teacher's name are BC. On still another occasion, a 6-year-old student spelled out on a computer keyboard that he wanted to tell his mother that UUU YOU RUDE. He then explained that he resented his teacher's not letting him play at the classroom water table.

Independence

Ultimately, skepticism about students' ability to communicate fades away as students become more or totally independent in their typing. Unfortunately, requiring this standard is a bit like saying that students should become less disabled before they can be believed. In any case, students do reveal different levels of independence. After 18 months of using facilitated communication in Syracuse, nine students were typing with just a light touch to the elbow. Several could type some things with just a touch to the shoulder. In Australia, I observed several students typing completely independently; of these, all had been facilitating for more than three years.

Different Personalities

One of the most exciting aspects of helping people to have a means of expression is the opportunity to find out what they think and feel and, in a deep sense, who they are. With facilitation, students reveal themselves to be quite different from one another. Their personalities become visible. Some students have poor self-confidence. Some feel depressed about their difficulties in communicating on their own and its consequences for social relations and friendships. Some express frustration at not being as good as nondisabled peers in physical activities. Others are enthusiastic, funny, sarcastic, and full of themselves. Indeed, most people are a mixture of these many feelings and emotions, but in different degrees. One student recently complained about another person, whom he did not want to sit next to during meals. When asked where the person should sit, he responded, SIT HIM IN THE CAR. When his facilitator remarked that he had made a joke, the student admitted to having a sense of humor.

CONCLUSION: CAUTIONARY NOTES

The fact that we can prove that facilitated communication is a valid means of communicating for many people does not remove all questions about the method or about the validity of particular communication. But in this regard, questions about facilitated communication are not altogether unlike questions we may raise about any communication.

The idea of testing students implies that ability to communicate and to communicate at particular levels resides solely or principally in the individual. This is not necessarily so. All communication is interactional and influenced by context, including the relationship of communicator and receiver. In fact, one could just as reasonably ask that the facilitators be tested. Hardly anyone has observed certain facilitators without commenting, "She (or he) is really good." By this the observer means that the facilitator works well with the student, ignoring extraneous behavior such as slapping or screeching, gently redirecting the person to the task of communication, treating the person as fully competent and understanding, expecting good communication from the person, praising successes and making little of communication difficulties, and showing genuine interest in the person. Not surprisingly, such qualities of interaction elicit excellent communication, often including personal feelings and complex content. I am not suggesting that we test for good or bad qualities in facilitators, although it does seem important for us to identify the good qualities and train or educate ourselves to exhibit them.

Also, testing students' ability to communicate, whether done obtrusively or unobtrusively, may or may not reveal the person's true ability. Failure to prove a student's ability to communicate with facilitation or any other method does not prove that the person cannot communicate, only that the person did not do so when tested. Further, an individual's performance on a given test may or may not be reflective of the person's best effort. Poor performance or failure to produce words or thoughts does not necessarily mean the person has no thoughts or no potential to express them, only that the person did not reveal his or her thoughts at a particular time under particular circumstances.

If communication does occur, what does it mean? Among other

things, testing and verifying that students' words are their own (i.e., intended by them) does not guarantee their truthfulness. Similarly, verifying that one's words are one's own and that they are correct or truthful in one situation does not verify the correctness or honesty of future communication. This is true for everyone, whether using facilitated communication or not. For example, a teacher's aide/facilitator repeatedly asked one high school student, who had bruises on the sides of his face, who hit him and if his father hit him. Eventually, the student typed YES. Later, when child welfare officials investigated the case, the student typed that his father slapped him on his hands, but that his other bruises were from his hitting himself, something he had done since he was a young child. In reference to his father, he typed to a child welfare investigator (with his speech therapist serving as his facilitator) that his father had slapped his hands when he had grabbed and pulled on his sister's hair. Naturally, the case was dropped. But the fact that the matter was ever brought up and that the parents were investigated was terribly upsetting to the family. When the father asked his son why he had told the teacher's aide that he had been hit by the father, the son typed, BECAUSE HE WANTED ME TO. Here was an instance in which the student's typing was his own, but reflective of the facilitator's ideas. Interestingly, as this student typed his explanation to his father, he spoke one of his unusual, unrelated phrases simultaneously, repeatedly: "Did you cut the mayonnaise horse with scissors?"

Within the first year and a half of our using facilitated communication in the Syracuse area, 10 students out of approximately 75 who were using the method—we were following only 45 for our research at the time but more had been introduced to the method as teachers and parents learned how to facilitate—alleged that they had been sexually abused. In at least six cases there was corroborating evidence. In two instances, corroborating evidence of abuse was provided by child welfare investigations of the students' homes. In another case, a teaching assistant admitted to touching a girl in her crotch. And in three instances there was corroborating physical evidence that the children making allegations had been abused. Each case of abuse raised fears in teachers/facilitators: Were the students' words their own? Were the students telling the truth or responding to leading questions? If the case went to a grand jury, would the students be able to give testimony? Would family members and others get angry with the facilitators for being the messengers of bad news?

One elementary school student began to reveal his story of abuse slowly and enigmatically. He typed to his teacher that he needed to be cautious. She asked, "Cautious about what?" He typed, ABOUT SEX.

Fortunately, at least from the standpoint of validating his communication, he told the same information to his classroom teacher and to his speech therapist independently. It was only when they compared notes that they realized this. So in this instance, there was never a question about the validity of the communication. To his speech therapist, he was more specific: `i need to tell you about my sex with my dad. he makes me stick my finger in bh, his butt. i dmn dont nox know rights of chi;ld. talk to mrs.c. go to the police.` His speech therapist/facilitator encouraged him, telling him that it was good that he could share his feelings like this, that he should not be ashamed or feel that it was his fault, that, unfortunately, similar things happened to lots of children and that he was therefore not alone, and that, if he wanted, the therapist would be glad to talk to his mother so she could help keep him safe from this happening again. The next day, this student typed, `i am feeling good. i am happy i am not a bad kid. I AM very glhad i can talk with you it is not easy ij feel glad i have teachers wbho rite with me. i have jno other things to say.` When he was told that his father was coming to the school to talk to the speech therapist and teacher, he typed, `do you know i my idea sex to my xdad is my.` The therapist asked him to explain. He typed, `is sit my dads ideaga?` The therapist explained that she did not know: "I never see your Dad. I don't know his ideas." Then the student typed, `i think its petes idea.` She asked him "which Pete?" but the student ran from the communication device. Later, when asked if the therapist should tell his Dad anything, he typed, `tell him that i want him to be good to me. i feel better now that he dis lcoming here.` His father is divorced from the boy's mother and does not live with the son. When he came to the school that afternoon, he expressed outrage that his son might have been abused. He did not question that his son was communicating by typing, even though this was the first time he had actually seen it. Subsequently the father made regular trips to the school to learn how to facilitate with his son. A week after the father's visit, the student repeated the name of "Pete" as the person who had bothered him: `i throw the typewriter because i feel really fruightened abo bfcut sex with pete.` And a few days later, he typed, `opete . . . he msx makes sex and he sxcares me.` When asked if he understood why he needed to go to the doctor, he typed, `i have to go to the doctor because of the man wit h pecker in my mouth.` When his speech therapist asked what he thought about going to the doctor, he answered, `i bf am not happy because they hav e t o be looking at my body.` She asked if there was anything he wanted her to tell them. He typed, i want them to kno thz ati am not crazy. The speech therapist gave his typing to his mother to take to the doctor's office.

He had originally named his father as the abuser, perhaps because this was a "safe" person to name or perhaps because he felt his father could protect him in a way that others had not. It is hard to know. As with anyone in this situation, therapists can try to be supportive and encourage the abused persons to express themselves on the matter, to "get it out," but they cannot force their recollections and feelings from them, particularly if they have repressed these feelings or memories.

In talking with a child welfare investigator about how she could get at the truth with this boy, I suggested that she needed to be supportive of his sharing what he felt he could share, but I warned against leading him. She wanted to know if it would be all right to show him a series of pictures, one of which would include a picture of a distant relative who was believed to be the perpetrator. While he might indeed have pointed to this relative's picture if shown it, I warned against such a strategy. He might point at one of the pictures simply because he understood that the child welfare worker wanted him to point to at least one. He might point simply as an impulsive act, perhaps pointing at a color that fascinated him. He might point at someone he knew did not do it, but who he believed would protect him and show concern for him, someone he might be able to talk to about it. Rather than displaying pictures or asking leading questions, I encouraged the caseworker to try to be sure the child was safe *and* to keep creating conditions in which he could share information and feelings related to what had happened. He did not become much more explanatory of his abuse, but medical tests did reveal that he had been sexually assaulted.

From this case and others we eventually developed a recommendation for confirming allegations of abuse revealed by people who communicate with facilitation. Naturally, social welfare officials and police investigators want to know if the person with the communication disability actually typed the words that comprise the allegation. The procedure we recommend in these situations is to invite another experienced facilitator to facilitate with the individual and ask the individual to explain what he or she conveyed to the first facilitator. In effect, this is a version of message passing. Of course it is important to remember that if the person does not report the same information to a second person, it does not automatically mean that the person did not type the original allegation; nevertheless it may be difficult to proceed with legal action unless the person's communication has been validated or unless there is corroborating evidence.

A final caution concerns facilitators and the expectations one should have of them. Facilitated communication, particularly at the training level, requires ethical people. Anyone can move another's hands to, in effect, put words in their mouths. This would be terribly difficult—perhaps impossible—to do when facilitating someone far back on the forearm, at the elbow, or with a light touch to the shoulder or some other irrelevant part of the body (e.g., waist, back). But in the earliest stages, when students are typically supported at the hand or wrist, it is possible for students to be controlled, and thus for words to be put in their mouths (i.e., hands). The unobtrusive validation measures outlined in the previous section can be employed by observers or by facilitators in doubt about an individual's communication.

Recently, we became aware of a case of manipulation. For each of the students we were following, we had videotaped examples of their typing. In this case, I had observed that right from the first week when he was introduced to facilitation, Eddie was able to point to letters and write words with facilitation to his forearm. It surprised me, therefore, when I noticed that Eddie was being facilitated hand over hand by one of his teaching assistants. Upon seeing that, I spoke to Eddie's speech therapist and encouraged her to make sure that students were given only the level of support necessary; that all the facilitators work on fading support back to the elbow and then to the shoulder, with the expectation that students would ultimately become independent; and that facilitators make sure that students focused their eyes on the letters. If the latter was not insisted upon, the students would get used to the facilitators' protecting them from errors; worse, facilitators might inadvertently guide them to the letters. I was relieved when our next videotaping sessions revealed a different teaching assistant facilitating from the forearm, with Eddie making forceful movements to letters and numbers, obviously his own selections. But, as it turned out, my original concerns were warranted. At the end of this past school year, a teaching assistant announced to one of our university students that "facilitated communication is a lot of bullshit. Eddie's really an airhead. I've been doing his work for him all year long." This was the teaching assistant whom I had observed facilitating at the hand, long after Eddie had demonstrated the ability to type with support only to his forearm. So here the question was not whether the student was capable of communicating his own thoughts, but why a facilitator would fake his communication. We could accept the person's explanation at face value—that he simply did not believe facilitated communication made any sense and that Eddie was really not capable of communicating. But more likely, this teaching assistant must have realized that he was expected to facilitate and probably felt under pressure to have it work. Lacking confidence, he may have pretended in order to look competent himself. Perhaps he worried that he would lose his job if he could not do facilitation or if he refused to do it. Perhaps he worried that he would have low status among his peers if he admitted he was having difficulty with it. Conversely, perhaps he saw high status bestowed on those who claimed success with it. Whatever the explanation(s), this case of manipulation suggests the importance of creating conditions where lack of success with facilitation is tolerated and supported by being acknowledged and responded to, where people are encouraged to share their self-doubts, and where people support each other in learning how to facilitate. Further, and equally important, all of us, no matter how accustomed we are to facilitation, must remember that facilitated communication is a training method as well as means of communication and that for most people, fading back to the elbow, then to the shoulder, and ultimately to independence is a realizable goal and one we must persistently pursue.

NOTES

1. Some critics of facilitated communication appear to approach it from a positivist perspective. The tradition of positivism attempts to address social science questions as if human experience could be understood in cause and effect terms, much as one understands the natural science of physics. This perspective contradicts the perspective to which I hold, which is that objects, events, observation, and understanding are by definition socially constructed. As we will see, two prominent critics of facilitated communication, Cummins and Prior (1991), adopt a view of autism and disability that prevents them from accepting the particular neuromotor difficulties and lack of confidence that we have hypothesized as explanations for the communicative difficulties of people using autism. (For a discussion of positivism, see Mills, 1967, p. 460.)

2. The father did not have custody over his daughter but remained concerned about her education; the mother had given permission for the daughter to use facilitated communication and to be observed as part of our research project.

3. Freeman and Ritvo (1976, p. 32) discuss the difficulties of administering the Stanford-Binet to people with autism; their analysis preceded development of facilitated communication.

Part III

RETHINKING DISABILITY

CHAPTER 6

Typing to Talk, Typing to Dream

INTRODUCTION

March 13, 1991
Dear Mom,
DO YOU MIND IF TWO OF MY FRIENDS AT SCHOOL STYLE MY HAIR
NEXT W WEEK? KATHLEEN AND MOLLY WILL PUT SOME INTEREST-
ING THINGS IN MY HAIR LIKE A PONY TAIL AND CURL MY BANGS
UP IN THE AIR. THEY ARE NICE FRIENDS THAT HAVE BEEN
TEACHING ME HOW TO DANCE AND ALL ABOUT MUSIC AND THEIR
TAPES. THEY TELL ME ABOUT THE THINGS THEY DO AT HOME AND
TOGETHER. I WISH I COULD TELL THEM ABOUT MY LIFE. WE DO
SOME SHARING WHEN WE PLAY GAMES BUT ITS NOT THE SAME AS
REAL FRIENDS. IT IS SO HARD FOR ME TO DEVELOP NORMAL
FRIENDS SINCE I CANT LAUGH AND TALK ABOUT CLOTHES I WEAR
AND BOYS I LIKE OR THE CONCERTS I'VE BEEN TO. SO I WISH
I WAS NOT AUTISTIC. I WISH I COULD DO ALL THE THINGS
THAT THE OTHER KIDS DO. I GUESS I'M GETTING CLOSER TO
NORMAL BUT I AM STILL SO FAR AWAY. PLEASE KEEP PUSHING
ME FORWARD. I NEED YOUR SUPPORT AND STRENGTH. GETTING
THE MOST OUT OF LIFE AND PRODUCING THE MOST GOOD IS MY
GOAL. I WANT TO BE A N ACTIVE MEMBER OF SOCIETY AND JUST
NOT GET DRAGGED DOWN BY MY HANDICAP. I LOVE YOU MOM.

Maggie

Maggie was 15 when she wrote this letter. She cannot *speak* the words that she wants to say, although she can speak many of the words that she hears others say (i.e., echolalia). When she wrote this letter, she had been typing with facilitation for a year, and she was then able to type with just a light touch to the elbow. She could type stereotyped or usual expressions such as her name and the date and even sentences such as I LOVE YOU MOM with just a hand on her shoulder. Her speech has not improved—she can greet people but she cannot carry on a conversation. People who knew her before she began facilitating say that she speaks a bit less now than she did before. She herself reports that she speaks less now; she feels that her speech often makes her look silly. She wants people to take her seriously, to know that she is intelligent and that what she thinks is often different than what she can say. She still *does* speak greetings, names, and a few other words that she can use in contextually correct ways.

In her letter Maggie touches on most of the themes that emerge from the typed comments of the many students using facilitation: that facilitated communication gives her a means of communicating about ordinary everyday concerns, for example, DO YOU MIND IF TWO OF MY FRIENDS . . . STYLE MY HAIR . . . ?; that communication makes more possible the idea of having friends but that for a variety of reasons, making friends is still not easy (e.g., SINCE I CANT LAUGH AND TALK ABOUT CLOTHES I WEAR AND BOYS I LIKE); that facilitated communication allows people to talk about their feelings (I WISH I WAS NOT AUTISTIC); and that certain conditions help communication and personal growth along—Maggie implores her mother to KEEP PUSHING ME FORWARD. Since difficult behavior such as screaming, hitting, and biting has not been a problem for her, Maggie does not mention it. Finally, Maggie's letter implies at least one overarching theme: that with the newfound communication, people who are communication users as well as communication receivers/listeners change their perspectives about each other and about what is possible.

This chapter explores these themes, in part through our observations of people using facilitated communication in schools, at home, and at work, but primarily through the words of the communication users themselves.

CHANGING PERSPECTIVES:
SELVES, PARENTS, TEACHERS, FRIENDS, OTHERS

During my study in Australia neither I nor anyone could force skeptics to accept or appreciate facilitated communication. Often I wanted to stand up and shout or at least sternly lecture people to understand and act on this new way of thinking about ability and communication, but I knew that real understanding does not happen that way; it needs time to sink in; people have to be allowed to discover it for themselves, albeit with a great deal of guidance. After all, I was living proof of this. Day after day, night after night, I observed students using facilitated communication, asked Crossley and her colleagues many questions, often the same questions in only a slightly different form or even the same form, and pondered the contradictions of what I observed with what I had previously believed about autism and developmental disabilities. Eventually, I found myself adopting the new point of view, seeing the communication difficulties in autism as arising from a neuromotor problem rather than a problem of cognition. I began to see how the students' behavior, their responses to events and situations, their ability or inability to respond to requests, and their echoed words, whether spoken or typed, were not indicative of their thinking. Through facilitation, I could see that they had more than screeches and tantrums inside of them.

The problem of shifting perspectives arises often, usually with each new observer to facilitation. On one particular occasion, when I observed Crossley working with a high school–age student named Margaret for the first time—she is mentioned briefly in Chapter 1—I recall feeling impatient about the time it took for people to make the transition from thinking one way about a person (i.e., in prefacilitation terms) to adopting an entirely different framework, one in which the communication user is recognized as having sophisticated thoughts. I recall wishing that the transformation could be hurried along.

Margaret Reilly is nonspeaking except for individual words that she repeats after hearing them from others. I asked Margaret if I could tape-record the session. Her mother answered "yes." I asked Margaret if *she* was indicating yes. "Is that a 'yes'?" Her mother answered for her again: "I don't think she could comprehend the implications of that."

Margaret's mother first noticed that Margaret seemed different from her other children when Margaret was between one and two months old. Now, a teenager, Margaret attends a special school for children with disabilities. She has many of the features of children labeled "autistic." She does not look people in the eyes. She engages in stereotyped behavior—a favorite pastime is filling crossword puzzles with words that are provided, fitting words into available spaces without respect to *where* the words are supposed to go. Her mother informed Crossley and me that Margaret takes a sedative medication twice a day. She explained that Margaret is dexterous with her hands, that she gets along reasonably well with family members and rarely "raises any problems in public." Occasionally she will have temper tantrums, but these are "very few and far between." In response to Crossley's question about whether Margaret watches television, her mother indicated that "she watches but is not really interested. She doesn't seem to register much." And when Crossley asked Margaret how many words she could say, her mother answered "*no* is the one. She makes an approximation of *hello*."

As we spoke, Margaret penciled words into a crossword puzzle, her mother explaining that she fits them into the spaces rather than thinking about which words go where.

Crossley led Margaret through a series of questions on the talking computer, having her point to various words and then letters. Placing her hand only on Margaret's shoulder, she asked Margaret to point to the word *on*. She did. In all the other instances up to this point, Crossley had facilitated Margaret's communication by slipping her finger under the top of Margaret's sleeve and, in essence, slowing down her arm and pulling it back when Margaret went to point at words repetitively. Crossley constructed the sentence: "The cat and the dog are by the tree," telling Margaret she had "made a story" and asking her if she would make up her own story. With Crossley facilitating her arm movements by holding on to the top of her sleeve, Margaret pointed to the words *I, see, green,* and *grass;* then she hesitated. Crossley encouraged her, saying "terrific" and noting that the talking computer has an American voice. Margaret pressed her pointer on another word, *and.* Her mother remarked, "it's lovely," apparently referring to the computer's ability to voice the words pressed. Then she offered what seemed like a self-conscious apology for Margaret: "It takes a long time for her to get a word." Crossley allowed that this was okay, as Margaret continued to press words, *a, yellow, flower, and, cat, and, small,* and *car.* Crossley read the entire sentence: "I see green grass and a yellow flower and cat and small car."

At this point Crossley announced: "We're not going to do any more of that. It's far too babyish for you." She told Margaret that she had two choices: "First, you can talk to me using this [a Canon Communicator], or second, I'll ask you questions. So it's die or die," she joked. Here Crossley put aside the Talking Computer on which Margaret had been shown preexisting words and introduced the Canon Communicator on which one can create one's own words. Margaret typed the word TALK–ING. Crossley asked her what she would like to say. Margaret typed the word GRASS. Crossley said, "I'm not going to accept this rubbish, ho ho, what would you like to do ?" Margaret typed LIKE. Crossley said, "Okay, go on," and Margaret typed GOT NOTHING TO SAY.

Crossley explained to Margaret's mother that she has a tendency to retype the last word, saying, "It's like echolalia of the hands. Sometimes people like Margaret will go to type a sentence but the pattern of the last word of a previous sentence comes out again and again and again."

Crossley pulled out a picture and had Margaret write a story about it. The picture was of a man and a suitcase with yellow smoke coming out of it. The man held a switch. Crossley asked, "Okay, what do you think is going on?" To this, Margaret typed THE MAN HAS BLOWN UP THE SUITCASE. Crossley asked "Why?" Margaret answered, BECAUSE IT HAS STOLEN MONEY IN IT. She hesitated before typing the last part of the sentence IN IT, but did so when Crossley said "go on." Crossley explained that her holding of Margaret's sleeve is "a security blanket and it is slowing you down, deliberately slowing you down."

Margaret's mother seemed astonished and said as much: "I'm surprised she even knows the word *stolen*." She asked what Crossley thought about Margaret's vocalizations. Crossley explained how she interpreted Margaret's speech, answering Margaret's mother's question by speaking directly to Margaret: "Margaret, if you can't say words, you probably aren't going to say them at your age. If you can say words, but they are not clear, you may get to be able to say them more clearly. But, Margaret, you will probably tend to get spontaneous words but they won't say all that you need to say." And then to her mother, and to me: "We're looking at someone with significant word-finding problems." Crossley explained to Margaret that one of her difficulties is that when she nervously hunts for words she comes up with stereotyped patterns whether in typing or in speech, hence the value of Crossley's slowing her hand movements down so that she can get the letters and words she is searching for.

Next Crossley gave Margaret a story-completion activity. Margaret began to type, filling in the blanks: "It was a dark and stormy NIGHT. A SHOT rang out. The door BANGED. The fire FLICKERED." Crossley asked her if she could try to say the word, and Margaret said what sounded like "da da dum." At this point Crossley asked if Margaret would like to do the work with "mum or Doug?" Margaret typed YOU, meaning Crossley. "I'm not an option," Crossley declared. Margaret typed MUMMY. Margaret continued to type: "Inside the HOUSE a MAN and a CHILD were SITTING." Crossley said to Margaret at this point: "They felt _____. How do they feel?" Margaret said "da da dum" and typed the word FEEL, to which Crossley responded, "All right that's just the word feel." And then Crossley said, "How did they feel?" adding "you can do it." Margaret typed NER and then hesitated. Crossley said she wanted to see the rest of it, and Margaret typed VOUS, making the word *nervous*. Her mother noted that Margaret had needed a bit of a "hint." Crossley preferred to think of it as "shepherding over a hard spot." Margaret continued to fill in the story: "They did not know if they should GO OUT. There was something STRANGE moving outside the window. What was it? Was it a SICKMAN or a GPHOST?" Margaret then went back and eliminated the P herself. As she did this, Crossley said: "I thought you were off the planet there. I was surprised by the GP." Margaret continued to fill in the story: "How could they FIND OUT?" "They were too SCARED to GOING." Crossley commented: "That's the breaking of the pattern we need to work on, getting rid of the *ing* which you are so familiar with." Presumably what Margaret had intended to type was *go out*. Margaret continued to type words to fill the blanks in the story: "At last MOURNING CHAME." Crossley said, "Oh, bad luck, that's okay. You've just got an extra H in there; and, Margaret, *mourning*—you have spelt this perfectly, but the *mourning* you have spelt is when you are sad. The morning that starts the day is the same except it doesn't have the U." Margaret finished the story: "When they opened the DOOR, they were SURE to find it was A DEDMANM." Crossley explained that "*dead* is one of those crazy words like *head*. But if you fed the horses it would just be F E D. This is terrific, this is great. Do you think they really found a dead man?" Margaret pointed to the word *yes*.

Margaret then typed that she wanted to come again to DEAL, whereupon Crossley turned to me and said, "She's great, she'll be fine."

After Margaret and her mother had left, I mentioned to Crossley that I felt ambivalent watching Margaret's mother try to make sense of what was happening in the session. It was natural that she would not shed all previous interpretations and beliefs about autism and about Margaret's limited speech. Yet at the same time, I felt like turning to Margaret's mother and saying, "What you are witnessing is extraordinary. It conflicts with traditional notions about people who are non-speaking, particularly about people classified as having autism. It will surely change your life." Crossley reminded me that it was equally extraordinary for Margaret: "This is the first time in her life she's used sentences." Crossley seems to follow the principle of allowing the person who is developing communication abilities to set the pace for self-disclosure and personal reflection: "I'm very careful not to ask anything personal of people the first time out." But at the same time, Crossley anticipated Margaret's future unfolding, particularly in light of her facility with the communication: "She's a cinch; she'll be really easy."

Back in Syracuse, similar scenes have occurred over and over, in terms of the struggle for parents, teachers, and others to grasp the remarkable change that attends the unfolding of communication (even though student and facilitator do not always have such enormous success on the first try). The mother of a 9-year-old girl, Nancy, asked me several times, "How should I treat her now that she can do this?" Nancy has poor posture, appears floppy, and is described by her speech teacher as having low muscle tone "almost like cerebral palsy." She often makes groaning sounds. Her mother had always thought her daughter understood more than most people gave her credit for and that she could even read a little, but prior to using facilitation, she had no idea that Nancy could understand nearly everything she heard. This mother was facing the fact that she had been speaking to her daughter as if she were a much younger child: "not . . . like a baby, but I talked to her like a 5-year-old." Even so, many of the mother's friends, and particularly strangers, wondered why she spoke so much to her at all; they found it hard to believe that Nancy understood her mother's words. In the early stages of facilitation, this mother found it hard to make a quick change in the tone and content of her speech. "It was hard to talk to her like a 9-year-old. I didn't know how. . . . I tried very hard not to repeat the same thing over and over again. . . . She understood it the first time— I knew that. She may not be able to respond to it immediately, but I realized that she did understand me. I didn't have to repeat things or talk down to her." Now she would try to say things once, "and touch her on the elbow to help her move along to follow the direction that I was asking her to do, rather than acting like she didn't know what I wanted from her."

Another parent recalls being terribly excited when she asked her 6-year-old son where his classmate had gone on vacation and he typed MIAMI. She told me,

> It was like a shock for me. It was a shock for a lot of people. Even though she didn't go to Miami, he probably heard that she went to Florida. It was so hard for me to believe that I asked him the same question two or three times, and he would again spell the same thing. When I told that to my husband, he said, "Come on. You're just making up all these things. How can Mark know how to spell something like that?"

She remembers feeling discouraged that her husband did not share her enthusiasm. "He was like a cold shower," she said. Prior to Mark's being introduced to facilitated communication, his parents would show him photographs and ask him to point to make choices, for example, between a cracker and cookie. As his mother explains it: "We thought that symbols were too hard for him. Now we know that was kind of silly." As they began to use facilitated communication, this mother continued to be "shocked" by her son's words. One day he came home from school and complained about another student in his class. The student made noises that bothered him. When his mother asked why the student made noises, Mark answered with a single typed word, AUTISTIC. Within several months, her husband also became convinced of Mark's genuine communication through typing.

Similarly, most other families slowly made the transition, forced to reckon with their children's words. A few parents, although they expressed interest in the communication method, did not see it as crucial to their interactions with their children. Sam's mother, for example, said that she did not push the communication method with her son at home because "he has a really short attention span with me" and because she could already understand him and judge what he wanted, for example, types of food:

> I always just about know what he wants . . . he takes me to what he wants. . . . If I think he wants cereal and I bring it down and if he don't want it he will push it back, and I know that's not what he wants. So he'll reach up . . . and if it's crackers or something, I will take it down and if that's what he wants I'll give it to him. I'm rather proud of him.

The reference to a "short attention span" suggests a difficulty that many parents seem to encounter. In school, students are expected to participate in activities, and it is the teachers' *job* to help them do that. At home, things are usually less structured; the idea of sitting down with a child to facilitate and to practice communication is a new activity, a different way of doing things for many families. Those families that *have* achieved success with facilitated communication at home have introduced it as something that is *always* available; they have communication boards everywhere in the home and frequently ask their children to make choices and to express themselves, telling them that without words, they have difficulty knowing what the child wants or is thinking. Sam's mother has ordered a Canon Communicator but is waiting on health insurance approval.

In the classroom, teachers and teaching assistants go through a similar process of acculturation to the idea of facilitation and its implications. In Syracuse, it took months before some speech therapists and teachers would try it. When they did, they did so hesitantly. A few saw language coming from the students that immediately convinced them of the method's value. Others remained skeptical for months. Many teaching assistants adopted the method quickly, but others continued to relate to the students as if they could not understand the world around them or as if they were purposefully noncompliant with classroom and school rules. In such cases, the teaching assistants would speak to the students, respond to their speech as if it were the extent of the students' thinking, and demand better behavior before allowing involvement in schoolwork. None of these strategies worked, for they effectively denied the students' communication. Slowly, nearly all of those who resisted the method came to use it and understand it.

Interestingly, the adults nearly always changed because of something the students did—the students modified the adults' behavior! For example, students began to refuse to work with or be with certain teaching assistants or teachers because they did not think the student was smart or did not believe the student could spell. Lenny, a 7-year-old, told his speech therapist that he was sick of always having to listen and of not having enough people typing with him. Mark told his therapist, ITS A BAD DAY BECAUSE FLT . . . SAID TO SOMEBODY THAT I WAS STUPID. I ARM [i.e., am] NOT STUPID AND THJE NEW TEACHERS DONT KNOW THAT. When his facilitator asked if this was really true, if it really happened, the student typed, YES IFACT YES. And Alicia, age 6, told one of her facilitators at school that she no longer wanted to share a Canon Communicator. Her teacher had promised her one for herself, and she wanted it. Further, she wanted the therapist to help more people learn to communicate with her. As the students asserted themselves, more and more teachers, teaching assistants, and speech therapists began to take them seriously.

While focusing on the changes in perspective experienced by teachers, parents, teacher assistants, and others, it is easy to forget that students' own expectations and opportunities change rapidly once they are able to communicate their wishes. This was exemplified in a conversation between Maggie and her speech therapist/facilitator, a typed conversation—both Maggie and her therapist typed their communication—that took place only a few months after Maggie had first begun to type original, nonechoed language:

MAGGIE: YOU AN LIKE MY MOM BECAUSE YOU BOTH HAPPY.
THERAPIST: YOUR MOM AND I ARE BOTH HAPPY?
MAGGIE: YES.
THERAPIST: WE'RE BOTH DELIGHTED ABOUT YOUR TYPING. ITS A
    WHOLE NEW SIDE OF YOU WE'RE GETTING TO HEAR FROM!
MAGGIE: I AM SO PLEAED TO SHOW IT TO YOU.

. . .

MAGGIE: THE TIME IS GETTIBNG CLLOSE FOR MY MEETI NG
    WITH ALL THE PEOOPLE WHO PLACE ME IN SCHOOL. . . .
    I WANT TO GO TO MRS SOHMS CLASS NEST YEAR.
THERAPIST: YOU HAVE A NICE AMBITION. HAVE YOU DISCUSSED
    ANY OTHER THINGS ABOUT NEXT YEAR [i.e., with her parents]?

MAGGIE: I WANT TO GO TO MATH CLASS AND LEARN SIXTH
     GRAXDE MATH.
THERAPIST: WOULDN'T THAT BE SPECIAL?
MAGGIE: I ALSO WANT TO GO TO ME.
THERAPIST: WHOOPS. WHAT DID YOU MEAN?
MAGGIE: I MEANT SCIENCE CLASS.
THERAPIST: I ADMIRE YOUR AMBITION.
MAGGIE: I WANT TO GO TKO SOCIAL STUDKIES.
THERAPIST: YOU ARE THINKING OF QUITE A CHALLENGING LOAD.
MAGGIE: I CAN DO IT.
THERAPIST: HOW DO YOU SEE YOURSELF DOING THE WORK?
MAGGIE: I WOULD NEED A TYPEAEWRITEER. . . . I ALSO HAVE
     TO HAVE PEOPLE TO HOLD MY ARM.
THERAPIST: DO YOU THINK YOU'LL BE ABLE TO TYPE WITH
     OTHER PEOPLE BY NEXT YEAR?
MAGGIE: YES. I TRY IT NOW.
THERAPIST: I'M SO PROUD OF YOU!
MAGGIE: I AM TOO.
THERAPIST: IF YOU WORKED SO HARD TO LEARN SCIENCE, SO-
     CIAL STUDIES, MATH, READING, WRITING, AND SPELLING,
     YOU WOULDN'T HAVE TIME TO BE INVOLVED IN PENNY-
     SAVER, SWIMMING, AND SO ON.
MAGGIE: I THINK THE PENNYSAVER IS NOT APPROPRIATE FOR
     ME.
THERAPIST: WHAT ABOUT THE SWIMMING, BOWLING, BREAK TIMES
     AT RESTAURANTS, ETC.?
MAGGIE: I LIKE THEM, BUT THEY ARENT RIGHT FOR NMRE [i.e.,
     me].
THERAPIST: WELL, WE'LL HAVE TO DISCUSS YOUR IDEAS WITH
     MANY PEOPLE. I WILL LET THEM KNOW WHAT YOU HAVE
     TOLD ME. IS THERE ANYTHING ELSE YOU WANT THEM TO
     KNOW?
MAGGIE: THE TYOPEWRITER HAS CHANGED MY L,IFE. I CAN
     TALK TO PEOPLE AND TELL THEM WHAT I THINKL.
THERAPIST: ANY OTHER MESSAGES?
MAGGIE: PLEASDE DONT LOCK ME UP AGAIN.

SCHOOLWORK AND THE COMMUNICATION CONTEXT

Two-thirds of the students with whom we have worked are doing
some academic work at their grade levels; an equal percentage attend

regular academic classes for part or all of the schoolday. Some of the students do some grade-level academic work but are not yet integrated into regular classes; and a few students in regular classes are not yet doing work typical for their age level. (See Table A.1 in the Appendix for a brief description of students' communication with and without facilitation). Some of the classroom work can be accomplished through completion of structured activities, such as typing the week's spelling words, solving math problems, answering specific questions, and doing multiple-choice and fill-in-the-blanks exercises. The particular activities are selected by teachers in keeping with the regular class curriculum; where a classroom activity calls for open-ended typed responses or compositions, the activity is modified for students who are not yet doing open-ended work.

In elementary school classes, teachers typically have students read passages from books and then describe something that has happened or respond to questions, for example, "Where did Frog sit when he was waiting for Toad?" or "The boy held up the _____." For math, students are simply asked to do the same problems as the rest of the class; for complex calculations in later elementary years or in secondary school, students can do each calculation in steps or, as is the case with a number of students using facilitation, with calculators.

For almost any age level, teachers can develop games that are well suited to students who have different means of expressing themselves. For example, at the secondary level, the game "fictionary" works well. One student finds a word in the dictionary that he or she believes the other students will not know. The word is read aloud, and each person writes down a made-up definition. The person with the dictionary writes down the correct definition. This person then collects all the definitions and reads them aloud or writes them on an overhead transparency or on a chalkboard. The students then vote for the one they believe is correct. The author wins the votes of anyone voting for his or her definition. Since this is a language game, and because the definitions are necessarily brief, it lends itself to participation by someone using facilitation. At the elementary level, students often compose commercials, write group letters, write alternative endings to stories, and do other activities that rely on written communication. In a first-grade class, Mark made up clues for an object. Other classroom members had to guess what food it was. He typed, NUT IXTS ROUND CAN EAT ITT CAN CUT IT IN TRIANGLES ITS HOT IT HAS A CRUST CAN PUT SAUUCE AND CHEESSEYES YOU CAN PUTTNING ON IT PEPRONI. One day in Mark's reading group, the students learned about homonyms, for example *ate/eight* and *one/won*. Students had to match the words to pictures. Also, they were asked to put the words into sentences. Students who could speak could say their sentences. Mark typed his: I ATE DINNER. In another first-grade class, students were asked to give words that have a "short U" sound in them. A student who has echolalic speech but has difficulty saying whole words typed BUN and BUS. In a preschool class, 4-year-old Charles was asked to spell out what he wanted for snack. He had a choice of Ritz crackers and "fish" (i.e., fish-shaped) crackers. He pointed to F repeatedly and then to the whole word *MORE*. In a high school biology laboratory, Todd reviewed the previous day's work by answering questions from Larry, his teaching assistant/facilitator, with facilitation at the wrist and under his palm:

> LARRY: WHAT WAS THE PROBLEM?
> TODD: WHAT IS THE FUNCTION OF THE EARTHWORM
> LARRY: WHAT WAS THE PROCEDURE?
> TODD: THE PROCEDURE WAS WORM AND LOOK AT THE INTERNAL ORGANS
> ASSISTANT: WHAT IS THE CONCLUSION?
> TODD: THAT THE WORM LIVES IN THE GROUND HE FEEDS OFF THE DIRT

Mary, a student who often makes loud groaning noises and occasionally hits herself and gets up and down from her chair in the middle of a lesson is not yet producing open-ended communication consistently. Yet in a seventh-grade science class, she was observed to be the first to respond to her science teacher's request for the metric measure of weight; she typed out GRAM. Other examples of structured schoolwork included a true/false test on prime numbers, a test in which students were to write out the names of elements when given the element's letter symbol (e.g., Hg, U), a laboratory sheet calling for students to identify the parts of a microscope, exercise in matching synonyms, comprehension checks for reading class, and math problems.

Obviously, not all schoolwork can be completed with single words or phrases. In facilitated communication training, one-word or multiple-word expressions are seen as an early stage of responding, with students being encouraged and supported to move on to more complex expressions—namely, sentences, paragraphs, and essays. This can be accomplished through modeling of sentences, for example, asking students to type or point to letters to spell out part of a sentence stated orally by the facilitator and then to complete the sentence on their own. Other students, however, produce sentences spontaneously in dialogue. For some students who respond in dialogue with phrases or single words, a simple request to put their thoughts into full sentences yields sentences.

Many teachers used the regular classroom curriculum, especially reading and language arts, to evoke sentences. Thus the students produced conversational work as part of their schooling. For example, a second-grade student, after reading the book *Sammy the Seal*, responded to the teacher's question about what he liked best about the book by typing: THE SEAL GOES TO SCHOOL. HE DOES NOT LIKE IT IN MY SCHOOL BECAUSE HE WANTS TO BE LIKE THE OTHER KIDS. ME TOO SIIIILLY. Another second-grader wrote the following poem:

```
PLEASE HEED MY NEED
I NEED TO HEED
OTHERS
I THIS REASON THINK
THE WORLD
THEY NEED HEED
LIKE WE HEED
BROTHERS
```

And a third second-grader wrote,

```
I AM THANKFUL FOR THE LIBRARY
I LOVE BOOKS BECAUSE THEY TELL UPON MY MIND GOOD THINGS
   TO LEARN
I PLAY UPON THE WORDS LIKE FRIENDS
YOU ARE MY FRIED TOO
TICKLE ME
```

A key element in any teaching/learning/communicating situation is the degree to which people feel supported, secure, and safe. The younger students are quite explicit on this matter; 6-year-old William typed, for example, i need hugs to do my job. One means of creating a supportive, caring atmosphere is to provide students a sense of control over it. In some schools, students were given the opportunity to select other students with whom they wanted to be paired or grouped for classroom activities. In many classrooms, we observed that teachers encouraged students to select the books that they wanted to read. It was not uncommon for students to complain that a book that had been selected by a teacher was too easy. Conversely, 14-year-old Evan complained that he was having difficulty with English because he got behind in the reading; he typed that science was his best subject. Maggie and Evan both participated in the Individualized Education Plan meeting with teachers, psychologist, and parents to decide on their academic programs. Later, after Maggie had been given a completely typical academic schedule for the first time in her life, except for math, I asked her why she was not taking math. She spoke an echo, saying, "What you did," but typed, I DONT KNOW. NOBODY LISTENS TO ME. I TOLD THEM I WANTED TO BE IN MATH. EVERYONE IS WORRIED ABOUT PUTTING ME UNDER TOO MUCH PRESSURE. WHAT DO YOU THINK? I jokingly told her that she was going to get me in trouble by making me her advocate with the school officials. Maggie then said, "Pressure of [unintelligible]. What you talking about boy?" Then she typed a request for me to speak with her mother about getting her into math class. I promised to do this. Several weeks later, she entered math.

Another element of security and comfortableness within a learning/communicating context involves social relations. Unfortunately, despite students' enormous success in communicating through typing, no matter how good they became, none of the students with whom we worked could actually start a conversation on their own. They all needed a facilitator. On a few occasions, students seemed to go and stand near other students, but again they required facilitation in order to say something. Many initiated conversations when facilitated.

Sam has echolalic speech; he can greet people with "hi," but then often continues to say "hi" repeatedly while in the presence of a group of people. His other echoes are often partially formed, for example, "bu" for *bus* or *balloons*. He cannot speak in sentences and cannot use spoken words for conversation. Before using facilitated communication, he had a picture book and communication board with pictures on it to express his wants (e.g., food, drink, bathroom), but his communication was limited mainly to labeling. The communication book included pictures of objects and activities. He would not initiate using it, but if presented with the book, he could point to pictures; this seemed to work as a way to label activities or things in which he might be interested. Prior to using facilitated communication, there was no evidence that Sam could read. In his first-grade class, at "morning meeting," he participates through typing with facilitation. One day, for example, a student named Liza gave her contribution to the morning news: "We are going to a party." Sam initiated his own comment on that, typing: ME TOO. On other days, Sam gave his news, I HAVEE BLUE PANT, and I CUT A KEY and I GO IN TRRUCK. One day, his teacher initiated "peer conversations." Sam typed, MOLLY I LIKE YOU. Upon hearing from Sam's facilitator what he had typed, Molly responded, "I like you too, Sam."

The desire to have friends and to lead a normal social life in school are common themes for the students who communicate with facilitation. A second-grader, Gerry, typed to his facilitator, I WET MY PANTS BECAUSE MY MOM WONT LET ME GO TO MY FRIENDS HOUSE. Gerry does not speak and had no effective alternative means of communication prior to learning facilitated communication. His parents report that they believed he could read from the age of 2½, but professionals would not verify his reading abilities until he began to communicate through typing. On another day, Gerry typed, I WANTT TTO HAVE TIME TO PLAY WITH THE KIDS. I WANT TO TALK WITH KIDS. I LIKE LORI. Gerry's classmate Raul expressed similar sentiments: I HATE VACATION. I CANST GO TO SCHOOL. (Raul, age 10, has some functional speech as well as echolalia and was able to use several hundred signs prior to learning to type with facilitation, but only for labeling, choosing, or requesting; he had not been able to use signs or spoken words to formulate sentences.) And Lenny, whose parents were planning to move to a different community, wrote to Rosemary Crossley and asked, DEAR ROSE MAARIE DO YOU THINK I CAN SHOW BAD BEHAVIOR AOND STILL BE IN REGULAR CLASS ?

CONVERSATIONAL COMMUNICATION WITH PEERS

At the Ed Smith School, teachers, speech therapists, and teaching assistants have used a variety of strategies to encourage students to converse with each other, including cooperative learning groups, morning news time, pairing students, word and number games with teams, small reading and math groups, "peer conversations," letter writing between students, and role plays. In kindergarten and first-grade classes, many nondisabled classmates asked their teachers for letter boards like those used by students who had no speech or only echoed speech.

For any lengthy conversations, the nondisabled students as well as those with speech difficulties had trouble maintaining dialogue unless it was encouraged and arranged. Thus second-grader Gerry was urged to invite a friend to his daily, half-hour "speech/language" sessions with a speech therapist. As noted above, Gerry does not speak. He often claps his hands, pushes his desk away with his feet, and gazes around the room, seeming not to pay attention. During one speech class, the speech therapist, Ms. Bloch, facilitated with Gerry in a structured role-play between Gerry and his friend Lori. The role-play was designed to foster communication, to help Gerry's classmates learn how to converse with him, and to help Gerry become more independent in his communicating. Interestingly, Lori needed as much or more prompting as Gerry. The role-play involved Gerry pretending as a patient and Lori as a doctor. The speech therapist asked Lori what she wanted to ask Gerry. Lori said, "I don't know." The speech therapist encouraged her, saying, "Well, if you are the doctor, what would you want to know?" Lori said, "What hurts?" Facilitated alternately at the hand and under his wrist, Gerry typed, I HAVE A HEADACHE. The speech therapist then asked and helped Gerry to give the tape of typing from the Canon Communicator to Lori. She did this each time Gerry typed something; on one occasion, when Lori reached to get the tape, the speech therapist said, "Let Gerry do it; it's good practice." The role-play conversation continued. The speech therapist asked Lori, "So what are you going to do, doctor? Ask some more questions? Do something?" "Where does you head hurt?" Lori asked. The speech therapist praised her for her question: "Lori's a good doctor. She has good questions to ask." Gerry told her that it hurt AT THE BACK. Lori seemed to have difficulty thinking of what to ask. When she asked if his head hurt a lot, she learned little more about Gerry's imaginary problem, for he answered, NO. Ms. Bloch noted that sometimes doctors want to take a patient's temperature. Lori did this, telling him that he had a temperature of "10." Ms. Bloch looked amused. She then said to Lori, "If you are the doctor, what would you do now?" Lori responded, "I would tell him that he has the flu." "Okay, tell him that," the speech therapist encouraged. Up until this point, Lori had been standing opposite Gerry. Now she moved and stood beside him, to his left, with a hand on his chair. Ms. Bloch facilitated Gerry's typing, supporting, and thus stabilizing, his hand as he typed.

LORI: Gerry you have the flu.
Ms BLOCH: Do you have some questions for the doctor about that?
GERRY: WHAT SHOULD I DO?
LORI: Take medicine.
Ms. BLOCH: She says you need medicine. Do you have any questions about the medicine?
LORI: I have a question. Do you want liquid or pill? (*She sat down on the floor beside Gerry.*)
GERRY: I DONT LIKE EITHER BUT I WILL TAKE LIQUID.
Ms. BLOCH: Do you have any questions about the liquid medicine? (*Gerry began to type and then hesitated.*)
LORI (*holding Gerry's other hand*): Come on Gerry finish it.
GERRY: HOW MUCH MEDICINE DO I TAKE?

Lori and Gerry "talked" some more about the medicine. Then, before finishing up, the speech therapist asked Gerry if he had anything else to say. He typed, I WAS ONLY PLAYING.

During the role-play conversation, the speech therapist modeled for Lori how to converse with Gerry and for Gerry how to hand his communication to Lori. It took a while for Lori to catch on about how to ask questions that would elicit useful information, how to speak directly to Gerry, and how to support Gerry in his responding. But at the point where Gerry asked her, WHAT SHOULD I DO?, Lori made the transition to direct, naturally flowing communication with Gerry.

This conversation occurred in March. At the beginning of the same school year, in September, before being introduced to facilitated communication, Gerry had never had a conversation with another person.

The task of facilitating conversations is similar with older communication users in that the facilitator must initiate dialogue, but it is different in that the facilitators may also be co-workers or other peers—of course, younger students can become facilitators with their peers as well, something with which we are just now beginning to experiment.

Neil is 24. He works mornings in a university office, where he photocopies and collates papers. He receives support from a full-time job coach as part of a vocational rehabilitation program. He has been labeled "autistic" and "severely mentally retarded." He sometimes makes screeching sounds, slams his desk with his hand, and hits himself or other people; he often manipulates poker chips in his hand or in his mouth. When people are conversing with him, he often looks away or straight ahead; he appears not to be listening. His muscle tone is poor and his gait is haphazard; occasionally he almost looks as if he might tip over. He learned how to read at an early age. His mother spent many hours instructing him at home with flashcards. She also insisted that he be placed in a regular class, but in fact most of his schooling took place in a separate school for students with moderate and severe retardation.

In the early stages of using facilitated communication, Neil's co-workers posed questions that he could answer with yes/no responses. Next they asked him to indicate choices of what he wanted, for example, "to use the Canon; to go home; to drink; to visit; to take a break; to work; to be alone; to use the men's room." Similarly, his job coach and other co-workers listed words that he could select to let them know his feelings: *angry, happy, frightened, lonely, hungry, hot, cold, sad, thirsty, amused, tired,* and *sick.*

It took several months before the co-workers realized that they could have conversations with Neil and that he did not need prewritten words to cue his contributions. Recently, for example, his job coach,

Lorriane, asked if he had seen two adult friends of his over the weekend. He responded, YES AND BABY. The couple had a newborn baby.
Often Joanne, his afternoon support person, asks him if she can smoke,
to which he responds variously, NO SMOKING, I DO NOT LIKE SMOK-
ING, DONT SMOKE IN THE CAR, and BAD GIRL FOR SMOKING. In each
of these conversational situations, the content of the conversation concerned topics of interest to both participants.

TYPING TO COMMUNICATE: SELF-DETERMINATION

In one way or another, all communication promotes the self, de-
fines the self, makes the self known to others. Aside from its relevance
as a means of doing schoolwork and getting educated, or of expressing
feelings, facilitated communication has enabled students to convey their
needs, wants, and aspirations.

Many of their communications about needs or wants appear mundane but nevertheless are important to them. Evan, for example, asked
if the television crew that visited his classroom could turn off its bright
lights; he was bothered by the lights. A first-grade student indicated
that she did not want to be videotaped by our research project: I THINK
IRT WOULD BE PITS TO TAPE ME. I RIGHBT ABOUT SEYING NO. I
JUST DONT WANT TO BE VIDEOTAPED. Several months later, she asked
to be videotaped. Another first-grader typed to his teacher that he
wanted her to speak with his mother to get her to send permission slips
to the school to allow him to participate in afterschool activities:

> i was talking about the kides having fun rollerskating.
> i want to go rollfersikalting .i dont have the persmis-
> sion slip. i want you to talk to my mom to tel,l her i
> am yelling for help. i read the notices and my mom igpl.
> ignores them.
>
>   . . .
>
> i want her tolp learn to talk with me. on your type-
> writer.

A third first-grader typed that he wished he could be in a Canadian
school with a Canadian teacher because, he believed, A CANADIAN
WOULD NOT MAKE KIDS SSIT AT DESKS. A second-grader typed to his
mother that he wanted her to stop buying margarine and start buying
REAL BUTTER. In the classroom, students could use facilitated communication to indicate which books they wanted to read, which students

they wanted to be grouped with, and what part they wanted to take in cooperative learning activities. At the secondary level, students could use facilitation to indicate which classes they wanted to take as part of their schedules.

The ability to communicate also allowed students to express themselves on crucial, even life-threatening, matters such as sexual abuse, fears, and health problems. One student asked his speech therapist/ facilitator to HYDE MY DIGGIHNG . . . PUT MY PZapers away, referring to his desire to have his communication about sexual abuse kept from other students or teachers (it had already been shared with child welfare officials). A kindergarten student typed, iwant a daad so he can help mom. This same student was able to communicate how he happened to fall off a swing in the playground and hurt his nose: i fell forward kid let me go the swing. Another student typed that, TUF GIESC . . . ARE AT SCHKOOL. . . . THEY PUSH OTHER PEOPLE AROUND. I SAW THE GUYS IN THE HALL.THEY USED THEIR HANDS. (Here the teacher had explained to him how to spell *guys* so that when he typed it a second time, he had the spelling correct.) And one student complained that his teachers did not talk enough with him. i dont thinkk people . . . lget happy about me talking, he typed. When asked to explain who he meant, he typed, people at school. He further elaborated that the teachers let him sit in his seat and tmhey dont ask hme to do my work. Later he clarified that he was referring to the teacher assistants. He typed to his speech therapist that she could TELL HER [his teacher] BUTT DONT TELL SISTANTS. A classmate of this student's who also uses facilitation made a similar complaint about his mother, spelling out on a spelling board, HOME IS CRAZY. MY MOM IS TOO BUSY. SHE IS NOT HOME ENOUGH. . . . SHE HAS TO TAKE MORE TIME TO SPELL WITH ME. A third-grade student used communication to explain to his speech therapist/facilitator that he did not like the person who takes care of him at his home:

> I FEEL SCARED WHEN I AM WITH JANE AND A THERE IS NOTHING
> I CAN DO ABOUT IT. . . . SHE YELLS AT ME AND SPEECH SHE
> SPEAKS HARSHLY ABOUT MY MOM.

It is still too early in the process of using facilitation for us to see what most students have to say about their futures, but already, 6-year-old Alicia has typed about her desire to become a writer by the time she is 25. A middle school student who is two years older than most of his classmates spelled, I RDEADTY TO TALK ABOUT NEXT YEAR I WANT TO GO TO NOTTINGAN [Nottingham High School] I WANT TO GO TO

CLAXSSES. Evan spelled out his desire to go to college. Marny, a 21-year-old student who is described in a later section of this chapter, has already enrolled in a college course, only a year after typing her first words.

FEELINGS

```
my name is Alicia. i am 6 years old. ig go to ed.smith
school. i talk best by typing. i really like to type be-
cause i am very good spieaking that way. i only talk
with my voice on occsion because w it doesn't work
right. i get very angry because of this. i want you to
know i am very smart and only can't talk.
    i am really the only child in my class who uses a
typewriter. i feel very proud of my typing. i will be a
writer when i am 25 years old . i x want people to re-
spect children with autism. we are bright and want to be
just like opther kids.
    Alicia april 19,1991
```

Alicia's speech is highly echolalic and conversationally limited to single words or phrases, not sentences. Her typing has none of these problems. She can type sentences free of pronoun reversals, incorrect verb tense, and other communication difficulties associated with autism. Also, her written thoughts and her choice of vocabulary are unusual for a 6-year-old, although not inconsistent with observations of the typed language of other young students with autism who have been introduced to facilitated communication. Perhaps because this was a public document, written for an awards contest, Alicia's words are positive and commanding.

Alicia and other students using facilitated communication often share personal feelings. While some of their thoughts exude enthusiasm and hope, others bespeak frustration, sadness, and anger. They cover nearly every conceivable topic, with clusters of comments about people they love and people who are supportive, jealousy toward other students with whom they feel competitive for their teachers' attention, their thoughts on autism, and their desire for independence and often their lack of it.

Since the teachers, therapists, and teaching assistants are the students' most frequent and often most effective facilitators, many students feel they can share personal thoughts with them. One second-grade student, who had been counseled by his therapist after communicating with her about having been sexually abused by a family member, typed: `i am feeling good. i am happy i am not a bad kid. I AM very glhad i can talk with you it is not easy ij feel glad i have teachers wbho rite with me.` A first-grade student told his speech therapist/facilitator that he did not want his family to move to another state, typing `I WANT HERE` [his mother] `TO STOOP BEINGG HAPPYY ABOUT MOVING.` But realizing that he was in fact going to have to move, he then asked his teacher to `TELL . . . THE TENNESEE PPEOPLE I AM IDEAL FOR FIRST GRADE.` He was concerned that he would get to Tennessee and find that people would not use facilitated communication with him and would not know or believe that he could do academic schoolwork.

The desire for people with whom to facilitate recurs often in the students' typing. Many of them ask the teachers to have their parents come to school to learn how to facilitate. All of them express concern when they move to new classrooms and new teachers. The statement of one second-grader that `i worry about myn time with new teacher` is a common refrain; will the new teachers be good at facilitation; will new teachers know they are smart?

Other student expressions of feelings concern war (some thought the war in Iraq was good and necessary, others were against it), family strife, loneliness, frustration, friends, and joy. The following two examples typify such expressions, although admittedly they are by two very articulate students. Writing about happiness as part of a school assignment, a 7-year-old boy, wrote:

> `it makes me happy tthafgt you wlork wigth nme here. it makes me happy that youn g rjtsters` ["Do you mean youngsters?" he was asked] `yes are hdere at school and that i am wyth thenm. it jusgt isv good to be here. i am the hqappiest jyoungster in greadt big w orld. i am finished.`

He said he was finished, but then started up again:

> `i think peopleb should eatmore good food. i eat good food and that helps me stay open to teachers.. i dont restle` [he probably means "get restless"] `when i foofd is good for meur.`

Asked what was good food, he answered, `i mean eggs and toast. and hyrw hamburgers and potatoes. i stquand by eating tjhe` best. Also in a happy mood, Mark, a second-grade student, had the following interchange with his teacher, Betty:

> BETTY: Good morning Mark.
> MARK: GOOD MORNING BETTY HOW ARE YOU TODAY?
> BETTY: I'm fine. How are you?
> MARK: I AM FINE THANK YOU.
> BETTY: Do you have any news?
> MARK: I CANT THINK OF ANYTHING ELSE TO SAY I HOPE THAT
>   IT IS OKAY WITH YOU.
> BETTY: Yes, it is fine.
> MARK: I AM HAPPY TO HEAR THAT. I DECIDED THAT I SHOULD
>   BE NICE TO YOU FOR A CHANGE.
> BETTY: Why?
> MARK: THOUGHT IT WOULD BE GOOD THING BECAUSE CHRISTMAS
>   IS COMING.

This same student told his teacher that his mother was sad because of his tantrums and of his failure to sleep well at night; this student also typed that he was worried about his teacher, who had been absent for several weeks because of medical problems.

Feelings of Jealousy and Love

Among the frequent topics in discussions of feelings is student jealousy, mainly over teacher attention and expressed primarily by elementary school students. Occasionally high school students hit each other, yelled, or complained via typing that they wanted their teachers for themselves, but this was relatively rare in contrast to elementary students' insistence on the matter. I AM UPSET BECAUSE I THINK THAT YOU DONT LI KE ME I THINK YOU LIKE ANDREW AND MARK BETTER, 6-year-old Alicia typed. She continued:

> I THINK THAT IT IS TRUER BECAUSE YOU DPERND MORD TIME
> WITH THEM. I WIOSH THST YOU WOULD TALK WITH ME MO%E AND
> :PLAY WITY ME MORE. aLO DONE THANKS FOR LISTENING. i
> hope that I DIDNOT HURT YOUR FEELINGS BUT I FELT YOU
> SHOULD KNLW HOW I FEEL. ARE WE STILL FRIENDS

Similarly, William, age 6, complained that his teacher had gone outside with a classmate of his and that he wanted to go out himself. i liketo go outside so ican enjoy the breezesbb, he typed, uu . . . went with jermayne can not i go it is not fair and i need you to no how i think. Another student in the same class complained, YOZ LOVE JERMAY MORE THAN ME. Interestingly, the student about whom they complained is one who requires a great deal of the teacher's and teacher assistant's time to keep calm. In a second-grade class, still another student typed, I FEEL MAD AT MY TEACXHER BECAUSE SHE LIKES GERRYP NOT ENOUGH LIKING ME. And one student typed that he WAS REALLY UPSET BECAUSE I AM MAD ABOUT LIZA ALWAYS KISS ANDREW I WANT TO KISS LIZA. Students ask for hugs from their teachers and often want reassurance that their teachers love them. Mark typed with his mother, I BELIEVE BLOCH [his speech therapist/facilitator] IS VERY CARING AND I LOVE HER. Before he developed a facility to type with his mother, he had typed to his speech therapist, I LOVE HER [his mother] BUT I CFANT TALK WITTHH HER. On this same theme of love for parents and teachers, William typed, MMY MOM IS HAPPY TODAY SHE LOVE ME MUCH SHE TTTRY HARD FORR ME . . . DDO YOUP LOVE ME TO.

Like most other students, William expresses dismay at requests for him to generalize his typing to more facilitators. i need someone who knows mee, he complained, and he does not want certain people who, he claims, don't like him. A classmate of his echoed these sentiments when he typed, NO NEW SAPEECH TEACHER. Asked if he would at least be able to try with a new teacher, he typed back, NO I CANT. BECAUSE I DONT KNOW HER. I DONT WANT TO. I DONT THINK IT IS GOOD. A middle school student apparently felt so strongly about who could and could not be his facilitator that he hit and broke one facilitator's nose; he did this only after a month of telling his favorite facilitator and his parents that he did not want to work with that particular teaching assistant. After he broke the woman's nose, he was assigned a new assistant, a rather large man.

Feelings About Autism and Independence

The primary message of students about autism is that they want to be rid of it. None of the students with whom we have worked have communicated that they have accepted autism. While the students think of themselves as good people, deserving of understanding, friendship, and love, they nevertheless do not like having autism. They describe life with autism as often lonely and difficult. The difficulties they describe concern their problems with communication, specifically with not being able to talk like other people, and their lack of indepen-

FIGURE 6.1 On Not Wanting Autism

Charles, age 4

II WWAANNTT TTOO TTAALLKK LLIIKKEE TTHHEE OOTTHHEERR
KKIIDDSS.... I MAD XCH   I PISED BECAUSE I CANT TALK

William, age 6

i need help people do not under stand about authism mom talks
tto the doctor about me i want to be like the other kid it is
hard to be oautisitc mo prays i can not helpp it when i get out
ofcontrool... I LIKEE YOU I NEED HELP HELP MEMORE HUG ME LOVE
ME.

Peter, age 8

i regular person. i dont like hosw people treat me. they tell me
i am stupid. [When asked who does this, he responded] tjj the people on
the street.... i feel bad bny h xer because myh teacher is not
her e. i feel terrible because people hate me.

Andrew, age 6

I CRY A LOT ABOUT MY DISABILTIY.... IT MAKES ME FEEL BAD WHEN I
CANT DO MY WORK BY MYSELF.... i want tqailk ab out the kind ijn my
classroom, they are reqally excited about my worki.i feel utmost
hapl/2piness with... my improved hewqalth.... i like it [here he refers
to the fact that he is typing with the facilitator supporting his forearm and elbow rather
than at the wrist or hand] b ecause it is more independent.... i think ogf
beooing indgtependent i am feeling very proud of myself.

Mark, age 7

I WWANT TO BELIKE NORMFAL KIDDSS [When asked what it means to be like
normal kids, he responded] BBBNG [being] FHF [?] AHBLE OOOTO TALLLLK...
I AI DONT WANT TO BE AUTISTIC... NOBODY REALLY ZUNDSERSTANDS WHAT
IT FEELS LIKE.... [When asked how it felt, he replied] IT IS VERY LONELY AND
I OFTEN FEEL LOUSY. MY MOOD IS BAD A LOT. I FEEL LESS LONLI WHEN
I AM WITH KIDS.... i am autistic and ssick of iut because i cando
anything if i am nnot autistic. i know it is always going to be
there... I AM VERY UPSET BEC AUSE I NEED FA CILITASION. I DONT WANT
TO DEPEND ON PEOPLE.

Alicia, age 6

i want to talk about lonley chidr en.... I feel lonely at times
when i   am uninterested in writing. it means that i fdeel very
lonely when tALKING IS HARD.... IFEEL BAD AT SCHOOL WHEN I CANT DO
THINGS BY MYSELF. I FEEL BAD WHEN CHILDREN DID NOT TALK TO ME
BECAUSE I CANT TALK TO THEM. I FEEL BAD AT ASCHOOL WHEN I CANT
TALK WITH THE OTHER KIDS [This statement was written in response to a
sentence-completion exercise beginning with the phrase, "I feel bad _____"]

(Continues)

FIGURE 6.1 *Continued*

Sam, age 6

I THINK IT IS HARD [referring to a game] BECAUSE I CANT DOO IT BY MYSELF.

Mary, age 12

LONELY AM MAD [Facilitator asked why, to which Mary responded] BECAUSE MARY STUPID.

Todd, age 17

THANK YOU FOR TALKING TO ME LIKE I UNDERSTAND. I LIKE YOU. DO YOU THINK I WILL EVER BE LIKE YOU? YOU ARE SO CALM.

Neil, age 25

[Neil's support person asked him to complete the sentence, "When people see me they think I probably _____," to which he responded] AM MEAN. [When asked why, Neil typed] HOW I LOOK. [When asked to complete the sentence, "The thing I'd like others to know about my handicap is _____," Neil typed] I CANNOT HIDE IT.

---

dence. Figure 6.1 lists examples of student comments about wishing they could be free of autism.

NOT A CURE FOR AUTISM: BEHAVIOR PERSISTS

Despite the normal quality of language that students often produce using facilitated communication, students' complaints about autism demonstrate that their new communication abilities have not resulted in the complete eradication of all their other autistic-like behaviors. Maggie, age 13, told us that facilitated communication *does* change her life, if not her autism. She wrote in a letter, mentioned in Chapter 3, that she could now tell people how intelligent she is, what she plans for herself, what she likes and dislikes, and her dreams. In another letter, she explained that facilitated communication HAS MADE MARVELOUS CHANGES IN MY LIFE AND THAT OF MMANY INDIVIDUALS WHO ARE STRANGERS IN THIS WORLD. Yet as we saw in her letter to her mother, quoted at the beginning of this chapter, Maggie is frustrated by her autism. In the same vein, an elementary school student told his speech therapist/facilitator that he did not type a lot for his mother because he did not want her to OD [overdose] ON MY PROBLEMS. Another student typed:

```
i cry a lot because i SN cant talk NN. i am older than
my brotherbrand heb can do more than me. I feel awful
aubout that. i think a speech teacher should be helping
me talk. i am thinking of talking with my mouth
```

None of the students' ritualized, stereotypical, or unusual behaviors disappeared entirely. While all but one of the students over 5 years of age revealed an ability to type for extended periods of time, ranging from 15 minutes to several hours, all continued to respond to the environment in unusual ways (e.g., not appearing to respond to sudden noise or seemingly not attending to other people). Others typed out complaints about being bothered by certain noises, revealing a heightened auditory sensitivity.[1] A few students could be observed putting their hands over their ears to keep out the unwanted sounds. Through their typing, all revealed an ability to hear and process the language of people around them. The unusual behaviors, which persisted and which masked the students' competence, could be observed first-hand and are also seen or heard on our research videotapes, including the following: seeming to gaze over a broad range of objects quickly; staring; seeming to use peripheral vision; desire for order; hand flicking; spinning objects and other repetitive movements; jumping up and down; hand clapping; getting up and down from a sitting position; echolalic speech; walking tentatively, almost as if blind and in need of feeling where to put the next foot; general instability; biting the fat at the base of the thumbs; screeching; seeming lack of affect; apparently excessive affect, including laughing at unusual times; hitting oneself or others; eating chalk and other objects; pulling the hair of other students or teachers; and delayed responses to events. Our study of facilitated communication did not specifically examine or measure increases or decreases in such behavior, but the researchers could not help noticing them and thinking about them.

As the students became more fluent and open in their communication, they began to comment on their behavior. It appears that behavior such as crying, hair pulling, biting, screaming, and hitting occur for one of two reasons: (1) out of frustration, where the difficult behavior is a form of communication and (2) in response to an unknown, physical feeling or as a compulsive behavior. It may be that these two "reasons" overlap, with frustration precipitating a physical feeling of being out of control or, conversely, with a physical feeling of being out of control resulting in frustration.

The most common source of behavioral outbursts seems to be related to frustration and an attempt to communicate something. For example, a 7-year-old told us that his tantrums were in response to his being upset about specific events or situations, such as school cancellation due to snow, being told to go to bed when he did not want to, or not being included in music class. A middle school student told his teacher and speech therapist that he had hit a fellow student because I WAS MAD. When asked why he was mad, he explained that he did not like going to the store with his classmates. Another middle school student explained that he was upset because his parents told him he could no longer play with pieces of string, one of his stereotyped behaviors. An elementary school student explained that he acted out because his school program was boring:

```
i set oupset because i
want to read
i get job done in the morning
end in the afternoon i set boorrjed
```

This 6-year-old attends both halves of a split session kindergarten program in which the afternoon session duplicates the morning session. When asked why he had a tantrum, this same student typed, I DONT HAVE THE CONTROL. Figure 6.2 includes additional examples of students' comments on the communicative intent of their behavior.

The communicative intent of a particular behavior is often hard to interpret on the basis of the behavior alone. For example, a speech therapist/facilitator worked with a student for several months, having him do set work such as fill-in-the-blanks exercises; throughout, he would often slap his desk and try to pull her hair. Then one day he was observed running from one side of the room to the other, knocking up against the wall. When the facilitator asked him what was the matter, he typed, I WAS HAPPY.

Evan's behavior appears more physical in origin, although perhaps not exclusively so. He has been known to hit facilitators. His teachers permit him to get up and pace in the school hallway if he feels he is about to hit someone. As he explains it in one of his poems, controlling his own behavior is a struggle in which he is not always successful:

```
BLACK HOLE
ALONE IN ME
FEARING, RIPPING STRETCHING
PLEASE LET ME BE FREE FROM YOUR GRIP
DEADEN
(EVAN, OCTOBER 30, 1990)
```

FIGURE 6.2 Communicative Intent of Behavior

Sam, age 6

I SCREAM ... I NEED YOU TO BE YELLING AT ME AND TO BE EBP A NASTY
TEACHER. I I NEED YOU TO IHG HUG ME WHE N I AM DOING WELL.

Andrew, age 6

I AM TIRED BECAUSE I HAD A SHORT NIGHT. IW WENT TO BED LATE
BECAUSUSE I WAGTCHED TV.I WILL CATCH UP WITH MY SLEEP TONIGHT. I
DONT GO TO BED ON TIME.... ["What do you do when your parents tell you to go
to bed?"] I HAVE A TANTRUM....
I AM SORRY ABOUT HURTING YOU. ["Why are you upset?"] it's too noisy....
i in trlouble because zi f iqght the other teachders azll the
time. i only fight to ell them i am mad. ["What could you do that would
help?"] i could talk wiqth them. i think it would bec hard. it
would be hard because thefy domnt know how to talk w.ith me....
i feel terribl e about mthe teacher no t wo rking with me.... i
captain i tell you how to try to cap my mean fighti ng....
I FEEL GOOD ABOUT THE CLASSROOM. I DIDNTB YELL. I STRUGGKLED
WITH ROSA MND DEY ZBECAQUSE RI WANT HER TO KNOW THAT I DECIDE TO
TRY MNY PQW TO BE GE GOOD.... I AM BONOM NOT HAPPY ZBOUT MY
BEHAVIOR.

Mark, age 7

[Mark was hitting his face. He was upset for 10 minutes.] I AM UPSET BECAUSE I
WANT TO GO HOMEW BECAUSE READING IS BORING I LIKE TO READ BY
MYSELF L... I AM BORED BECAUSE READING IS EASY....
[At lunch Mark began hitting his face and crying. When asked why, he typed] I I
DIDN'T WANT FRANCOISE SITTING NEXT TO ME. SHE... BUGS ME AND I
DON'T LIKE IT SO PLEASE DON'T LET HER SIT AT THE SAME TABLE.

Lenny, age 6

[Lenny did not want to participate in a "backwards" activity, that is, doing things
backwards.] I DIDNT WANT TO DO THE WORK BECAUSE IT IS STUPID IT IS
STUYPID TO HAVE BACKWARS DAY IT IS NOT NECESSARY TO DO I DONT
LIKE IT AND I WONT DO ANYTHING ELSE FOR IT ... I ENJOY GIVING YOU A
HARD TIME BECAUSE I GET ATTENTION

Nancy, age 9

[Nancy left her classroom and went into the kindergarten classroom next door and
would not return when her first-grade teacher asked her to, explaining] i did want
to talkk to mrs rrruffallore....
I threw some stuff in the classroom. I was mad at Mr. Rea because
he was talking with Mrs. Franklyn. ["Do you think you can tell Mr. Rea in a
different way without throwing things?"] I can give him my sopelling bord.

When Evan found himself overcome by the out-of-control feeling during one of my visits with him, he subsequently wrote me a letter,
saying,

```
YOU  ARE  SO  KIND  TO  METREATING  ME  AS  AN  INTELLIGENT
FRIENDWUITH A MATURE SENSE OF VHUMOR. I FELT RUHDEWHGEN
I LEFTBECASE YOUI CAME TO TALK TOME. I WENT OUT IN RE-
ACTION TIO WHATR I WAS EXPERIENVCING INSIXDE MY BODY. I
FELT AN TENSION BUILDING UP. IT HASD NOTHING TO DO WITH
YOU, MBUT EWITH MY SEARCH FOR C ONTROL. COME BACK.
```

In another poem, Evan hints at the physical sensations that may
partly explain his difficulties with behavior. He seems to describe his
hypersensitivity to certain sound frequencies—he has complained several times to me about sounds bothering him—and also describes having a headache:

```
DO YOLU HEATR NOISE IN YOUR HEAD?
IT PONDS AND SCHREECHES
LIKEA TRAIN RUMBINGF THROJGH YOUR EARS
DO YUOU HEAR NOIXSE IN YOUR HEAD?

DO YOU SEE COLORS
SSWIRLING TWIXSTIBNG STABBING AT YOUJ
LIKE CUTS ON A MOVIE SCREEN HURLING AT YOU
DO YOU SEE CO,LORS?

DO YOU FEEL PAIN
IIT INVADES EVERHY CELL

LIKE AN ENEMY UNWANTED
DO YOU FEEL PAIN?²
```

It appears that for some people, behaviors such as hitting and hair
pulling may both reflect communicative intent and be the result of physical feelings or a compulsive act. Such seems to be the case with 24-year-
old Neil, who has autism and had been defined as severely retarded
until he began to communicate with facilitation. Neil, whom we met
earlier in this chapter in the context of his part-time job, does not yet
type voluminously, but he has begun to use facilitation to express his
needs, wants, and thoughts. Joanne, a support person who spends each
afternoon with Neil at home, at first had a difficult time interpreting his

occasional shrill screaming, his rapid hand flapping, his tendency to slap people on the shoulder or arm, his hitting and hair pulling. When he grabbed and pulled her hair, was he being playful, was he excited, was he acting on impulse, or was he trying to hurt her? When asked to explain the behavior, he typed, I DONT MEAN TO DO IT. Yet on another occasion, he typed, I LIKE TO SEE YOU JUMP. It is hard to know exactly how to interpret this, but it could be that he is attempting to make light of behavior that embarrasses him and that he really cannot explain. Similarly, Todd, a high school student, sometimes makes growling sounds, which he explains he does to annoy the people around him; on several occasions he has typed that he growled because he was mad about something in particular. The growling could also be a nervous habit, a compulsive activity. Dan, a third-grade student, explained that he makes "woof" sounds BECAUSE IT IS FUN AND I AM SAFE AGAIN. On several occasions when Neil has made loud sounds and slapped tables or himself, he has typed, for example, I AM UPSET, and then provided explanations like I DONT WANT TO GO FOR A WALK or I DONT WANT TO GO IN THE CAR because someone has assumed without asking whether he wanted to do so. In another instance, Neil was at his part-time job, sitting with a group of co-workers who were having a conversation, when he began to slap his hands together and rock back and forth; when one of the co-workers coaxed Neil into his office, in effect placing him in "time-out" because she thought he was upset, he became *really* upset and threw a full coffee cup and yelled, typing: I WANTED TO BE WITH THE OTHERS . . . I WAS LISTENING.

Several young students have also described their behavior as somewhat impulsive, but at the same time cued by the context. Peter, age 8, described his vacation in terms of his "behavior":

> PETER: i huffed [i.e., upset about] in the tv in my house. i
>   goygy got very bothderecd zydeds by the crazy boy
>   running through h thde housde.
> TEACHER: What is the boy's name?
> PETER: his name is Peter. i do it becausede i cant stop
>   myself.
> TEACHER: How can people help you?
> PETER: they can tell me to do something else.
> TEACHER: What did you mean by "huffed in the tv"?
> PETER: i didnt like the tv programs.[3]

Later he suggested what would help him: i need lots kohm cahm . . . people. [His teacher asked if he meant *calm*, which she spelled for him.] calm people help me vget calmer. Similarly, a kindergarten student, William, typed, i like to run and play help me get in control it is hard to sit i can do it if u r by me to help. Mark, who is in the second grade, has typed that he has a worse time controlling his behavior at home than at school, although he hits himself both at home and at school. He typed, I AM CRYING BECAUSE I EFED . . . UP WIT H BEING AED AUTISTIC. . . . I CANT STOP INITIALML OUTBURST. On one occasion he typed that he was hitting himself because he was tired and that he was tired because he is autistic and can not sleep properly. I AM DIFFERENT, he typed.

We have not been able to determine whether the sensitivity of some students to certain noises is a factor in their behavior. We have observed a number of students putting their hands over their ears to block out unwanted noise; some have typed that they are bothered by certain noises—I DO NOT LJIKE NOISE, explained Nancy at age 11—such as the screeching of fellow students and certain music. One student explained that he was bothered by his family's new stereo in the dining room. i dolnt llikrre myuusi [i.e., "I don't like music"], he typed.

Some students hit their facilitators even while they are typing. One speech therapist wrote a phrase on a student's laminated letter board—"hands are for typing, not for hitting"—and encouraged him to point to these words whenever he felt himself getting upset or frustrated. Periodically, this student slaps his teacher's hands; tries to rearrange her sleeves, pulling them down; and screams or yelps. Such behavior can lead to confusion, fear, and anger in people around him. A teacher explains:

> Last week in the cafeteria, he got up and, you know how he always wants to straighten people's clothes, he was doing that and there was a girl and she got upset and pushed him away and his fingers slipped under her golden chain and broke it.

Another student, one who has periodically hit, bitten, pinched, and slapped people near her, asked one of the researchers why she had turned off the videocamera during such a hitting and biting incident. The researcher explained that she thought the student probably would rather not be seen behaving this way. But to the contrary, the student asked for the camera to be turned back on, typing, SHOW PEOPLE. IT WILL HELP TEACHERS TO SEE YOU [the facilitator] BE CALM. She explained further that she appreciated people who facilitate her communication *and* who can stay calm, even when she tries to hit them.

Several students have managed to lessen their hitting and screeching, possibly as a response to their interest in attending regular academic classes. Others have persisted with their difficult behavior; their teachers have had to allow them to leave the classroom when they become upset. Some teachers tolerate occasional loud noises, echoed speech, and even some self-hitting so that the students can remain in the regular academic classes. With several students, behavioral improvement is obvious. One student who a year earlier could be observed hitting himself, getting up and down from his seat a great deal, chewing chalk, fidgeting with pieces of cloth, and throwing objects can now be observed staying calm in regular middle school classes. For example, he attended science labs, typed answers to the instructor's questions, sat with other students and a teaching assistant, and did not upset the lab equipment, including a Bunsen burner with its flame lit. Some teachers, parents, school administrators, and teaching assistants, as revealed to the researchers during classroom observations, have the subjective impression that many of the students do seem to be calmer and more in control of their behavior.

CONCLUSIONS: MAKING THE CONDITIONS RIGHT

The data in this chapter are based on observations and interviews with teachers, parents, students, and others whose lives have been affected by facilitated communication. The study focuses on everyday use of facilitation for communicating—when it works as well as when and how it breaks down. From these case examples, nine factors for fostering successful use of facilitated communication in everyday settings have emerged:

1. People who rely on facilitation for communication need to have both facilitators and communication devices—such as letter boards, electronic communicators, computers, or electronic typewriters—available to them *constantly*, whether at home, in the classroom, at work, or in social situations.
2. People in the communication user's environment must appreciate that he or she has ideas and may want to convey them; people must initiate conversations and be willing to wait for responses; communication users need to have access to the same communication opportunities available to others.
3. To communicate in typical environments—such as regular classes, the workplace, home, and social settings—communication users need to be supported to be in those environments; this may involve

adapting classrooms and other settings to be flexible enough to accommodate some of the unusual behaviors created by certain disabilities.

4. The facilitator and others in the environment need to be able to ignore unusual or difficult behaviors, to calm the person, and to redirect the person to communication or other activities.
5. The facilitator and others in a setting need to select activities or approaches to tasks that encourage collaboration and interaction.
6. Facilitators can foster improved typing fluency in training as well as work or social situations by conveying a positive, expectant attitude in the person's ability to become an effective communicator; the communication user generally responds best when other people in the setting understand and accept alternative communication methods, when they are included in conversations, when they are spoken to in a normal tone of voice and not patronized, and when they are assumed to be competent. Difficulty with communicating or not responding does not mean that the person has nothing to say.
7. Nearly anyone can learn to be an effective facilitator—often the method can be learned in a few hours or days; while some communication users have difficulty generalizing their fluency of typing to new facilitators, persistence on the part of both the communication user and facilitator is important.
8. Communication users benefit by having multiple facilitators; this increases opportunities to use the method in a variety of settings and also hastens independence in communication.
9. Communication users want respect and communicate best when given it, for example not having people speak in front of them as if they are not present, not being tested on their competence, and being guaranteed the choice of having their communication remain private or, conversely, of having it shared.

NOTES

1. For additional information on sensitivity to certain sound frequencies and possible treatment approaches, see Stehli (1991) and also Rimland and Edelson (1991).

2. The typographical errors in this poem are typical of those that many students produced. In this case, Evan's finger tends to veer to a letter above, below, or next to the intended target. Note that the extra letters are all next to or below the intended letters, for example the H in EVERHY occurs because he hit the H when going for the Y. Similarly, he hit the comma below the L in CO,LORS and so on. The problem of striking unintended letters next to in-

tended ones could be partially remedied by providing a key guard to the electronic typewriter he uses and perhaps also by slowing him down more as he types or by asking him to try slowing down; a combination of these is necessary most of the time, although he is able to slow himself down voluntarily on some other occasions.

3. It was not uncommon for students to create words to describe their feelings. One first-grade student, for example, typed, I AM HASSY, and then explained that he was MAD at his teachers for insisting that he walk all the way to the library. Then he typed, I AM HARPY ABOUT MY TEACHERS BECAUSE THEY MADE ME WALK. By HARPY he meant he was harping about it.

CHAPTER 7

Ending the Ability/Disability Dichotomy

LEARNING ABOUT THE ABILITY/DISABILITY DICHOTOMY

> My "pre-racialized" sons, then aged 3 and 5, observed that we call pink people white and brown people black. But the media dichotomize the human continuum by failing to distinguish between ethnic heritage—in which we are African Americans, Native Americans, Asian Americans, Latin Americans and, heaven forbid, European Americans—and racial/racist ideology in which we are suddenly "black" and "white." In such a charged, racialized environment, it seems almost impossible to view others as individuals rather than stereotypes. (Hare, 1990, B1)

A number of years ago, I had a similar experience regarding disability. After my 4-year-old daughter had been attending the Jowonio school—a preschool program that includes students classified by the State as "severely handicapped" and "nondisabled"—for more than half a year, she asked me, "what's *handicapped* mean?" She had overheard me use the term. It was an innocent question. Apparently, she had not yet been "handicapized." She had not adopted certain "handicapist" attitudes (Biklen, 1992a; Bogdan & Biklen, 1977). She had attended this school for more than six months and not learned the meaning of *handicapped*. Apparently that was because the school staff studiously avoided using the term. Although the staff struggled for alternatives, sometimes using the not altogether satisfactory terminology of *special needs, labeled,* or *severely involved* to describe the children to others, in the classroom, they referred to them by name, not by ability or disability. The school does not organize students into ability groups. The teachers and administrators had judged the idea of "handicap" unhelpful, indeed harmful.

When I explained to my daughter what the term *handicapped* meant, she was able to apply it: "Oh, like Billy. He uses a wheelchair." I did not feel very good about the part I played in this bit of my daughter's education, for this marked the beginning of her learning that society dichotomizes people into the "disabled" and "normal" (i.e., nondisabled). In retrospect, I felt bad that I did not communicate more forcefully to her the arbitrariness and wrongmindedness of the concepts of "disability" and "handicap."

One of the most important and inescapable questions raised by facilitated communication is: What does disability mean? This question comes up either because individuals' typing forces us to ask it or because the idea of disability and its social connotations often seem to get in the way of our being able to see and appreciate communicative ability.

FORCED TO ABANDON THE BLINDERS OF "DISABILITY"

During the course of the study of facilitated communication that I conducted in Melbourne, Australia, I observed several people classified as having cerebral palsy and Down syndrome who had no "autistic behaviors." But since it seemed conceptually easier to report my study of facilitated communication in terms of "autism and autistic behaviors," I dropped these individuals and these observations from my report (Biklen, 1990). Nevertheless, in a number of instances my observations of these individuals were as astonishing and eye opening to me as any of my other observations.

Two observations stand out particularly. They were of a young man named David and of an older man named Ben. Both have Down syndrome. I met David and Ben at the same adult training center where I had met Louis, the man whose first session with Rosemary Crossley is described in Chapter 1.

On August 1, 1989, Rosemary Crossley and I traveled to the adult training center where she was to conduct six "first sessions" (i.e., assessment sessions) with adults at the training center. The adults had been selected by the staff of the Center for communication assessments. David was the first person we saw that day. He is heavyset, has pudgy hands, and was wearing a white jersey and green sweat pants. He spoke very little, saying only one or two words when he did speak; it was hard to understand his speech. Crossley began the session with her usual introductory refrain: "I work with people who have difficulty speaking. I help find other ways for them to communicate." Then she began to get some insights into his use of speech as she engaged him in conversation. She asked, "What kinds of things do you like? Do you like watching TV?" He responded softly, "Ya." "What's your favorite program?" she asked. He made a sound that Crossley thought was "football," and then said another word that was also hard for me to understand but that Crossley apparently picked up, for she said,

"Collingwood?" David nodded his head in agreement; Collingwood is the name of an Australian football team. "Terrific," Crossley said, "you can't do better than that." Actually his speech was very difficult to understand. He seemed to mumble and have difficulty getting words out. When I asked him how old he was, I could not understand his answer. He is in his early 20s. Other than "ya" for yes, for the rest of the session, David did not speak any words that were distinctly understandable.

Using a "talking computer," Crossley asked David to point to pictures, for example, a blue fish, yellow bird, blue fish again, brown car and red car respectively. He pointed correctly to these, as he also did when asked to discriminate among triangles, circles, and squares. David did not talk during this part of the assessment. Crossley held onto his wrist, slowing down his already slow pointing. Next she showed him a series of sentences, including "Is my dog in the car?" Crossley now held just his sleeve end from above his forearm to stabilize and slow him as he pointed to the words *in* and *the* on request. When Crossley asked him to make a sentence out of words that were on a picture, he pointed to the following sequence, "I see a bird and small car cat and dog." David also was able to point correctly to particular letters in the alphabet upon request. With a Canon Communicator, Crossley asked David if he could spell his name. He spelled out, DAVID. Finally, Crossley asked, "Is there anything you'd like to tell me?" This was the point at which one expected to see a person's first sentence, constructed of letters and words that he or she had selected (i.e., not preselected as is the case with the talking computer and many augmentative communication language boards.) For his first sentence, David typed, HOW AB (it appeared he was headed for a consonant so Crossley pulled his arm back, still holding onto his sleeve end only, and said, "Come back, I'm not sure where you are going, try again") OUT (Crossley showed him the space bar) COFFEE. By this point in my study I was no longer shocked that people were often able to spell and construct sentences with typing, yet were seemingly unable to speak these same thoughts. Casually, I asked David if he wanted milk and sugar; he typed, WHITE. Crossley asked if he wanted sugar and told him to type Y for "yes" and N for "no." David typed N.

As I got the coffee, Crossley asked David, "Where did you learn to read?" He did not respond verbally but typed, SCHOOL. Crossley asked if he would like to join a communication group. He typed Y. "What would you like to be able to do most?" Crossley asked. David spelled, FIND A GIRLFRIEND. Crossley commented, "My goodness, and extremely well spelt. Right, and you'd like to find a girlfriend. Well at least you will be able to use this to talk to some of the girls in the group. Are there any that you really like particularly?" David nodded yes but typed, NOT SPECIALLY.

Before the session with David was over, Crossley asked a few more questions. She said, "I'd just like to ask you a couple of really silly questions, just because I'm curious. Um, do you know the name of the prime minister?" David said nothing and typed, BOB H, whereupon Crossley said, "Okay, Bob Hawke." Crossley hesitated a moment, thinking, then asked, "Okay, now you get top marks if you can tell me the name of the Opposition and any one of his 20 nicknames." Without hesitation, David typed, PEACOCK. Crossley commented that it was interesting and amusing that the two leading politicians had birds names. I pointed out that, "we have a Bush and a Quayle." Crossley told David that "quails are these tiny little birds that hide in bushes," and laughed. Crossley then said to David, "I don't suppose, . . . do you know any of Peacock's nicknames?" David hesitated for a moment and then typed, SHOW–PONY. Crossley congratulated him and added, "The 'Gucci kid' is another one."

Later that same morning, after meeting several other adults and going through assessment/conversation routines similar to the one with David, Crossley and I took a stroll through the training center. In one part of the building, half a dozen people were working at tables, packaging children's games. In the corner, rocking, sat a sandy- haired man about 55 years old. He was wearing gray pants and a brown jacket. He had Down syndrome. This was Ben. As we approached him, he stopped rocking. Rosemary said hello to him and asked him how he was doing. He typed on her Canon, FINE ROSIE. HOW ARE YOU. His alert greeting, including his use of the diminutive *Rosie*, surprised me, for his facial expression was nearly blank. Like David, he had little expression. Ben and Crossley spoke for a few minutes before Crossley introduced me, whereupon Ben surprised me by typing, DOUG BIKLEN I SAW YOU YEARS AGO. He was able to type without support. It turned out that we had met three years earlier when I had visited the school attached to the adult training center. I was amazed that Ben would know the spelling of my name. Often, people add a C or place the L before the K. He told me that he had met me when I had visited the center with Mary Dalmau, a Ministry of Education official. When I told Ben that I would be seeing Mary the next day, he asked if he could send her a message, typing, HELLO MARY. I CAN TYPE BUT I GET LAZY. LOVE BEN.

It did not surprise me that a person with Down syndrome could read, but Ben's conversational ability in typing contrasted dramatically with his spoken language. The same was true of David. In David's case, until I saw him type, I would have thought that perhaps he could not speak effectively because it was too difficult a cognitive task or because he had difficulty processing the complex sentences of the people around him. Neither seemed to be the case. Yet, even after seeing David, I found myself believing that his responses to questions and therefore his literacy/thinking abilities might be "more concrete" than those of other individuals I had observed during the Melbourne study. After all, his question, HOW ABOUT COFFEE, and his wish to FIND A GIRLFRIEND were indeed concrete, different from Louis's first sentence that day, IM NOT RETARDED (see Chapter 1). But labeling him a "concrete" thinker was presumptuous. David had demonstrated that he could form sentences, that he could spell difficult words such as *friend*, that he could read, and that he also knew a bit about politicians. In fact, I could not then know the extent of David's thinking, the nature of his personality, or a great many other things. But the fact that I was ready to believe that he might be more limited than other people was testimony to my disability blinders, to my attributing mental retardation to the condition of Down syndrome, and to my retrieving its associated stereotypes. I had seized on David's asking for coffee as evidence of lesser than great competence. Yet what I had in fact observed was that David and Ben possessed literacy competence far in excess of my expectations. The social meaning of "disability"—in other words, the stereotypes of incompetence, of concrete thinking, of difficulty with anything abstract—was getting in the way of my being able to see and understand people. It was time to shed the false dichotomy of "ability" and "disability."

My interactions with David and Ben were evidence again that a person not saying anything is not the same as a person not having anything to say. I have been learning this lesson over and over through the use of facilitated communication. Toward the end of the first year of using the method in Syracuse, preschool teachers introduced the method to a student with Down syndrome, a student named Melanie. At the age of 4 she has revealed that she can read—she has typed, for example, television, camera, chair, crown, typriter, boat, and elefant—and that she can use typing to communicate. Like David and Ben, her speech is limited to a few sounds that approximate simple words but that are often extremely difficult to understand. Several months after Melanie first began to type, she had the following conversation with her teacher:

TEACHER: What do you want to tell me today?
MELANIE: MOMMY ISNT DEAD NO DADDY ISNT DEAD IEJ IDD
MOMMY ISNT DEAD MOMMY ISNT DEAD

TEACHER: Is there someone you know who died?
MELANIE: NATHAN
TEACHER: Who is Nathan?
MELANIE: MOMMYS DANDD
TEACHER: Your mom's dad?
MELANIE: YES
TEACHER: How do you feel about that?
MELANIE: SCARED MS.
TEACHER: Is there anything else you want to say?
MELANIE: MOMMY ISNT DEAD

In another conversation, Melanie told her teacher that MOMMY IS MAD
NOT HAPPY because YESTERDAY IK I I HAD A BAD DAY BECAUSE I
NNOT HAVE GUMS. She was upset because she was not allowed to chew
gum that day. On another day, without any question to prompt her,
Melanie typed, i am happy i not ignorent. The next day, she told
her teacher, tell mommy i am smart. A day later, she repeated these
themes, typing, MOMMY IS IGNORENTT MOMMY HATEES ME BECAUSE I H
HAVE DOWN SYNDROME TELL MOM I IO AM SMART. She typed this
quickly and walked away from her teacher. Later when her teacher
asked Melanie what *ignorant* meant she typed, STUPID. It is noteworthy
that Melanie typed on this same topic several times, complaining that
her mom was mad because she has Down syndrome and that she (Melanie) was mad that her mom was sad not happy. The fact that she repeated her thoughts on this topic, each time in slightly different form,
and always coherently, suggests that she was using written language in
much the same way that children who are learning to speak use spoken
words; they often simultaneously convey a thought *and* practice their
language, looking for how others respond to their language and learning through the interaction. In fact, Melanie's typing, like Ben's and David's, should force us to see the inherent artificiality and illogic of defining people according to the categories "ability" and "disability."

WHAT IS REQUIRED IN ORDER TO SEE THE PERSON?

No matter our claims to the contrary, we all engage in "perspective
taking." That is, to any situation, we bring a lens, a way of looking and
of understanding. Perhaps one of the most classic examples of this can
be seen in Itard's account of *The Wild Boy of Aveyron* (*L'Enfant sauvage
d'Aveyron*). Accounts of the child's early history vary. Itard's (1894/1962)
account is of a child from the wild:

A child of eleven or twelve, who some years before had been seen completely naked in the Caune Woods seeking acorns and roots to eat, was met in the same place toward the end of September 1799 by three sportsmen who seized him as he was climbing into a tree to escape from their pursuit. Conducted to a neighboring hamlet and confided to the care of a widow, he broke loose at the end of a week and gained the mountain, where he wandered during the most rigorous winter weather, draped rather than covered with a tattered shirt. At night he retired to solitary places but during the day he approached the neighboring villages, where of his own accord he entered an inhabited house . . . there he was retaken. (p. 3)

When brought to Paris for professional observation, he came under the view of a gawking public. But, according to Itard, the public saw only a

disgustingly dirty child affected with spasmodic movements and often convulsions who swayed back and forth ceaselessly like certain animals in the menagerie, who bit and scratched those who opposed him, who showed no sort of affection for those who attended him; and who was in short, indifferent to everything and attentive to nothing. (p. 4)

In his report of the "wild child," whom he called Victor, Itard describes the public as having rushed to view the child, only to "see him without observing him," and to pass "judgment on him without knowing him" (p. 4). The public saw an image of a child, a backward image, and lost interest.

Itard's account of his first observations might have led some people to be pessimistic about his potential: "There was a profound indifference to the objects of our pleasures and of our fictitious needs" (p. 8); "his locomotion was extraordinary, literally heavy after he wore shoes, . . . always remarkable because of his difficulty in adjusting himself to our sober and measured gait, . . . [with] his constant tendency to trot and to gallop" (p. 8), Itard notes "it would have been necessary for me to run with him or else to use most tiring violence in order to make him walk in step with me" (p. 23); he was mute except for a guttural sound; "except for the occasions when hunger took him to the kitchen, he was always to be found squatting in a corner of the garden or hidden in the attic behind some builders' rubbish" (p. 11); in his room he could be observed "swaying with a tiresome monotony, turning is eyes constantly towards the window," but "if . . . a stormy wind chanced to blow, if the sun behind the clouds showed itself suddenly illuminating the atmosphere more brightly, there were loud bursts of laughter, an almost convulsive joy, during which all his movements backwards and forwards very much resembled a kind of leap he would like to take (p. 12); "sometimes instead of these joyous movements there was a kind of frantic rage, he writhed his arms, pressed his closed fists upon his eyes, gnashed his teeth audibly and became dangerous to those who were near him" (p. 12); "his mastication was equally astonishing, executed as it was solely by the sudden action of the incisors . . . a sufficient indication that our savage . . . lived on vegetable products" (p. 8); "he had an obstinate habit of smelling at anything that was given to him, even the things which we consider void of smell" (p. 8). But even seeing and reporting these qualities and behaviors, Itard remained optimistic for Victor.

Several factors account for Itard's ability to observe these qualities of behavior and nevertheless proceed further to observe, educate, and understand Victor with optimism. Itard believed in a notion of educability—even the person thought to be an "idiot" could benefit from instruction. He entertained multiple possible explanations for what he observed, rarely being satisfied with the first or most common interpretation. Itard seized upon evidence of competence and presumed that other abilities of a similar nature could and would follow: One word indicated the potential unleashing of many words; if Victor fulfilled one of Itard's requests, the teacher counted on his discharging many other future requests. Perhaps most important, Itard believed that whatever Victor did or did not do was as much a reflection on Itard the teacher as on Victor's innate or learned qualities.

Several examples of Itard's work should suffice to demonstrate his persistent openness and insistence on implicating himself in Victor's actions. Teaching Victor to read and to use language is a case in point. Itard was never able to make much progress with Victor's verbal expression. Victor remained essentially mute save for occasional words, sometimes uttered without seeming intentionality: For example, Victor might utter the word for "milk" (*lait*) a considerable time after having milk or in his sleep; sometimes he said words automatically, as when he would "let . . . escape [the statement] 'Oh Dieu!' in moments of great happiness. He pronounces it by leaving out the *u* in Dieu, and laying stress on the *i* as if it were double . . . Oh Diie! Oh Diie!" (pp. 33–34).

While Itard never credited Victor with being able to speak his thoughts, he pointed to many instances of communication. There was the pulling and miming that one can observe in many children labeled "autistic" or as having other disabilities as well as in unlabeled children. For example, Victor apparently enjoyed being carted about in a wheelbarrow. So, on evenings where no one initiated this activity and when he was so inclined, he returns to the house, takes someone by the arm, leads him to the garden and puts in his hands the handles of the wheelbarrow, into which he then climbs. If this first invitation is resisted he leaves his seat, turns to the handles of the wheelbarrow, rolls it for some turns, and places himself in it again; imagining doubtless, that if his desires are not fulfilled after all this, it is not because they are not clearly expressed. (p. 35)

If Victor was hungry or impatient for dinner, he put on the tablecloth and handed out the dishes to the housekeeper.

Itard observed progress with symbolized communication as well. Victor responded quickly to exercises that required him to match objects to pictures. When Victor failed to respond as intended or desired, Itard often took heart nevertheless. For instance, when Victor was asked to bring an object from among three possibilities and brought all three— and only the one requested matched the drawing shown him—Itard did not assume that this response reflected inability or lack of understanding. He knew that it was equally likely that the task was too simple and, after all, possibly silly or boring. "I am convinced," Itard wrote, "that this was merely calculated laziness which did not let him do in detail what he found quite simple to do all at once" (p. 38). Sometimes Itard's requests to Victor were met not with overcompletion but with resistance and even tantrums, sometimes precipitating "convulsions . . . like those of epilepsy" (p. 43). Itard recognized such rage as equal to his persistence and was "finally overcome by [Victor's] independence of character" (p. 43).

When first shown the word *lait* (i.e., "milk"), with individual letters so displayed as Itard pretended to drink milk, Victor seemed to catch on. But when given the letters and shown a jug of milk, Victor placed them in reverse order (p. 47). But after having been shown the correct display five or six times, Victor was able to spell the word on each future request and would display the letters at a neighbor's house when sent to pick up the day's milk. One glimpse of an accomplishment unveiled a landscape of possible others: "I had completely established in Victor's mind the connection of the objects with their signs, it only remained for me to increase the number gradually" (p. 79).

Itard marveled at Victor. When working with Itard on verbs, Victor seemed capable of genuine creativity. Asked to demonstrate the actions "to tear stone, to cut cup, to eat broom" (p. 82), Victor took a hammer to a stone and dropped a cup. Then, "not being able to find any word to replace" the verb *eat*, Victor "looked for something else to serve" (p. 82) in place of its object. He made bread the broom and ate it.

At first, it appeared that writing would prove as difficult for Victor as speaking. He evidenced what I have termed *apraxia* in both speech and physical action. Standing at a blackboard, each with a piece of chalk in hand, Itard and then Victor drew lines, with Victor "dividing his attention between his line and mine, looking without intermission from the one to the other as if he wished to compare them successively at all points" (p. 83). Eventually, Victor was able to copy words of which he knew the meaning, reproduce them from memory, and use them to secure his desires. His writing remained "entirely unformed" (p. 83).

With regard to personal feelings, especially the ability to reveal interest in and concern for others, it is necessary to turn to an example other than language communication. At one point when Victor left the house and ran to the forest, he was captured some distance from the community in which he was being educated. Local authorities locked him up in jail for a fortnight before he was recognized and returned to Itard. Upon seeing Madame Guerin, his guardian, he is reported to have lost consciousness momentarily and then, upon gaining consciousness, "showed his delight by sharp cries, convulsive clenching of his hands and a radiant expression" (p. 90). Itard concluded from this that Victor appeared not like a fugitive but rather like an appreciative, affectionate son.

One cannot but observe that it was certainly Madame Guerin's warm, persistent spirit and that of Itard that helped elicit Victor's unfolding as a caring, expressive, competent person in their eyes and possibly in his own as well. This notion of the importance of warmth, encouragement, and optimism—so embodied in these two and revealed in Itard's account—is not new; rather it recurs in any account of educational breakthrough (e.g., Ashton-Warner, 1963/1986; Crossley & McDonald, 1980; Grandin & Scariano, 1986; Oppenheim, 1974; Park, 1967, 1982). What *is* startling is that it does not command a more central place in the literature on learning.

WHY IS IT SO HARD TO BELIEVE THE COMMUNICATION OF PEOPLE PRESUMED RETARDED?

Itard surely encountered people in his day who must have wondered why he would expend his creative talents on the education of Victor. People must have wondered about Itard, just as many people question the sense of spending public funds on the education of students labeled "handicapped" today. Hopefully, Itard's and Victor's progress together was sufficient to justify effort spent on this kind of education. But what happens when the results of educating a student thought to be retarded produce unexpectedly good results? How are such findings received?

As I recounted in Chapter 4, successes with facilitated communication have often met with skepticism and outright disbelief and have even evoked charges of deceit and deception. Interestingly, others have encountered similar doubt and rejection before us. When Bogdan and Taylor (1976) published an interview/autobiographical account of a man named Ed Murphy, who was labeled "retarded" and who had lived a number of years in state institutions for retarded people, some readers disputed Murphy's classification as "retarded." Murphy's insights and sentence structure were thought not to be those of a "retarded" man. Yet he tested solidly in the range of retarded. Similarly, when May Seagoe (1964) attempted to publish the diary of Paul Scott, a man with Down syndrome, she encountered hurdle after hurdle in the publishing industry and in the field of mental retardation from people who questioned its authenticity.

Blatt (1987) was one of the experts to whom the Seagoe/Scott manuscript was sent by its publisher for an authenticity check. In *The Conquest of Mental Retardation*, he tells the story of Seagoe's struggle to have Scott's words accepted and publicly available. Blatt (1987) provides a few examples of Scott's diary entries from his travels around the globe, including the following:

> June 13. About 12 miles from Amsterdam is the home of the famous Edam Cheese: we went to the factory in Edam but it is a poor outfit; I put on wooden shoes and dutch trousers for a picture with dutch gals; I was in Dutch; our guide was a lad about 20 who had 7 brothers and 3 sisters; he spoke very fair English picked up from tourists; a remarkable individual and most likeable. . . .

> June 18. Paris is mobbed prices in hotels high and merchandise is about on the same level with U.S.A.: the great and historic boulevards and squares are still beautiful illuminated at night: . . . (quoted in Blatt, 1987, p. 105)

The question that Blatt had to answer was whether the manuscript was authentic. Had Paul Scott written the words, words such as *illuminated* and *remarkable*. Had he conceived of the ideas? Blatt does not explain how he became convinced of their authenticity, but in telling Scott's and Seagoe's story it is obvious that he became convinced of Seagoe's honesty and came to understand that Scott lived with and was educated by people who believed in his ability to learn and express himself. The more important question for Blatt did not concern Scott, it concerned Blatt himself. He asked himself:

Why was it that someone like me—someone engaged in the study of educability, someone who hypothesized that capability is educable—would find it difficult to believe that such a work could elicit anything but serious reservations if not outright belief? The answer to that question perhaps lies in the deeply embedded hopelessness associated with virtually everything connected with mental retardation. (p. 102)

Ultimately, Blatt determined that while Scott may still have tested as "retarded," his diary belied the tests.

Blatt concluded that one important message of Paul Scott's success was that intelligence is educable. Another way of looking at the same phenomenon—that is, Scott's writing—is that assumptions of inability and hopelessness associated with terms such as *retardation, disability,* and *handicap* convince experts in the field of mental retardation as well as the public that such coherent, thoughtful writing and expression such as Scott's are either anomalous—they are often characterized as unusual or unique cases or as islands of ability—or fraudulent. A third possibility sometimes entertained is that the author was not "disabled" in the first place.[1]

Expectations of hopelessness and inability undoubtedly cause many people labeled "disabled," especially those presumed retarded, to suffer discrimination in education. What Blatt apparently meant in suggesting that Scott benefitted from being educated was that all people may have Scott's potential. While his case may appear unique—Blatt suggested that it might be as important an example as that of Helen Keller's life—it may also be emblematic of the possibility residing in others, masked only by the implied hopelessness of labels such as "retarded" and "disabled." Similarly, regarding the literacy and ideas revealed by people using facilitated communication, at least some of the skepticism surrounding facilitated communication surely reflects the pessimistic beliefs of observers in people labeled "disabled" and the power of an ideology of hopelessness.

THE MEANINGS OF FACILITATED COMMUNICATION

Perceptions, understandings, and interpretations of facilitated communication, as with any events or text, have no truth unto themselves, only the meanings that people attribute to them. The way we understand facilitated communication or anything observable, indeed the very act of observing something and of describing it as something, necessarily reflects certain prior understandings, beliefs, and rules of observation and reporting (Foucault, 1972; Rabinow, 1984; Weedon, 1987). With facilitated communication, as with any event or circumstance that poses a potential challenge to traditional understandings, we have a choice. We can interpret facilitation in the context of current, dominant ways of thinking, for example, how society conceptualizes "disability," or we can understand it as a challenge to prevailing rules of discourse about disability, as a way of countering prevailing assumptions, practices, and ways of thinking about ability and disability.

Similarly, if facilitated communication is just a technical innovation, it can be provided wherever people are located, whether in institutions, sheltered workshops, special schools or regular schools, people's own homes, or regular workplaces; this view suggests that people's life circumstances need not necessarily change. But individuals using the method—that is, the communication users—suggest through their words and thoughts that they want more from the discovery of facilitated communication than a communication method.

The themes of people who use facilitated communication are of course not unidimensional. Yet there are a few that predominate in their communication and that challenge traditional, professional, and socially common ways of defining "disability." As in the fields of education and psychiatry during this century, societal understandings of intellectual and physical disability have been strongly shaped, even dominated, by professional power and professional knowledge (for discussion of the concept of professional knowledge and professional power, see Goodson & Dowbiggin, 1990; see also Foucault, 1972; Sampson, 1989). These themes concern identity, self-determination and independence (i.e., power), conditions of learning, and freedom of expression. Overall, these messages are in conflict with the notion of the individual as patient, as dependent, and as disabled.

Identity

Some of the most consistent and frequently heard declarations from people using facilitated communication are: "I'm not retarded"; "I wish I didn't have autism"; and "People need to treat me like I'm a human being." These statements convey several messages. Students are saying: Treat me as you would treat other people; see me as a person who has ideas, as a person who is interesting to know, as a person who can love and be loved, as someone who is good. These statements resist the notion that a person with autism or a similar condition must occupy marginal status. By saying, "I wish I didn't have autism," the person is not saying "I don't like myself," but rather that the physical effects of autism or other conditions get in the way of expression and of being able to do things that other people can do and therefore get in the way of being perceived as ordinary.

Of course it is more than physical or behavioral qualities with which the person must contend. "Disability" has rules and institutions to define it (Bogdan & Biklen, 1977; Dexter, 1964). University researchers make the ability/disability dichotomy real through their studies of "the disabled"; school psychologists create the "special" learner through elaborate, societally sanctioned processes of assessment, using "intelligence" and achievement tests; school organization further reifies disability through its divisions of education and special education, of classroom or subject area teachers and special education teachers, of regular and special schools, of regular school financing and special education supplements, of regular students and classified students, and of education law and special education law. One wonders if there would be so much disbelief about facilitated communication if the ability/disability dichotomy were not so ensconced in the culture, particularly in schools and in disability agencies.

The fact that people using facilitated communication challenge the definition of themselves as "the disabled" is consistent with autobiographical literature by people with disabilities (Bogdan & Taylor, 1982; Mairs, 1986; Mathews, 1983; Roth, 1981; Zola, 1982). In rejecting the master status of "the disabled," what people are saying is that they resent being defined as fundamentally different from other people and having their whole being defined as "disabled." Having seen themselves as like other people, they wonder at the inability of other people to accept this same viewpoint.

Self-Determination

If independence means having to communicate without support from other people—that is, without facilitation—then it is not a useful concept to the people with whom we have worked. To them, independence means being able to express themselves. They equate independence with having a measure of control over their lives. They reject prevailing social norms about independence that arbitrarily prohibit them from exercising self-determination. Within the dominant culture, the dividing line between the so-called able or normal and the so-called disabled is determined by physical prowess. The word *handicapped* refers to people who do not walk, people who have difficulty controlling their physical movements, and people who have difficulty speaking, among other things; handicaps are seen as creating a condition of dependence. It is ironic that while nearly everyone relies on other people in nearly every aspect of life (e.g., to get food, for housing, for travel, for education, in work, and for social recreation), certain kinds of interdependence (e.g., facilitated communication or support in personal care such as eating, hygiene, or mobility)—are defined as evidence of being "dependent." When people with disabilities speak of an "independent living" movement or of "independence" in communication, they do not necessarily mean doing things apart from facilitators or attendants, but rather enjoying what many other people take for granted—the chance to make choices about everyday matters, the chance to express themselves, and the opportunity to participate at the center of society rather than at its margins.

Conditions of Learning

One of the most personally disappointing aspects of our using facilitated communication or of seeing it used by other people is that for many professionals it *is* merely a new teaching or communication technique. This perspective on facilitation implies that society must now treat some individuals with autism and other conditions differently—many people who were previously thought to be dumb are now redefined as smart and therefore must be treated differently. It is a perspective that does not question the validity of treating people differently on the basis of perceived intelligence.

This perspective ignores the fact that time and again, students using facilitation refer to the importance of having teachers and others who believe in them and in their ability to think and express themselves. The implication is that all students, all people, should be treated as competent; ironically, for many students, many teachers, and many schools, this assumption seems to break with prevailing practice and assumptions. Treating people as capable learners reflects an ideology or belief that education should be fundamentally a process of interaction and support rather than one of testing and sorting. The latter creates a class system of schooling, with certain students, including those labeled "disabled," forced to the margins; the former, what we might term inclusive education, attempts to place traditionally marginalized students at the center of learning. Inclusive education assumes that students respond well to people who expect them to be able to communicate. And the good teacher has an uncanny ability to catch glimpses of sophisticated thinking when they appear, however fleetingly. The opposite also holds: Students generally do not communicate with people who are themselves not confident as facilitators or who doubt the students' abilities. The good teacher conveys a supportive confidence, perseveres, and exhibits genuine interest in the person and his or her communication. In so defining the good teacher, the communication user reveals a close relationship between emotion and learning.

Freedom of Expression

While controversy about facilitated communication continues, there can be little doubt that the method will survive, and almost certainly flourish. The words produced by people using the method are poignant and original, so much so that it will be hard to dismiss them. Individuals tell of both pain and determination that is at once poetic and demanding. Recently I invited a 22-year-old young man to speak before a graduate class of teachers. He has some echoed speech, but none of his echoed words convey his inner thoughts. During the presentation, a friend of his served as facilitator. The young man seemed nervous, repeatedly looking at his watch and several times interrupting his typing to pace from the front to the back of the lecture hall and then back to the front and to typing. Speaking of what it was like before he learned to communicate with facilitation, he typed, I WAS TRYING TO TALK BUT WAS ABLE TO MAKE ONLY ANGRY SOUNDS. Then, when one of the teachers asked him to comment on how he would have wanted schools to educate him if he had been able to use facilitation during his public school years, he explained, I AM SMART AND THEY SHOULD RUN THEIR SCHOOLS AS IF IT WERE SO.

Also recently, I received several letters from individuals who are mentioned in earlier chapters of this book. Their thoughts at once tell of their sense of themselves and of the kind of world in which they want to live. Chris, mentioned in Chapter 2, wrote about his deep loneliness:

IHANTEBEINGCAUTISTICJUSTFHEALLMEVLEMYLJMIFEISSTILLM
EANINGLESSTHEWORRLDDOESNOTKNOWMIEMYMMISZZONISSYINLI
FEISTTOTEACHMAINKINNDTMHINGSTHATONLYFEWOFUSFKNOWLIK
ELUONRLDINESMYLONLINESSREFAHLLONLINEXSXSINSIIDEMSIN
EECEDSOMEBODYUTONEEDMERESTOFTHEWORLRDONLYETAKEXSCAL
RIEOAFUSILOVEJUSTBALKINGYTOCINDYBECAUTSEYOUTAKENMME
SEIRIOUUSLY
["I hate being autistic. Just heal me. My life is still meaningless. The world does not know my mission is in life to teach mankind things that only a few of us know, like real loneliness inside. I need somebody to need me. The rest of the world only takes care of us. I just love talking to Cindy because you take me seriously."]

Another letter came from Evan, the teenager/poet mentioned previously. He commented on what facilitation has meant to him and what it means for his future, explaining that it can treat us to the worlds respect and warmth . . . freedom, friendship and confidence . . . freeing me from the frightful triangle of fear, frustration and failure. I want to help autistic people everywhere find reason and release. Positive reassurances and responses were white waters in dark tides of terror.

In a similar vein, Eve Hanf-Enos, mentioned in Chapter 4, wrote to me to say that with facilitation, people have found under our seething apparent wrong behavior, sense and sensitivity. She signed her letter, Yours in freedom.

These are voices filled with anguish but also of expectation and determination. A celebration of fiercely independent free speech, their words vividly portray both the horrors of being kept silent and the profound satisfaction—even joy—of achieving the ability to communicate.

NOTES

1. It is interesting to note, for example, that Harlan Lane (1977), author of an account of Itard and Victor, discounts suggestions that Victor might have been autistic, arguing that "unlike the autistic child, Victor was, within his limits, highly communicative" (p. 202), although his communication was mainly gestural.

APPENDIX
"How-To" Training Materials

When people first learn about facilitated communication, three questions seem to predominate in their thoughts: (1) "Does it work?" (i.e., are the words those of the person with the disability or are they created by the facilitator?); (2) "How does it work?"; and (3) "If it does work, why does it work?" Hopefully, the preceding seven chapters have addressed each of these questions. As a further resource, this appendix includes lists or guides that may be useful in learning the method. They address the second of the predominant questions, namely, "How does it work?"

I. Basic Elements of Facilitated Communication

The list below serves as a kind of short-form description of the method. It summarizes the basic principles of facilitation and also provides a brief overview for people who want to know something about the method but who may not want or need to know its intricacies.

1. *Physical support.* The facilitator provides physical support under the forearm or at the hand to help the person isolate the index finger and/or slow the movement of the hand to a selection, such as a letter on a keyboard. Physical support also helps the person initiate the movement—literally helping the person get started—while simultaneously conveying emotional support. The facilitator does not assist the student in making a selection of a letter or other target, such as a picture or shape.
2. *Initial training/introduction.* Students are encouraged to progress through a series of activities or choices successfully, being pulled back from incorrect selections. The initial activities include pointing to pictures from among several choices (e.g., "Point to the car"). Stu-

dents seem to have an easier time initially with set work such as fill-in-the-blanks activities, math problems, answers to questions based on materials read, or other activities in which the answers are more predictable than in open-ended dialogue. After the person has begun to develop fluency with facilitated communication, personal, open-ended communication is introduced and encouraged.

3. *Maintaining focus.* The method requires the facilitator to remind the person typing or pointing to keep his or her eyes on the targets, to find a position that makes pointing or typing relatively easy, to maintain isolation of the index finger, and to reduce such extraneous actions as screeching, slapping of objects, hand flapping, and pushing away the typing device or letter board. When students engage in extraneous actions, the facilitator ignores the behaviors and physically supports the student in redirecting to the typing or pointing. Similarly, if the person engages in echolalic speech, the facilitator asks the person to type what he or she wants to say, regardless of whether the speech is appropriate in the situation.

4. *Encouragement and avoiding testing for competence.* The facilitator attempts not to test the person but merely to provide support for typing or pointing, providing encouragement in a natural manner. It is important to treat the person being facilitated as competent.

5. *Fading.* Physical support can be faded over time; this may take a number of months or even years. Fading back support can begin even in the very first introductory session; similarly, facilitators can attempt to provide varying degrees of support during a single session.

II. Collecting Communication Data

A number of people ask why I do not attempt studies of facilitation involving control groups. There are are at least two reasons. First, anytime you have a means of assisting people for which you have good, solid evidence of efficacy, it is difficult and potentially unethical to withhold the method or approach. Second, the control condition is not necessarily what *other* people do when not using the method or when using other methods; rather, it may be what the same individual who uses facilitation can do or express when not using facilitated communication. Thus we can look at the communicative effectiveness of people before beginning facilitation and then with facilitation as the control and experimental conditions, respectively. The latter approach to conceptualizing research makes sense given the communication difficulties of the people with whom we have worked. At the same time, it is important to collect information about individuals' communication abilities under different circumstances and also to follow their progression toward independence.

The sample form shown in Figure A.1 lists some of the kinds of data that are helpful to facilitators as they attempt to understand the communicative difficulties and abilities of individuals. (For a sample tabulation such data, see Table A.1 at the end of this appendix.)

III. Assumptions About the Difficulties Experienced by People with Autism

One of the greatest barriers to success with facilitation is the tendency to underestimate people's abilities, based on prevailing paradigms or definitions of disability. It is not unusual to forget or to ignore the fact that many assumptions about disabilities are merely that, assumptions. Too often assumptions are treated as facts. Many of the assumptions that are often associated with autism and related developmental disabilities are listed below. Because so many people, myself included, initially had difficulty even considering the viability of facilitated communication with certain people because of what we "knew" about autism and related disabilities, I found it helpful to try to confront the contraditions posed by people's communication abilities when using facilitation and my prior assumptions about them. Typically, in training workshops, I contrast these prior assumptions with examples of individuals' typing, noting that nearly all the assumptions may be refuted, at least for the individual in question. On the other hand, it is important to note that certain descriptive qualities—for example, "tactile defensiveness" and demand for order or consistency—may still have some relevance. A number of individuals *do* report that they are sensitive to certain textures or touch. Similarly, many people with autism *do* demand order or the following of routines, although in their typing many people also explain that they cannot help themselves; such demands seem compulsive rather than intentional.

- Receptive problem
- Processing problem
- Global cognitive failure
- Specific cognitive failures
- Inability to use pronouns, verb tenses, and other forms of language appropriately
- Levels of deficit (i.e., people with no speech and who appear nonresponsive to instruction are generally severely retarded)

FIGURE A.1 Data Collection Form

Name . . . .

Street address . . . .

City . . . . State . . . . ZIP . . . . Date of birth . . . .

Description of communication without facilitation (verbal and written); provide examples:

. . . .

. . . .

. . . .

. . . .

Alternative communication system prior to facilitation: . . . .

. . . .

. . . .

. . . .

Description of communication with facilitation (e.g., words/phrases/sentences; set work or fluent conversation); provide examples: . . . .

. . . .

. . . .

. . . .

. . . .

Degree of physical support in facilitation (least amount of support required: e.g., hand, wrist, forearm, shoulder, no support): . . . .

. . . .

. . . .

Numbers of people and roles of people (e.g., parents, teachers) with whom the person facilitates:

. . . .

. . . .

Settings in which facilitation is used: . . . .

. . . .

. . . .

Other comments: . . . .

. . . .

. . . .

. . . .

- Rote learning and reproduction of language without understanding (e.g., echolalia, stereotyped speech)
- Lack of interest in social contact
- Lack of normal affect/emotional responses
- Favoring objects rather than people; greater interest in objects than in people
- Lack of internal language
- Lack of prerequisite skills for language development (e.g., inability to understand and manipulate symbols; inability to play with toys or objects or to engage in imaginative play)
- Demand for order; poor tolerance of change; failure to understand change
- Tactile defensiveness (some students appear uncomfortable with the touch of certain textures, including human touch and may pull away when touched)

IV. Criteria for Candidates to Use Facilitated Communication

Among the other questions commonly asked about facilitated communication is the one concerning candidates: "With whom should we try the method?" Obviously, no method will prove useful for all people. And for some people, the approach would seem unnecessary—for example, some people may have excellent speaking skills or already be able to type or write effectively and independently. On the other hand, it is important not to prematurely narrow the group for whom the method might prove useful. Consequently, the proposed criteria that follow are purposefully broad.

1. Individuals with autism or related developmental disabilities who do not speak *or* whose speech is not very functional.
2. Individuals who have these problems with speech *and* who may be presumed to have severe intellectual disabilities.
3. Individuals who have these problems with speech and for whom we may have no evidence of literacy and numeracy skills.
4. Individuals who have these problems with speech and who may also exhibit poor eye-hand coordination; low or high muscle tone; problems with index finger isolation and extension problems; perseveration; the use of two hands to do a task requiring only one; tremor; instability of the finger, hand, and arm; problems of initiating an action (long delays); and unusual responses to what is going on around them (Crossley, 1990).

V. Getting Started

In order to begin using the method with anyone, it seems essential to follow a process of steps, moving from structured work toward fluency or open-ended communication. The following list describes the aspects of getting started.

- Explain what you are doing. Explain that you are going to show the person a way to communicate that has been useful for other people who have difficulty saying what they want to say with speech.
- Apologize in advance for the fact that many of the exercises you are about to use may be simple, explaining that these are often helpful just to get started.
- Treat the student as perfectly competent; assume that the student understands everything you are saying, even if he or she does not always respond as if this is the case. Remember that the problems a person has with saying words or pointing to letters also carry over into other actions that require purposeful movement; thus the person may appear to be not attending or not responsive when in fact he or she *does* understand what is being said. By treating the student as competent, you will convey your confidence in him or her.
- Try to speak in a normal, supportive way, avoiding unusual tones of voice (e.g., babying the person). The attitude of the facilitator is very important and the success of this method depends on the facilitator's building a relationship with the student. It is also helpful to work in a supportive environment, where the person's competence is accepted and respected.
- Identify right- or left-handedness. An easy way to do so is to hand the student an object, such as a pen, to see which hand he or she uses to accept it. Use the hand that a student has expressed as a preference. Some students may not have a preference; this is referred to as being "nonlateralized." It is noteworthy that a higher proportion of people with autism than of the whole population are nonlateralized.
- Determine how much support the person needs. Watch for poor muscle tone, shakiness/tremor, movement of the index finger to one side or another when pointing, tendency to hit keys next to the ones desired, and other problems that may require support. Also watch for the tendency to hit a key or other target repeatedly; pull the hand or arm back after each choice if necessary. Provide only as much support as is needed.
- Make sure the seating is comfortable, with a table that is low enough (or a seat that is high enough) that the student can easily type or point to choices.

- Select a variety of activities, beginning with pictures or symbols (e.g., triangles, squares, circles) but also including letters, words, and, where appropriate, sentences.
- Maximize the student's success by helping him or her *not* make mistakes.
- Pace the activities. When the student completes one activity, move on to the next. Try not to repeat the same material; once a student demonstrates a skill, move on to another activity. With set work, or structured activities, you know the range of possible responses; this kind of work proves more useful in early sessions than completely open-ended conversation. (Examples of set work are included in the next section.) But allow the student to progress from simple activities to more complex ones, including an opportunity to demonstrate literacy skills with words and sentences. It is helpful to use or adapt materials from the regular education curricula that students would be exposed to if they did not have disabilities. Such materials can be very motivating, although you need to work up to them; in other words, try not to frustrate the student by moving too quickly. Before completing any session, ask the student: "Is there anything else you would like to say?"
- If the person types echoed words or letters, just ask the person to try again and feel free to pull the person back from incorrect or echoed selections.
- If the person gets up in the middle of a session, slaps the table, screeches, pulls away, hits, or engages in other challenging behavior, try to ignore it. Redirect the person to the task at hand. Avoid moralizing to the person, but feel free to be firm in a supportive fashion, saying, for example, "I know this isn't easy, but I want you to complete this before we stop."
- Even in the first session(s), experiment with fading hand or arm support where appropriate. Continue enough hand, wrist, arm, or shoulder support for the person to continue to feel confident and to communicate. Fading too quickly can lead to frustration and to failing confidence; it can lead to a breakdown in communication.
- Make sure that the people you are working with have access to communication boards or typing devices all the time.
- Encourage the student to let you know when and if they want anything kept confidential. Assure the student that you will abide by this request.
- Videotape the first and even subsequent sessions if possible. Looking at the videotapes will help you examine your own facilitative techniques and will also enable you to become more aware of the student's unique style of typing, etc.

VI. Examples of Set Work

Since structured activities with predictable answers are a standard and effective part of the getting started process, it is valuable to consider the many kinds of such activities (i.e., set work) available. Anyone who uses facilitation will need to develop set work. Typically, in initial sessions the facilitator may ask the person to point to certain people or objects in pictures or to point to different geometic shapes and then to move on to identifying letters and words. Other kinds of set work include choosing from several words (e.g., "What would you like to eat—a hamburger, an egg sandwich, or a slice of pizza?"), typing out the names of objects, spelling words, and answering comprehension questions based on a reading passage; in the latter instance, the comprehension questions should be fill-in-the-blanks or multiple-choice exercises rather than open-ended questions, since anything open-ended may prove too difficult initially and may dash the person's confidence. Having said that, even in a first session, some people will be able to progress through set work to open-ended communication. The following is a list of types of set work:

Typing own name and family members' names
Pointing to objects, shapes, people, or things in pictures
Multiple-choice exercises
Crossword puzzles
Matching exercises
Spelling words
Fill-in-the-blanks exercises
Math problems
Comprehension questions
Labeling objects
Completing sentences

VII. Individuals with Echolalic Language

As indicated in Chapter 3, a number of unique issues arise with respect to enabling people with echoed language to communicate. Indeed, it may be fair to say that we have sometimes found it more difficult to work with people who have echoed speech than to work with people who do not speak. In part the difficulty arises from our not wanting to offend people by ignoring their speaking, however repetitive and nonsensical it may seem. But the other major problem seems to be the difficulty that some individuals encounter when they try to stop typing echoes and to begin typing what they want to type, that is, natural language. For many, echolalia is a formidable barrier. Practices and assumptions about facilitating with people who have echolalic language are listed below. The various items derive from my observations of and discussions with Rosemary Crossley and from observations in our own use of facilitated communication in the United States.

- Echolalic language may be different from typed language.
- People with echolalic speech or typing may have difficulty believing they can type ordinary language; you can help them overcome this by explaining that typing is another channel for language and that other people who have the same problem as theirs have been able to say what they want through facilitation.
- People may initially type echoes; over time we expect the person can be helped to type ordinary language.
- Before people have been introduced to training in facilitated communication, independent typing will generally be echolalic; such typing *does not* predict the quality of what people will type when facilitated.
- Explain that you understand how frustrating the echoes must be.
- Encourage the person not to speak and instead to type.
- Give the person structured work (e.g., fill-in-the-blanks exercises, synonym matching, bingo, math problems, and other predictable activities).
- Explain that you are going to stop or minimize your own talking while the two of you type to each other.
- Over time, as the person types with fewer or no echoes, or types without repeating words that you say, you can resume speaking.

VIII. Generalizing Facilitation to Additional Facilitators

It is quite common for students to become fluent communicators with one or several facilitators and yet have difficulty communicating with other facilitators. This may result from the student's lack of confidence, inexperience of the new facilitator, nervousness on the part of the student, or other factors. The following principles seem to help ensure that a student will communicate with more than one or two facilitators:

- We should convey to students that we have confidence in their ability to communicate and that we expect them to be able to communicate with many facilitators. Related to this, we should affirm the importance of a student's being able to communicate with a variety of facilitators.

- Students will find it easier to do set work than open-ended conversation with new facilitators. In other words, begin with yes/no questions, choices from among two or three or four options, spelling exercises, fill-in-the-blanks work, cloze exercises (e.g., "Mom and Dad drive a _____"), and questions with a predictable range of answers (e.g., "Which book should we read?"). Then later you can move on to more open-ended conversational typing (e.g., "What did you do at school today? What should we do this weekend?").
- Students will need more physical support from a new facilitator than from one to whom they are already accustomed.
- It helps to be firm and supportive with a student. New facilitators should keep trying to facilitate a person. Be persistent. Do not give up. It may help to explain that you are going to keep trying regularly because you know this is important and you know the student will be able to do it.
- Try to use facilitated communication in a variety of functional, everyday situations. You can almost always use yes/no questions as a starting point. Similarly, you can ask a student to make choices by typing or pointing to the first letter of possible answers to your questions.
- If the person being facilitated is a student who is entering a new class for the first time, it will be helpful to inform him or her that several people will be serving as facilitators. There is no harm in having several people facilitate from the start. Approach this form of communication as a natural part of the educational process; in other words, some students can do some of their schoolwork by speaking, some by handwriting, and some by facilitated communication/typing.
- If a student does not facilitate equally well with each person, be sure not to blame the student. Just continue to express your optimism about the student's ability and persist with efforts to facilitate the student's communication.
- When introducing a new facilitator, it may be useful to begin by having the veteran facilitator place his or her hand over that of the new facilitator while the latter supports the student, progressively removing this extra support as the student becomes comfortable with the new facilitator.
- Avoid testing the student to see if he or she is comprehending what you are saying.
- Look for signs that the student wants to communicate in particular situations. For example, we have observed students take a language

board and bring it to a peer or to another teacher. Try to respond to the student's desire to communicate by providing facilitation at these times. It is important that the person have access to communication when he or she wants it.

• Remind the student periodically that the ultimate goal for the student is to become more independent. This can be accomplished by being able to communicate with a number of facilitators and with decreasing physical support to the hand or arm.

• If a student produces a series of letters that you do not understand, try not to label them "wrong." Instead, tell the student that you had difficulty understanding the word or statement and ask, "Could you try again?"

• Most important, try to be positive at all times.

IX. Fostering Communication

Finally, it would be a mistake to conceptualize facilitated communication as dependent only on the communication user's abilities and the facilitator's skill. Its usefulness and any individual's success with it also depend on the context in which it is used. For example, facilitated communication will prove more useful in settings in which people have constant access to communication devices and are expected and asked to communicate frequently, where communication through facilitation is respected, and where people are available to facilitate. Nine important factors that can foster the success of facilitated communication are listed below.

1. Constant availability of facilitators and communication devices (i.e., letter boards, electronic communicators, computers, or electronic typewriters)

2. People who want to interact and will initiate interaction with the person using facilitated communication; access by the person using facilitation to the same communication opportunities available to others

3. Opportunity to communicate in all typical environments, for example, regular classes, the workplace, home, and social settings; support in these environments must include accommodation of the unusual behaviors created by certain disabilities

4. Facilitators with the skill to ignore unusual or difficult behavior, to calm the person, and to redirect the person to communication or other activities

5. Facilitators who select activities or approaches to tasks that encourage collaboration and interaction
6. Facilitators who convey a positive, expectant attitude in the person's ability to become an effective communicator
7. Persistence on the part of both the communication user and facilitator
8. Availability of multiple facilitators; this increases opportunities to use the method in a variety of settings and also hastens independence in communication
9. Facilitators and others who demonstrate respect for the person who uses facilitated communication, for example, not speaking in front of people as if they are not present, not testing their competence, and guaranteeing them the choice of having their communication either kept private or shared.

TABLE A.1. Students' Communication Before and With Facilitated Communication*

Name	Age	Speech*	Other Communication System	Communication with facilitation	Support in facilitation
Bobby	3	Echolalia	Pictures; 2 signs: "more" and "all gone"	Words; sentence completion	Forearm, elbow, no support (sitting on teacher's lap)
Lauren	3	Echolalia (rare)		Words, labels, names	Wrist
Jacque	3	None		Pictures and objects	Hand
Henry	4	None	Pictures	Points and moves body toward correct choices of pictures and colors	
George	4	Echolalia		Points to pictures and whole words; copies words	Hand
Hassan	4	None		Phrases and some sentences; open-ended questions	Hand
Charles	4	None		Sentences	Hand
Shane	4	None	Few signs	Words and phrases; some sentences	Hand
Alan	4	Echolalia		Sentences	Hand
Ezekiel	5	Echolalia		Sentences	Forearm

(Continued overleaf)

*Students referred to as having echolalia all speak words or phrases they hear others say as well as, in some instances, greetings; where students who have speech are not identified as having alternative communication systems, this indicates that teachers were attempting to prompt functional speech.

TABLE A.1 *Continued*

Name	Age	Speech*	Other Communication System	Communication with facilitation	Support in facilitation
Sally	5	Echolalia	Few signs	Pictures, yes/no, and a few words	Hand
Jermayne	6	None	Picture book; 3 signs	Sentences	Hand
Lenny	6	Echolalia (rare)	Picture book	Sentences	Hand
Andrew	6	Echolalia	None	Sentences	Hand and wrist
William	6	Echolalia	Signs and pointing	Sentences	Wrist
Alicia	6	Echolalia	Signs	Words and phrases; sentences	Wrist
L.S.	6	Echolalia		Words	Hand
Sam	6	Echolalia	Picture board; 70 signs	Words and phrases; a few sentences	Hand
Gerry	7	None	2 signs	Sentences	Hand
Mark	7	None	Picture book; indicates 5 signs, imitates 15 signs	Sentences	Hand, finger isolation
Peter	8	Echolalia		Sentences	Hand
Jason	8	Echolalia	Word and sentence book	Sentences	Hand
Daniel	8	Echolalia	None	Sentences	Hand
Nancy	9	None (vowel sounds, "hi," and "no")	Picture book and 6 signs	Sentences	Hand and wrist

Name	Age		Communication aids	Speech	Body part
Eric	9	Echolalia	Picture schedule for activity choices	Words and phrases; a few sentences	Hand
Raul	10	Echolalia	500+ signs	Sentences	Wrist
Brett	10	Echolalia		Words	Hand
Fitz	10	Echolalia	3 or 4 signs	Words and sentences	Hand
Elwin	11	Echolalia	Phrases	Sentences	Wrist, forearm, and elbow
Mary	12	None	Picture book; 5 signs (e.g., "drink," "eat," "bathroom")	Sentences	Hand and wrist
Mustafa	12	Echolalia	Word and phrase book	Sentences	Hand
Maggie	13	Echolalia	None	Sentences	Wrist, forearm, and elbow
Eddie	14	None	Picture book	Sentences	Hand, wrist, and forearm
Abdul	14	Echolalia	Picture book	Sentences	Hand and wrist
Evan	14	None	Picture and functional words	Sentences	Wrist and forearm
Todd	17	Echolalia	Picture book	Sentences	Hand, wrist, forearm, and elbow
Erin	19	Echolalia		Sentences	Wrist
Edward	20	None	Pictures	Words	Wrist and arm
Jerome	21	Echolalia	None	Sentences	Wrist and forearm
Brendan	21	Echolalia		Sentences	Hand
Marny	21	Echolalia		Sentences	Hand/wrist and forearm
Neil	25	None	2 or 3 signs; pictures	Sentences	Hand and wrist

References

American Psychiatric Association. (1987). *Diagnostic and statistical manual of mental disorders* (3rd ed.). Washington, DC: Author.

Ashton-Warner, S. (1986). *Teacher*. New York: Simon & Schuster. (Original work published 1963)

Baltaxe, C. A. M., & Simmons, J. Q. (1977). Bedtime soliloquies and linguistic competence in autism. *Journal of Speech and Hearing Disorders, 42*, 376–393.

Barron, J., & Barron, S. (1992). *There's a boy in here*. New York: Simon & Schuster.

Bartak, L., Rutter, M., & Cox, A. (1977). A comparative study of infantile autism and specific developmental receptive language disorders: III. Discriminant function analysis. *Journal of Autism and Childhood Schizophrenia, 7*(4), 383–396.

Bauman, M. L. (1991, May). Microscopic neuroanatomic abnormalities in autism. *Pediatrics, 87*(5), 791–796.

Becker, H. S. (1969). Problems of inference and proof in participant observation. In G. J. McCall & J. L. Simmons (Eds.), *Issues in participant observation* (pp. 245-254). Reading, MA: Addison-Wesley.

Bettelheim, B. (1967). *The empty fortress: Infantile autism and the birth of the self*. New York: The Free Press.

Biklen, D. (1990). Communication unbound: Autism and praxis. *Harvard Educational Review, 60*, 291–314.

Biklen, D. (1991, March 17). There's more to DEAL methods than meets the eye. *The Sunday Age*, p. 15.

Biklen, D. (1992a). *Schooling without labels*. Philadelphia: Temple University Press.

Biklen, D. (1992b). Autism orthodoxy versus free speech: A reply to Cummins and Prior. *Harvard Educational Review, 62*(2), 242–256.

Biklen, D., Morton, M. W., Saha, S. N., Duncan, J., Gold, D., Hardardottir, M., Karna, E., O'Connor, S., & Rao, S. (1991). "I AMN NOT A UTISTIVC OH THJE TYP" ("I'm not autistic on the typewriter"). *Disability, Handicap & Society, 6*(3), 161–180.

Biklen, D., & Schubert, A. (1991). New words: The communication of students with autism. *Remedial and Special Education, 12*(6), 46–57.

Biklen, S., & Moseley, C. (1988). "Are you retarded?" "No, I'm Catholic": Qualitative methods in the study of people with severe handicaps. *Journal of the Association for Persons with Severe Handicaps, 13*, 155–162.

Blatt, B. (1987). *The conquest of mental retardation*. Austin, TX: Pro-Ed.

Bogdan, R., & Biklen, D. (1977). Handicapism. *Social Policy, 7*(5), 14–19.

Bogdan, R., & Biklen, S. (1991). *Qualitative research for education: An introduction to theory and methods*. Boston: Allyn & Bacon.

Bogdan, R., & Taylor, S. J. (1976). The judged, not the judges: An insider's view of mental retardation. *American Psychologist, 31*(1), 47–52.

Bogdan, R., & Taylor, S. J. (1982). *Inside out: The social meaning of mental retardation*. Toronto: University of Toronto Press.

Brown, C. (1970). *Down all the days*. London: Mandarin.

Courchesne, E. (1991, May). Neuroanatomic imaging in autism. *Pediatrics, 87*(5), 781–790.

Crossley, R. (1988, October). *Unexpected communication attainments by persons diagnosed as autistic and intellectually impaired*. Paper presented at International Society for Augmentative and Alternative Communication, Los Angeles.

Crossley, R. (1990, August). *Communication training involving facilitated communication*. Paper presented to the annual conference of the Australian Association of Special Education, Canberra.

Crossley, R., & McDonald, A. (1980). *Annie's coming out*. New York: Penguin Books.

Cummins, R. A., & Prior, M. P. (1992). Autism and assisted communication: A response to Biklen. *Harvard Educational Review, 62*(2), 228–241.

Darley, R. L., Aronson, A. E., & Brown, J. R. (1975). *Motor speech disorders*. Philadelphia: Saunders.

Dexter, L. (1964). *The tyranny of schooling*. New York: Basic Books.

Doake, D. B. (1988). *Reading begins at birth*. Richmond Hill, Ont.: Scholastic-TAB Publications.

Donnellan, A. M. (Ed.). (1985). *Classic readings in autism*. New York: Teachers College Press.

Eastham, M. (1992). *Silent words*. Ottawa: Oliver & Pate.

Eisenberg, L., & Kanner, L. (1956). Early infantile autism, 1943–1955. *American Journal of Orthopsychiatry, 26*, 556–566.

Ferreiro, E., & Teberosky, A. (1982). *Literacy before schooling*. Portsmouth, NH: Heinemann.

Foucault, M. (1972). *The archaeology of knowledge* (A. M. Sheridan Smith, Trans.). New York: Harper & Row.

Freeman, B. J., & Ritvo, E. R. (1976). Cognitive assessment. In E. R. Ritvo, B. J. Freeman, E. M. Ornitz, & P. E. Tanguay (Eds.), *Autism: Diagnosis, current research and Management* (pp. 27–34). New York: Spectrum Publications.

Glaser, B., & Strauss, A. L. (1967). *The discovery of grounded theory*. Chicago: Aldine.

Goetz, J. P., & LeCompte, M. D. (1984). *Ethnography and qualitative design in educational research*. New York: Academic Press.

Goldberg, T. E. (1987). On hermetic reading abilities. *Journal of Autism and Developmental Disorders, 17*(1), 29–43.

Goode, D. (1992). Who is Bobby?: Ideology and method in the discovery of a Down Syndrome person's competence. In P. M. Ferguson, D. L. Ferguson,

& S. J. Taylor (Eds.), *Interpreting disability: A qualitative reader* (pp. 197–212). New York: Teachers College Press.

Goodson, I., & Dowbiggin, I. (1990). Docile bodies: Commonalities in the history of psychiatry and schooling. In S. Ball (Ed.), *Foucault and education: Disciplines and knowledge* (pp. 105–132). New York: Routledge.

Goodwin, M. S., & Goodwin, T. C. (1969). In a dark mirror. *Mental Hygiene, 53*(4), 550–563.

Grandin, T., & Scariano, M. M. (1986). *Emergence: Labeled autistic.* Novato, CA: Arena.

Hagen, C. (1987). An approach to the treatment of mild to moderately severe apraxia. *Topics in Language Disorders, 8*(1), 34–50.

Hare, B. (1990, July 13). The changing face of racism in America. *Newsday,* p. B1.

Heinrichs, P. (1991, March 10). Experts slam disabled "charade." *The Sunday Age,* pp. 1, 6.

Holdaway, D. (1979). *The foundations of literacy.* Portsmouth, NH: Heinemann.

Intellectual Disability Review Panel. (1989). *Investigation into the reliability and validity of the assisted communication technique.* Melbourne, Australia: Department of Community Services, Victoria.

Interdisciplinary Working Party on Issues in Severe Communication Impairment. (1988). *D.E.A.L. Communication Centre operation. A statement of concern.* Melbourne, Australia: Author.

Itard, J. M. G. (1962). *The wild boy of Aveyron* (G. Humphrey & M. Humphrey, Trans.). New York: Appleton-Century-Crofts. (Translated from edition published in 1894)

James, A. L., & Barry, R. J. (1983). Developmental effects in the cerebral lateralization of autistic, retarded, and normal children. *Journal of Autism and Developmental Disorders, 13*(1), 43–55.

Johansen, L. (1988). *The Dinkum dictionary: A ripper guide to Aussie English.* Ringwood, Victoria: Viking O'Neill.

Johnson, I. (1989). "Hellish difficult to live in this world": The unexpected emergence of written communication in a group of severely mentally handicapped individuals. *Journal of Social Work Practice, 4*(1), 13–30.

Kanner, L. (1943). Autistic disturbances of affective contact. *Nervous Child, 2,* 217–250.

Kanner, L. (1971). Follow-up study of eleven autistic children originally reported in 1943. *Journal of Autism and Childhood Schizophrenia, 1,* 119–145.

Kelso, J. A. S., & Tuller, B. (1981). Toward a theory of apractic syndromes. *Brain and Language, 12,* 224–245.

L. vs. Public Schools, No. 91–09, Final Order (Tennessee Department of Education Due Process Hearing, June 28, 1991).

Lane, H. (1977). *The wild boy of Aveyron.* New York: Bantam.

Lash, J. P. (1980). *Helen and teacher.* New York: Delacorte Press/Seymour Lawrence.

Mairs, N. (1986). *Plaintext: Deciphering a woman's life.* New York: Harper & Row.

Mathews, G. F. (1983). *Voices from the shadows.* Toronto: Women's Educational Press.

Maurer, R. G., & Damasio, A. R. (1982). Childhood autism from the point of view of behavioral neurology. *Journal of Autism and Developmental Disorders*, 12 (2), 195–205.

Menyuk, P. (1978). Language: What's wrong and why. In M. Rutter & E. Schopler (Eds.), *Autism* (pp. 105–116). New York: Plenum.

Miller, N. (1986). *Dyspraxia and its management*. Rockville, MD: Aspen.

Miller, S. (1990). *Family pictures*. New York: Harper & Row.

Mills, C. W. (1967). Methodological consequences of the sociology of knowledge. In I. L. Horowitz (Ed.), *Power, politics, & people* (pp. 453–468). New York: Oxford University Press.

Mirenda, P. L., Donnellan, A. M., & Yoder, D. E. (1983). Gaze behavior: A new look at an old problem. *Journal of Autism and Developmental Disorders*, 13(4), 397–409.

Mirenda, P., & Schuler, A. L. (1988). Augmenting communication for persons with autism: Issues and strategies. *Topics in Language Disorders*, 9(1), 24–43.

Mishler, E. G. (1990). Validation in inquiry-guided research: The role of exemplars in narrative studies. *Harvard Educational Review*, 60, 415–442.

Nolan, C. (1987). *Under the eye of the clock*. New York: St. Martin's Press.

Oppenheim, R. (1974). *Effective teaching methods for autistic children*. Springfield, IL: Thomas.

Ornitz, E. M., & Ritvo, E. R. (1976). Medical assessment. In E. R. Ritvo, B. J. Freeman, E. M. Ornitz, & P. E. Tanguay (Eds.), *Autism: Diagnosis, current research, and management* (pp. 7–23). New York: Spectrum Publications.

Park, C. C. (1967). *The siege: The first eight years of an autistic child*. Boston: Little, Brown.

Park, C. C. (1982). *The siege: The first eight years of an autistic child; With an epilogue, fifteen years later*. Boston: Little, Brown.

Paul, R. (1987). Communication. In D. J. Cohen, A. M. Donnellan, & R. Paul (Eds.), *Handbook of autism and pervasive development disorders* (pp. 61–84). New York: John Wiley.

Prior, M. P. (1979). Cognitive abilities and disabilities in infantile autism: A review. *Journal of Abnormal Child Psychology*, 7, 357–380.

Prizant, B. M. (1983). Language acquisition and communicative behavior in autism: Toward an understanding of the "whole" of it. *Journal of Speech and Hearing Disorders*, 48, 296–307.

Prizant, B. M., & Duchan, J. F. (1981). The functions of immediate echolalia in autistic children. *Journal of Speech and Hearing Disorders*, 46, 241–249.

Prizant, B. M., & Rydell, P. J. (1984). Analysis of functions of delayed echolalia in autistic children. *Journal of speech and hearing research*, 27, 183–192.

Prizant, B., & Schuler, A. (1987). Facilitating communication: Theoretical foundations. In D. Cohen, A. Donnellan, & R. Paul (Eds.), *Handbook of autism and pervasive developmental disorders*. New York: Wiley.

Rabinow, P. (Ed.). (1984). *The Foucault reader*. New York: Pantheon Books.

Rapin, I. (1991). Autistic children: Diagnosis and clinical features. *Pediatrics*, 87(5), 751–760.

Remington-Gurney, J. (1989). *Some thoughts from a one-time skeptic* [Handout]. Melbourne, Australia: DEAL Communication Centre.

Ricks, D. M., & Wing, L. (1975). Language, communication, and the use of symbols in normal and autistic children. *Journal of Autism and Childhood Schizophrenia, 5,* 191–221.

Rimland, B. (1964). *Infantile autism.* New York: Appleton-Century-Crofts.

Rimland, B., & Edelson, S. (1991). *Audiometric testing of autistic children.* (ARI Publication No. 11). San Diego: Autism Research Institute.

Roth, W. (1981). *The handicapped speak.* Jefferson, NC: McFarland.

Rutter, M. (1968). Concepts of autism: A review of research. *Journal of Child Psychology and Psychiatry, 9,* 1–25.

Rutter, M. (1978). Etiology and treatment: Cause and cure. In M. Rutter & E. Schopler (Eds.), *Autism* (pp. 327–335). New York: Plenum.

Sacks, O. (1990). *Awakenings.* New York: HarperCollins.

Sampson, E. D. (1989). The deconstruction of the self. In J. Shotter & K. J. Gergen (Eds.), *Texts of identity* (pp. 1–19). Newbury Park, CA: Sage Publications.

Schawlow, A. L. (1985, July). *Computers for autistic people.* Address given at the National Society for Autistic Children annual conference, Los Angeles.

Schawlow, A. T., & Schawlow, A. L. (1985a). The endless search for help. In M. R. Brady & P. Gunther (Eds.), *Integrating moderately and severely handicapped learners: Strategies that work* (pp. 5–15). Springfield, IL: Thomas.

Schawlow, A. T., & Schawlow, A. L. (1985b, July). *Never too late: Communication with autistic adults.* Paper presented at the National Society for Autistic Children annual conference, Nashville, TN.

Schopler, E., Reichler, R. J., & Lansing, M. (1980). *Individualized assessment and treatment for autistic and developmentally disabled children.* Baltimore: University Park Press.

Schuler, A. L., & Baldwin, M. (1981). Nonspeech communication and childhood autism. *Language, Speech, and Hearing Services in Schools, 12,* 246–257.

Schuler, A. L., & Prizant, B. M. (1985). Echolalia: Kanner's early observations. In E. Schopler & G. B. Mesibov (Eds.), *Communication problems in autism* (pp. 163–184). New York: Plenum.

Seagoe, M. V. (1964). *Yesterday was Tuesday, all day and all night: The story of a unique education.* Boston: Little, Brown.

Sebeok, T. A., & Rosenthal, R. (Eds.). (1981). *The Clever Hans phenomenon: Communication with horses, whales, apes, and people.* New York: New York Academy of Sciences.

Sienkiewicz-Mercer, R., & Kaplan, S. B. (1989). *I raise my eyes to say yes.* Boston: Houghton Mifflin.

Silberberg, N., & Silberberg, M. (1967). Hyperlexia: Specific word recognition skills in young children. *Exceptional Children, 34,* 41–42.

Stehli, A. (1991). *The sound of a miracle.* Garden City, NY: Doubleday.

Sullivan, R. C. (1980). Why do autistic children . . . ? *Journal of Autism and Developmental Disorders, 10*(2), 231–241.

Tager-Flusberg, H. (1981a). On the nature of linguistic functioning in early infantile autism. *Journal of Autism and Developmental Disorders, 11*(1), 45–56.

Tager-Flusberg, H. (1981b). Sentence comprehension in autistic children. *Applied Psycholinguistics, 2*, 5–24.

Taylor, S., & Bogdan, R. (1984). *Introduction to qualitative research methods.* New York: John Wiley.

Weedon, C. (1987). *Feminist practice and poststructuralist theory.* New York: Basil Blackwell.

Wetherby, A. M. (1984). Possible neurolinguistic breakdown in autistic children. *Topics in Language Disorders, 4*, 19–33.

Wetherby, A. M., & Prutting, C. A. (1984). Profiles of communicative and cognitive-social abilities in autistic children. *Journal of Speech and Hearing Research, 27*, 364–377.

Whitehouse, D., & Harris, J. C. (1984). Hyperlexia in infantile autism. *Journal of Autism and Developmental Disorders, 14*, 281–289.

Wing, L. (1969). The handicaps of autistic children—A comparative study. *Journal of Child Psychology and Psychiatry, 10*, 1–40.

Wing, L. (1978). Social, behavioral, and cognitive characteristics: An epidemiological approach. In M. Rutter & E. Schopler (Eds.), *Autism* (pp. 27–46). New York: Plenum.

Zola, I. K. (Ed.). (1982). *Ordinary lives: Voices of disability and disease.* Cambridge, MA: Applewood Books.

Index

About the Author

Douglas Biklen is a Professor of Special Education and Director of the Facilitated Communication Institute in the School of Education at Syracuse University. He has published numerous other books, including *Schooling without Labels: Parents, Educators and Inclusive Education* (1992) and *Achieving the Complete School* (1985, co-authored with Robert Bogdan, Dianne L. Ferguson, Stanford J. Searl, and Steven J. Taylor). He teaches and does research on the sociology of disability, educational mainstreaming, and most recently, communication. His initial study of facilitated communication, funded by the World Rehabilitation Fund, appeared in the *Harvard Educational Review* (August, 1990). News accounts of his work have since appeared in *The New York Times Magazine, Newsweek, U.S. News & World Report, The Washington Post Magazine,* and on the *CBS Evening News* and *ABC's Primetime Live*.